LITTLE ERN!

LITTLE ERN!

The Authorized Biography of
Ernie Wise

Robert Sellers
& James Hogg

WINDSOR
PARAGON

First published 2011
by Sidgwick & Jackson
This Large Print edition published 2012
by AudioGO Ltd
by arrangement with
Pan Macmillan Limited

Hardcover   ISBN: 978 1 445 87891 1
Softcover   ISBN: 978 1 445 87892 8

British Library Cataloguing in Publication Data available

Printed and bound in Great Britain by
MPG Books Group Limited

To Ernie and Doreen

CONTENTS

'Ernie was unique in comedy. He was a "straight man" who was funny in his own right'

—Ron Moody

'Ernie wasn't just a foil to Eric he was so much more than that; he was the maypole around which Eric danced'

—Sir Michael Parkinson

'They became the Laurel and Hardy of television, didn't they? They were just magic'

—Des O'Connor, CBE

'Ernie was a hugely underrated performer. It didn't seem to bother him though. Unlike his TV character he didn't have much of an ego. You have to remember that Ernie was one equal half of the most successful British comedy partnership of all time. The fact that he's been ignored has to be addressed'

—Glenda Jackson, CBE

'It was fate. I pulled the Christmas cracker and he was in it'

—Eric Morecambe

Acknowledgements

The authors wish to express their sincere thanks to the following people. All of whom gave their time and assistance with great generosity of spirit.

Ant and Dec, Derek Appleyard, Lord Archer, Michael Barratt, Tim Bates, Alan J. W. Bell, Geoffrey Bell, Eddie Braben, Bryan Burdon, Ingrid Connell, Ray Cooney OBE, Ray Crawford, Barry Cryer OBE, Jack Culley, Maureen Culley, Alan Curtis, Dame Judi Dench, Kevin Eldon, Howard Ferguson, Lord Grade, Robert Hardy CBE, Miranda Hart, Jackie Hockridge, Indra Hogg, Laurie Holloway, Jack Hylton Jnr, Glenda Jackson CBE, Paul Jenkinson, Jan Kennedy, Marty Kristian, John Lloyd, Graham McCann, Joe McGrath, Gee Mackie, John Mackie CBE, Millicent Martin, Francis Matthews, Sylvan Mason, Ernest Maxin, Ben Miller, Ron Moody, Sir Roger Moore, Des O'Connor CBE, Ian Ogilvy, Sir Michael Parkinson, Eddie Plumley, Angharad Rees, Angela Rippon OBE, Stan Stennett MBE, Jeffrey Taylor, Carol Vorderman MBE, David Wiseman, Martin Wimbush.

Very special thanks to Doreen Wise for her patience, sense of humour, candour and coffee.

PROLOGUE

MORECAMBE AND MORLEY

It's a tale of two statues, really. There is no greater example of the disparity that has existed between Eric and Ernie, about how each was valued by the public, than the story of the two statues erected in their honour. Eric's statue, immortalizing in bronze his famous comedy dance pose, was unveiled in 1999 by Her Majesty the Queen and was the focal point of a £125,000 redevelopment scheme paid from lottery arts funding and Morecambe council. It has remained a fitting tribute, standing proud on the seafront and attracting thousands of visitors a year.

It wasn't until 2010 that Ernie finally got his own statue, and then only just. Originally to have been cast in bronze with a price tag of £38,000, a lottery fund application was refused. Local sculptor Melanie Wilks was approached and agreed to carve the statue out of Yorkshire stone for £8,000, but even this modest fee was beyond the authorities so Doreen Wise, looking for a suitable way to commemorate her husband, stumped up the cash herself. It stands in the Yorkshire town of Morley near the long ago defunct New Pavilion Theatre and the Railway pub where Ernie's dad Harry took his young son to clog-dance on the tables for pennies. Standing on a stone plinth, Ernie is depicted not in his familiar Morecambe and Wise garb, but as a song-and-dance man, something he always considered himself to be. The statue was officially unveiled by Doreen. The Queen was obviously otherwise engaged that afternoon.

It's ironic that the discrepancy between the two performers that existed in life is mirrored even in death. Of course it is the curse of the straight man to be overshadowed by his partner, but it was especially tough for Ernie since in Eric he was working with one of the most naturally funny men in the history of comedy. Take this story. Gene Kelly was guest of honour at a Variety Club luncheon. Ernie was in attendance, but not Eric. Gene stood up and near the end of his speech paid glowing tribute to the boys' *Singing in the Rain* parody, calling it, 'One of the funniest things I've ever seen.' Then turning to Ernie he raised his glass and said, 'Thank you, Eric.'

In 2004 Channel 4 asked more than 300 comedians, comedy writers, producers and directors (on both sides of the Atlantic) to list their all-time favourite comedians. In the top ten were Laurel and Hardy, Reeves and Mortimer and Eric Morecambe—not Morecambe and Wise, just Eric. Why? 'That is so sad,' feels Michael Grade. 'I'm not saying that the people they asked don't know what they're talking about, but it does highlight a general ignorance about Ernie's contribution to the partnership. It was Morecambe *and* Wise. The same as it was Laurel *and* Hardy and Reeves *and* Mortimer. Not that Ernie could have given two hoots of course, but it's still very wrong.'

Three years later in 2007 the UK TV Network aired *Morecambe and Wise's Greatest Moments*, which gave the great British public the chance to choose their all-time favourite Morecambe and Wise sketches. A prime-time extravaganza, the show would run with the usual collection of interviewees mixed with a potted biography and of course the chosen sketches.

What makes the programme interesting though is that Ernie barely gets a mention. The entire production, when not concentrating on a particular sketch, focuses almost solely on Eric —every interview and every clip. Subjects covered include Eric the child protégé, Eric the talented dancer, Eric the comic genius and even Eric the sex symbol! None of this is Eric's fault, of course. Had he been around you can bet your back teeth that he'd have put the producers right. Ernie's very few mentions come, as you'd expect, from an interview with his widow Doreen. Sadly even they last only a few seconds and are almost a token nod to his side of the partnership. From start to finish Ernie is treated almost as an afterthought.

As we aim to prove in this book Ernie was worth much more than that. He was not simply Eric's straight man. 'I always felt in his professional partnership with Eric that Ernie was never given as much credit as he deserved,' says Des O'Connor. 'Eric was such a dynamic personality, the spotlight was always more focused on him than Ernie, but I thought that Ernie was very very important because Morecambe and Wise were a team, but as brilliant as Eric was and as loved as he was, he was always going to be more comfortable and assured just knowing Ernie was there.'

ONE

CARSON AND KID

'I'll cut you off if you marry him. I'll make sure no worthless husband of yours gets a penny of my money.' Her father's ultimatum was like a dagger through her heart. 'You're my favourite daughter, but you'll get nowt from me!'

Connie Wright's romance with Harry Wiseman had been met with considerable alarm by her family, especially from her mill-owner father, a dour individual, 'and hard,' according to Ernie, 'of the sort only Yorkshire breeds.' How dare she fraternize with a man several notches below her station in life? Harry worked on the railways as a lamp man, which was a tough and hazardous occupation, walking the line come hail, sun or pelting rain, polishing all the lamps on the track, trimming their wick and refilling them with oil or paraffin. It was a job he'd blame for the chronic arthritis that blighted him later in life.

Harry's upbringing in the working-class slums of Leeds had been almost Dickensian. One of six children, the Wisemans were wretchedly poor as Harry's father George barely scraped together a living in an assortment of jobs from general labourer to publican's brewer and hotel waiter and died when Harry was just fourteen. It was a life soured almost from the beginning since George's father, Ernie's great-grandfather, John William Wiseman, was a bigamist who deserted his second wife and moved south to Hampshire to marry for a

1

third time. Ernie may not have been aware of this dark secret from his family's dim and distant past. In any case it didn't affect him directly because he was descended from his great-grandfather's first wife, who died in 1877.

Just as tragic, Harry's mother Mary was blind, the result of neglect by the midwife during one of her pregnancies, according to family lore. Years later she lived for a time with Harry's own family, occupying a back room in their modest house, and Ernie loved to visit her and jump up and down on her bed as she laughed. One day she sat her grandson down to ask, 'I hope you don't pee in your bath water?'

It was a very odd thing to say. 'Oh no, Nana,' said Ernie.

'Because that would give you creepy crawlies.'

Sound Victorian advice, which Ernie adhered to all his life. He never did pee in his bath water.

Connie hailed from Pudsey, a market town near Leeds, and was a shy and reserved woman who left school at thirteen and went straight into the mills, becoming, in Ernie's words, 'a skilled box-loom weaver, producing lovely soft serge and worsteds, at a wage of three pounds a week.' She was religious, too, Church of England, and from a reasonably comfortable background. She'd met Harry when they were both in their early twenties, quite by accident on a tram when he tripped over her protruding umbrella. Ernie always liked to think it was love at first sight.

Unlike her dour traditionalist father, Connie wished to marry for love as opposed to social position and bravely went against his wishes. If anything, it was her father's staunch opposition to

2

Harry that pushed her even more emphatically into his arms, or so Ernie liked to believe. But her father made good on his threat and Connie was shunned for years and his will changed in favour of her two sisters, Nellie and Annie; it was they who inherited everything when he died.

Connie left home with just the clothes she stood up in and one other item, a piano she'd saved long and hard to buy out of her own money. Ernie never forgot that piano; he knew how much it meant to his mother, that it represented something strong and special. It took pride of place in the house and most nights the family gathered round it to sing. Connie was never happier than when she was sitting playing a hymn like 'Jerusalem', her own personal favourite.

The piano was such a powerful symbol of Connie's personality and fortitude, and, in fact she never sold it. In her old age there it still stood in her flat in Leeds, its surface always lovingly varnished and adorned with framed photographs of her dear Harry, Ernie and her other children, and also Eric.

Marrying in 1924, Harry and Connie moved into a single room they rented for six shillings a week at 6 Atlanta Street, Bramley in Leeds. It was to this damp, nondescript dwelling that they brought back their first child, Ernie Wise, born Ernest Wiseman on 27 November 1925 at St James's Hospital, the famous Jimmy's. Determined he wouldn't have to live there long, after a few months Harry managed to get enough money together to rent a small one up, one down house in Warder Street. This was to be the first of several moves in the young life of Ernest Wiseman, always to the same kind of working-class areas in and around Leeds, which later came to be called slums, and it's no surprise to learn that in many cases his childhood homes fell prey to the developer's wrecking ball.

It's 35 Warder Street where Ernie's earliest childhood memories reside, and one incident in particular stood out in his mind. It occurred as the family rested indoors after lunch. There was a loud commotion from out in the street: a motorbike had crashed in front of the house throwing a girl out of its sidecar. A member of the St John's ambulance brigade, Harry rushed into the road and helped the stricken woman back inside the house where she was laid on the kitchen table. Fetching his first-aid kit Harry attended to the young woman's injuries as Ernie watched wide-eyed.

When Ernie was five the family moved again, travelling almost twenty miles across the city. Harry had won a promotion, leaving his job as a lamp man to become a railway porter. Their new home was 29 Tombridge Crescent in the rural village of Kinsley near Wakefield and the Wisemans were registered there from October 1931 to October 1935, by which time Ernie would have been around nine years old. Another working-class district close to several small collieries, remarkably the house still stands today.

It was a happy home for the most part, and when there was friction it was mostly about money—or the lack of it. Rows always seemed to revolve around how best to distribute what little they had. Connie was thrifty, and needed to be with what ended up as four hungry mouths to feed. Ernie had been joined in 1929 by a younger brother, Gordon, who would become a farmer in Cambridgeshire and then two sisters, Annie, later a teacher, and Constance, who emigrated to Australia. There was another brother

4

born in 1936, christened Arthur, but he tragically died of peritonitis aged two. By the time Arthur was born Ernie was either at school or out working and thus spent very little time with his youngest brother, which was a shame. In those days children didn't go to funerals so he never really got the opportunity to say hello or goodbye.

With just two pounds a week coming into the household by way of Harry's wages it could be a hardship sometimes to keep such a large family going, although they never went without, and the young Ernie never forgot this struggle, the experience shaping his own attitude to money. 'Save a little, spend a little and remember that your bank book is your best friend,' was Connie's constant advice and it was this kind of prudence Ernie adopted his whole adult life, living in near constant fear of debt and determined always to pay his own way. 'Money means security to me,' he once said. 'The more money I have, the more security I have.'

Harry's carefree nature meant he was rather less dutiful with the family finances, unable to save and wasting what little he did have on cigarettes and booze. He once made the hare-brained purchase of a home projector, sending off for it from an advertisement in the newspaper. Connie could scarcely believe it, but Harry used to delight in hand cranking the contraption into noisy life, projecting the only film he ever bought endlessly onto the wall of the pantry to the delight of the children. It was exactly this kind of reckless spending that drove Connie to distraction, which was only exacerbated by his near total lack of domesticity. Harry left his wife to virtually bring up the children alone and run the household, but then this was a typical male, working-class attitude at the time and the couple never divorced, staying together through thick and thin.

'It was obviously a love match to start off with because Connie gave up everything,' says Doreen. 'If they had any arguments it was always over money, but I don't remember them ever not getting on. Ultimately they were very close I think.'

Of course the young Ernie was unable to make sense of some of the domestic strife Harry fomented. All he saw was, 'this warm, immensely attractive man with a sunny personality and an optimistic disposition, which he passed on to me.' Harry always seemed to have a joke ready to hand or a funny story he could recount when pressed. But behind the happy facade lay a darkness that Ernie never penetrated. In 1915, when Harry was just sixteen, he had lied about his age in order to join the army and fight in the Great War. Although he won a medal for saving his sergeant's life, something of which to be justifiably proud, Harry never spoke about his experiences in the trenches. As Ernie grew older he'd press his father to talk about the war but Harry would always steadfastly refuse. One can only imagine the sights this young boy, for at sixteen a boy he still was, must have seen and what lasting damage those experiences caused.

Juggling with very little money Connie tried to create as welcoming a family environment as she could. The kitchen was really the heart of the house, thanks to a coal range that kept it splendidly warm. All the domestic chores were carried out here. It was where the children sat to have their hair cut. It was too expensive to go to a barber's so

6

Harry did it with a basin and kitchen scissors. 'We looked like a row of coconuts,' Ernie recalled. And on Saturday evenings a large tin bath would appear in front of the range. The kettle and an assortment of pots on the hob would boil the water and then one by one the children took their turn, the last one in having to bathe in the dirt left by the others.

Connie was a handy cook. Although breakfast was rather basic, just bread and dripping, dinner was a flavoursome stew with dumplings, maybe followed by rice pudding baked in the oven with a grating of nutmeg and vanilla flavouring. Sunday was the meal of the week and what Ernie looked forward to: Yorkshire pudding with gravy, then meat and vegetables, and caramel custard to finish. These were memories and smells that even in late middle-age Ernie would recall with fondness.

In his adult years Ernie always remained steadfastly loyal to his parents whenever he spoke or wrote about them, but the truth is something was missing from his childhood: human affection. Ernie's widow Doreen can't recall ever seeing Connie hug or display any love towards Ernie. 'I never once saw his mother put her arms around him or kiss him. Connie was very reserved with everybody. She wasn't a hard woman; she just wasn't at all loving. Her father was a very hard man and I think him disowning her had an effect. The only time I remember Connie's mask slipping was when Eric died. She said to Ernie, "Thank goodness it wasn't you."'

As a consequence, whenever anyone paid Ernie a compliment or did some little favour for him, he'd say, 'Aren't people nice?' It was an endearing quality, that he hadn't allowed an emotionally barren childhood to sour his personality, but it did make it difficult for him to accept love. 'When the *Morecambe and Wise* TV series took off, the whole country loved him,' says Doreen. 'But he wasn't used to affection so he didn't know how to deal with it. He was puzzled by it. He knew I loved him, of course he did, and he knew the pets we had did too. But he couldn't imagine anyone else loving him.'

Family evenings in the Wiseman household were spent relaxing in the front room playing games, chatting or enjoying a sing-along round the piano. Ernie loved to join in during these musical family gatherings and pretty quickly Harry sensed in the child a natural talent for performing. Luckily he was in a position to exploit it. For some years now he'd been an enthusiastic amateur entertainer, just like his own father before him, telling gags and singing in working-men's clubs. He'd taken to the life well enough, the performing and then sitting down afterwards with the punters nursing a pint and a cigarette, but the prime motivation was the money it earned him not treading the boards for its own sake. 'He performed out of a sense of duty and habit,' Ernie recalled, 'rather than from the pleasure of performing.'

By the age of six Ernie was pestering his mum to teach him the songs she played on the piano. He'd been on a couple of trips to see his dad perform and wanted to try his hand at it, too. 'Come on, Ma. Teach me a song.'

Together they went into the front room and sat at the piano. Connie looked through a large pile of sheet music. 'Well, what's it to be?' Ernie chose 'The Sheikh of Araby', a Tin Pan Alley hit of a few years earlier that had been composed in response to the huge success of Rudolph Valentino's film *The Sheikh*. Oblivious to all that romantic sand-dune nonsense, Ernie must have been intrigued by the theatrical exoticism of the song. Connie approved of the choice and they went through it a couple of times before she suggested he went off and practised it all by himself. 'Then when your father comes home, you can sing it for him.'

Harry came back at his usual time and had barely taken his hat and coat off when Connie ushered him into the front room, 'Ernest has something to show you,' she said before running outside into the hall and wrapping a tea towel round Ernie's little head and securing it with a piece of string. 'Wait for me to play the introduction,' she instructed. 'Then come in for the song and put your heart and soul into it.'

'OK, Ma.' So there he was, looking like T.E. Lawrence standing in a trench, his little heart pounding ten to the dozen. Hearing the opening chords Ernie bounded in, desperate to make an unforgettable entrance and achieving it by tripping over a chair and falling over.

'Go out and let's try it again,' reassured Connie.

This time Ernie entered more sedately, already he was getting the hang of this showbiz lark, and went into the song, giving it as much welly as his little frame could muster. 'I will never forget the reaction I got from my father,' he recalled. 'He was bowled over, so excited and thrilled that his eldest son had taken after him and had a spark of talent that there were tears in his eyes.'

Harry was quick to encourage his son's budding abilities, first by teaching him how to tap dance, accompanied by Connie on the piano. Diligently, Ernie practised for hours in the kitchen and soon picked up the basics, doing so well that Harry was sure he'd make an inspired addition to his act. Together they worked out a routine, cobbling together a few gags out of joke books and what they'd heard on the radio, coupled with song and dance numbers. After a couple of months' rehearsal they were ready for their first gig as father and son; Harry christened the act, 'Carson and Kid'. Ernie was no more than seven years old.

The kind of venues they played were local Labour or Conservative clubs, and working-men's clubs affiliated to a factory or a union; large rooms with a stage at one end and a bar that ran along the entire length of the space. With no microphone or speakers, performers sometimes fought hard to make themselves heard above the cacophony of noise, as people played snooker and darts in side rooms or settled down to eat their pie and sip their pint of bitter, barely able to see the act through a deep fog of cigarette smoke.

Weekends were always special nights when the rooms were heaving with the punters done up in all their finery and out to have a grand time. Carson and Kid performed on Saturday night and then twice on Sundays for a fee close on four pounds, almost double Harry's weekly pay packet. Arriving at the venue there was never any time for rehearsal, it was simply a case of handing over your sheet music to the resident pianist and after a few hasty instructions you'd be introduced to the audience by a man sitting on the side of the stage who rang a bell and shouted above the din, 'Now give order for the next act on the bill . . .'

Harry knew he was on to a winner using a child as part of the act, especially when word got around that it was his own son; immediately it endeared the duo to the audience. Who was going to jeer an infant? It was also quite a novelty to see a young lad engaging in sharp banter of an 'adult' nature. Some of their jokes were a bit on the risqué side, many of which Ernie loved to tell his mates like Derek Appleyard in the playground. 'We always used to go to my auntie's house at Christmas and one year she had a big party and I got up and told a story I'd heard. I didn't understand it but people always laughed when I told it. Anyway, when I told this story I didn't get the reaction I was expecting. All the grown ups let out a gasp and looked at each other—then at me. My aunt leant forward and said, "Where on earth did you hear that, Derek, it's filthy." "Ernest Wiseman told me," I replied. I never did find out what I'd actually said.'

Harry exploited his son's natural innocence to the full by making little Ernie wear a cute costume of a black bowler hat with the brim cut off, a cut-down evening dress suit sporting a white carnation on the left lapel, a white wing-collar shirt, a black bow tie and striped trousers. Later on there was the addition of a Chaplinesque drawn-on moustache and large comedy safety pin that appeared to be stopping his trousers from falling down.

Most sweet of all were the little red wooden clogs Ernie danced in and which cleverly harked back to the days of the nineteenth-century when many Yorkshire miners and factory labourers wore them and clog dancing was a well-loved form of entertainment. Even stranger was the old tradition of clog fighting when, believe it or not, two men, usually the worse for drink, climbed into a large open-ended barrel, sat on the rim, and kicked away at each other's shins until one submitted. Ernie's clog dancing wasn't nearly so violent, but it was certainly frenetic and usually brought the house down. 'He could dance like a whirlwind in his clogs,' says Doreen. 'And he always said, "The faster I danced the more coins they threw."' Some nights he was invited to dinner at a neighbour's house and once the food was eaten they'd clear the table and Ernie would get up and do a dance for everyone.'

In 1982 Ernie was invited to a reception in London hosted by Queen Beatrix of the Netherlands. Being the only theatre person in attendance Ernie enquired as to why he'd been invited. 'Because you are a famous English clog dancer!' came the reply. Praise indeed!

The standard Carson and Kid performance went something like this: first Harry came onstage to perform a shortened version of his old routine, then Ernie would arrive and do a little solo spot singing 'I'm Knee Deep in Daisies' and 'Let's Have a Tiddly at the Milk Bar.' Later in the show they'd both appear for their double act, cracking gags and dueting on tunes like, 'Walking in a Winter Wonderland'. One popular routine involved a blacked-up Harry with little Ernie on his knee singing the Al Jolson song, 'Little Pal'. Of course, in today's cynical times the sentimentality of a father asking his son to promise to be a good boy should he ever find himself being looked after by a new daddy would be laughed off the stage, but this wasn't long after the Great War and people still remembered loved ones who never came back home from the trenches. Years later Ernie could still recall how at the end of that number many faces in the audience would be wiping away tears.

It wasn't long before Carson and Kid became quite well established locally and Ernie adored performing. Almost from the first moment he stepped out on that stage, 'I had found my purpose in life.' What made it even more special was that he was side by side with his dad, and those nights out on the road created a deep and unbreakable bond between them; Ernie became devoted to Harry.

But there were few perks in the job since Harry always pocketed the fee and gave it to Connie for the housekeeping, well, most of it. Sometimes a cheery punter would look upon Ernie with sympathy and give him a few pennies or a small gift. On one memorable occasion it was a budgerigar in a cage, which Ernie carefully carried home. Hating to see the poor thing cooped up, he let it out in his bedroom and left it flying around while he went to school. The inevitable happened: Connie was cleaning the room and opened the window for fresh air and the bird shot out. Ernie was distraught when he came home and, along with Harry, walked the streets for hours crying, 'Budgie! Budgie!' It was a fruitless mission and Ernie returned in floods of tears, not for the lost bird but for having let down a stranger's kindness.

With no car father and son travelled to each venue by bus, necessitating a two-mile walk to the main road and the nearest bus stop. Catching the last bus back, Ernie always succumbed to tiredness, despite the raucous laughter and chat of the men returning from a night on the tiles, huddled against the comforting warmth of his dad. So exhausted he'd be that Harry would end up carrying Ernie all the way back to the house on his shoulders. Getting up for school the next morning was always torture after so exhausting a weekend. Ernie vividly recalled one particular Monday morning being lifted bodily out of bed and dressed by Connie while still virtually asleep. Remaining in a fairly comatose state he was sat at the table and his mouth opened and shut in order for his breakfast to find its destination. Then off to school he walked bleary eyed, eating as he usually did a stick of rhubarb and sugar, only to fall asleep in the classroom. Often the school sent angry letters to the family complaining that Ernie's extra-curricular activity as a performer was interfering with his education.

Ernie's first school was Thorpe Junior and Infants, located a mile away from his house. No great shakes academically, Ernie enjoyed his time there and fondly remembered the headmaster, a Mr Riley, who like his dad had fought in the Great War and suffered a medical complaint where his eyes were always weeping, the result of being gassed in the trenches. He was a kind man and often rewarded his pupils for good work. Ernie never forgot one class when Mr Riley posed the question: why do British coastal waters never freeze in winter? Mr Riley's peepers scanned the classroom and rested on Ernie. 'You, Ernest Wiseman. You answer that.'

Standing up confidently, Ernie said, 'Because of the Gulf Stream Drift from the Gulf of Mexico, sir.'

'Correct,' said Mr Riley and awarded Ernie with a ha'penny. Not a bad outcome since at the time Ernie's pocket money was a rather paltry penny.

As 1935 drew to a close the Wisemans moved again,

14

to 12 Station Terrace, East Ardsley, a small town situated between Leeds and Wakefield. Never one to forget his roots, Ernie paid a return visit to the place in 1966 when, along with Eric, he opened a Youth Club there. His house was a simple end-of-terrace cottage beside an embankment near the railway station that was on the branch line to Bradford. Sadly it is another of Ernie's early homes that no longer exists, having been demolished in the early seventies to make way for the new M62 motorway. So close were they to the tracks that whenever a train hurtled past it shook the rooms. Far from being a nuisance, young Ernie enjoyed the sensation of that locomotive thundering through the night, the noise and the power of it was intoxicating.

With the front room overlooking the railway, out back the view was scarcely any better—a turnip field and the unsightly hovel that was the outside lavatory where Ernie had to sit and whistle or sing because there wasn't a lock. No loo paper either, instead you made do with the *News of the World* cut into squares and hung on a nail.

As a kid Ernie whiled away the hours reading comics or playing in a shed made out of railway sleepers that stood in the front yard, where he also kept rabbits. In little Ernie's fervid imagination that plain old shed became a castle under siege or sometimes a Red Indian fort. Maybe there was a big powwow going on when Ernie lit a campfire inside it one day using old newspapers, or was it an effort to just keep warm? In either case, the result was a blaze that spread instantly among the dry timber and Ernie ran into the house for help, but no amount of effort prevented the shed from being totally destroyed. It was the only time Ernie recalled his father ever giving him a thick ear.

By this time Connie's father had retired and bought a pub, The New Inn at Farsley near Pudsey, which is still in operation today. The family used to visit them occasionally and Ernie never forgot this brash and austere man, and the constant living in hope that one day he might bend down to his size, open his little palm and drop some coins into it; no such luck. His grandmother was so desperate for money for the housekeeping she'd take it herself from the pub till.

When Connie's mother passed away the family all went up to Pudsey for the funeral. Her coffin stood supported by two chairs in the front room as the mourners paid their brief respects. Ernie, then in his early teens, walked up and on tiptoes looked inside. There she was, serenity itself, her hands placed as if in prayer, her soft white hair combed to frame a face that seemed almost young again. Ernie recalled thinking that she looked at total peace. Years later when Ernie's father died the thought of seeing him laid in an open coffin chilled his blood and he refused to enter the room where the coffin lay until after the lid had been fastened down. 'He had meant too much to me alive for me to be able to look on his waxen face in death.'

One of the most important venues to put on their act was the Holbeck working-men's club, close to the grounds of Leeds United FC. Here all the club secretaries and promoters in the greater Leeds area would turn up to watch and if they liked what they saw held up their hand and the performers would traipse round from table to table filling their little notebook with future club dates. As Carson and Kid, or as they later billed themselves Bert Carson and his Little

16

Wonder or sometimes even The Two Tetleys, named in honour of the local brew, Harry and Ernie were always in demand, but Harry knew that what he was doing was highly illegal. There were laws governing child entertainers and when he started at seven Ernie was well below the permitted age. Letters from school about his inattention and general malaise had increased and the local education authority sought to stop father and son performing. Harry was having none of it; the extra income Ernie helped bring in took priority over the damage it was clearly doing to his education. And so he arranged to play venues in towns further afield where they weren't so well known. Then, if the authorities caught up with them, next time they'd play somewhere like Wakefield before quietly slipping back into their old haunts in Leeds or Bradford. In the end Ernie was sure the authorities simply gave up on them.

For a while it became an elaborate game of cat and mouse. It was certainly fun for Ernie, but there is a disagreeable sense that Harry and also Connie exploited their son, almost to the point where they were using him as a meal ticket. It was obvious that Ernie was the selling point of the double act and the reason they were so heavily in demand, so in essence he'd become the family's main breadwinner. Both parents knew a good thing when they saw it and even the threat to Ernie's education didn't make them stop. 'He was out working at age seven. Slavery, really,' is how Doreen sees it. 'Both his mother and father just regarded him as a workhorse.'

Placid though Ernie might have appeared on the outside throughout his life, he was driven by a work ethic instilled in him from very early in

17

his childhood, a childhood that Doreen believes affected him immensely. This need to always work never left him. 'Everything was about work. Even towards the end of his life he was agonizing about where he could have done things better. One thing Ernie told me about those days I shall never, ever forget. The family were on holiday in Cleethorpes one year. Everyone else had a carefree time, but Ernie always had to leave the beach at 3 p.m. to go to work. He'd been booked at a local theatre to pay for their holiday.'

Seeing the profits they made being siphoned off by his dad, Ernie had arrived at the opinion that his endeavours should be rewarded in some way. And so he came up with a cunning plan. At one gig he arranged for some of his friends to mingle with the audience and at the point in the act where he delivered his frenetic clog dance to start throwing coins onto the stage. As he'd hoped, the rest of the audience followed suit and pretty soon the stage was raining pennies. 'Not copper, silver!' yelled Ernie, getting perhaps a bit too cocky. By the close he'd collected two shillings, which he kept in a drawer in his bedroom. It was the first money he ever earned as a performer.

In the early spring of 1936, when Ernie was eleven years old, he was launched for the first time into the legitimate theatre. Every year Bradford's Alhambra Theatre staged a charity show that celebrated the region's child entertainers. Entitled, rather unfortunately, the Nignog Revue, it was a big social event, sponsored by the local newspaper the *Bradford Telegraph and Argus*, and played to packed houses, with all profits going to the King George Memorial Playing Fields Fund. Such was Ernie's growing reputation that he was asked to participate,

18

an appearance that warranted his first notice. The critic of the *Stage* newspaper, the entertainment profession's very own periodical, remarked that 'comedian, Ernest Wiseman, scores with the house'. What always remained vivid in Ernie's memory about that show was not his performance but the party for the young cast held afterwards, with cake and jelly and orange squash in abundance and every child left with a present to take home.

The organization behind the revue was the Nignog Club, which was extremely popular throughout the 1930s and 1940s. Thousands of children were members, joining for a small sixpenny fee and getting in return an enamelled brass badge, a newsletter and a gift on their birthday, a real treat for those many children who came from disadvantaged backgrounds, like Ernie. One volunteer took such pity on Ernie, seeing he was always turning up for club events in just his wellies, that she went out and bought him a proper pair of shoes.

Growing up in a household where money was scarce, Ernie did without many things that most other children took for granted. 'There was never a birthday cake, for instance,' claims Doreen. 'And very few presents because he was away working so much. That's why in later life I would always try to make his birthday special. I made sure he always had plenty of parcels to open, even if some of them came from our dog.'

Doreen believes that Ernie's passion for cars—at one point he had four in the garage, including a yellow Rolls-Royce—stemmed from his years growing up with very little to play with. 'To him they were just like belated toys. The Teddy Bear

Society wrote to him once. They asked him for one of his bears to auction for charity; they assumed every child had a teddy bear. But Ernie never had one, so I had to go out and buy one.'

The club also organized sports events and taught youngsters to swim. And there were outdoor activities like cycling trips, which for many kids growing up in grimy, factory-clogged areas was possibly their first exposure to the beauty of the Yorkshire countryside. For children like Ernie, with an artistic bent, there was, of course, the club's annual revue at the Alhambra. But Ernie did other shows for them, too. Leslie Sands, a contemporary of his from that time who went on to carve out a modest career as a stage and television actor, recalled that he and the young Ernie were part of a theatrical troupe who entertained at the opening of an old people's home in Morecambe where the guest of honour was the distinguished playwright J.B. Priestley. After the performance Priestley made a point of gathering up the youngsters and then sitting down with them at the side of the small makeshift stage to talk about his life in the theatre.

For the next two years Ernie performed in the annual Nignog Revue, while still appearing in the clubs with his dad, gaining huge experience and building up his self-confidence appearing in front of houses that regularly topped 2,000. Given his own little routine, Ernie would come onstage leading a Shetland pony before launching into, 'The Lambeth Walk'. Other times he dressed in drag as a little girl to sing, 'A Little Bit Independent'.

On the same bill in 1937 was a budding young performer by the name of Harold Gilderdale who in the late 1970s recalled to his local newspaper, 'I can always remember Ernie because his hands and face were scrubbed so clean that they almost shone. And his flair for comedy was blatantly obvious.' Gilderdale then took out a yellowing piece of paper to show the reporter, on it was scrawled a humorous rhyme that Ernie had written and that Harold had kept ever since. It read:

The boy stood on the burning deck
Selling peas penny a peck
Did he ever wash his neck?
Did he heck.

TWO

KNEE DEEP IN SUCCESS

Harry always rather fancied that Ernie might follow in his footsteps and go into the railways: 'Start by shovelling coal and in a few years you'll be an engine driver, my son.' It was a far more secure profession than show business. But show business was where it appeared little Ernie was headed and certainly his parents didn't stand in his way. There was the occasion when father and son were travelling to a gig by train and overheard two theatricals talking in the next carriage. Wasting no time, Harry gatecrashed the pair's conversation and made Ernie perform an impromptu audition in the cramped compartment. 'Rather barefaced cheek, perhaps,' recalled Ernie. 'But a measure of how keen Dad was to get me onstage.'

This continuing success was offset by

unhappiness at school, thanks to a brutal teacher who took perverse pleasure in humiliating him. Ernie had left the infant school, which he'd enjoyed and been happy at, and was now attending East Ardsley Boys School. It was a large, Gothic-looking Victorian building and the staff upheld a rigid discipline, including a Mr Lodge who, according to Ernie's classmate, Geoffrey Bell, had an interesting method of punishment. 'His form of torture, as it were, if he caught you misbehaving, was to get his knuckle and brush it straight across your forehead which could really hurt.'

As for the headmaster, he made a habit of sneaking up behind any pupil in his class not paying attention and pulling hard on their ears. As Ernie tended to drift off during lessons, especially on Mondays after a weekend busy performing, he was often on the receiving end of this harsh treatment. He was also on intimate terms with the cane, administered because of his lack of attention. But such physical abuse was as nothing to the psychological mistreatment meted out by one specific teacher who knew of Ernie's local fame as a performer. Nicknamed The Toad, this teacher took real delight in making Ernie stand in front of the class for the duration of the lesson. 'Come out, tap dancer!' he'd say malevolently. Ernie never forgot it. 'Whatever he hoped to achieve by such public ridicule I do not know. But its effect was to turn me against the school and all it stood for and to alienate me from my classmates.'

A strange incident made The Toad stop. One of Ernie's classmates was a boy with serious learning difficulties, but one day The Toad viciously caned him for producing poor homework. He was in huge distress afterwards and Ernie and a few others observed large bloody stripes on the back of his thighs. Worried about more injuries they slowly removed the lad's trousers to see that his backside looked as if Captain Bligh had gone to town on it with a cat-o'-nine-tails. Ernie was so outraged that after lessons he took the boy up and down the streets of East Ardsley and showed the aftermath of his caning to parents who had children at the school. In adult life Ernie was to look back on that incident and find it hard to believe he had the gumption to do it.

In class the next morning The Toad remained silent on the matter; Ernie knew he knew what had happened, but nothing was said. And from that day on he no longer mocked Ernie in front of his classmates.

It didn't alter his overall impression of school much. It probably didn't help that Ernie was not the most upwardly mobile of pupils, or in his own words, 'just plain dumb'. So if schooling wasn't moulding his personality, what was? Performing, of course. 'Entertaining was a personality prop which helped me to cover up a deep-rooted shyness and sense of inadequacy.' Performing onstage allowed Ernie to break out of his shell and become the kind of person he wanted to be, without fear of ridicule; it was a safe environment. 'I was able to step out of my very private little world and be an entirely different person, a cheeky chappie.'

There's a good example of this. Often at the end of their act he and his dad would sometimes be invited by punters to sit with them and share a drink: fruit juice for Ernie, a half pint of Tetley's for Harry. One time the house band was playing a popular tune of the day, 'The Greatest Mistake of my Life'. Everyone was singing along when a man at the table looked at Ernie and said, 'Heh, your flies are undone.'

Ernie looked down and saw the awful evidence. 'Yes,' he said. And then, quick as a flash, 'It's the greatest mistake of my life.'

The whole table cracked up. That single incident left a huge impression on Ernie, not only because of the laugh he got, but also because of the realization that it was only because he was still in his stage costume that he had the nerve to make a joke.

Talent shows were another useful tool to build up confidence and experience and when Harry learned that a week-long revue was being staged at the Pavilion Theatre in nearby Morley, which also included a talent contest for local performers, he wasted little time entering Ernie. Held between 14–19 March 1938, *Chuse Ow*, as the revue was called, had on the bill your typical variety performers, singers, comics and dancing girls, but it was the 'discoveries' element that seemed to catch the public's interest, not least because of the fact that it wasn't a panel of experts doing the judging, but the audience themselves. On entering the theatre everyone was issued with voting papers and asked to choose their favourite act of the evening. During the week all the slips were collected and counted, so it was the audience who determined which five performers made it through to the grand final on Saturday night. You could say it was an early version of *The X Factor*.

With ages ranging from six to twenty-nine and acts as varied as ventriloquists, acrobats and impersonators, Ernie certainly had his work cut out to make an impact in the preliminary rounds. Instead of his usual gear, Ernie walked onstage in short trousers and a flat cap but his routine was more or less the same: a tap dance and a quick volley of jokes. One in particular is of note. It went like this: 'When I awake in the morning I toss a coin. If it comes down heads I go out to play. If it comes down tails I go to the pictures. If it comes down on its edge I go to school.'

The joke is significant because years later it was recycled by Eric and Ernie during one of their very first performances together as a double act. This time Ernie posed the question: 'What shall we do today?' to which Eric replied: 'Let's toss a coin. Heads we'll go to the dog racing. Tails we'll go to a football match. If it comes down on its edge we'll go to work.' What's interesting here is that not only had Ernie fallen very quickly into the role of the straight man, but was also happy to feed Eric a punchline that had once been his own.

Come Saturday night Ernie found himself in the final, but if he'd hoped to win over the sympathy of the audience because of his tender age, one look at his fellow finalists soon scuppered that idea; none of them was over the age of thirteen.

While the voting was close, in the end it was Ernie's comedy song-and-tap-dance routine that, according to reports, 'brought the house down' and won him a first prize of three guineas. This in spite of losing one of his clogs over the course of the evening and having to make do with one clog and one rubber-soled shoe. But his elation over winning was cut short when his father took the three guineas off him. The runners-up prize of a box of chocolates now looked much more inviting, especially as he watched the other kids merrily tucking into them as he was led outside by Harry.

In the autumn of 1938 Ernie's big break arrived. Bryan Michie was a leading show-business impresario who toured the British Isles searching for juvenile talent to feature in his variety shows. His job was also to bring such performers to the attention of the celebrated bandleader Jack Hylton, who also produced theatrical entertainments in London. A former actor, Michie was well known for his ability to spot and develop young talent. When Harry got to hear that Michie was holding open auditions at the Leeds Empire he sent Ernie down there.

Feeling he'd done enough to impress, Ernie sweated for weeks to hear any news. None was forthcoming. Dispirited he went back to performing with his dad; there was also the added bonus of being asked to perform on local BBC radio. Singing 'Let's Have a Tiddly at the Milk Bar', Ernie was rewarded with a two-guinea fee and was so proud that he kept the contract his entire life, where it held pride of place in a frame on the wall of his study at home. Harry, of course, kept the two guineas.

As the months passed Ernie had all but forgotten about his audition, when in December a letter arrived from none other than Jack Hylton himself. As he began reading Ernie could scarcely contain his excitement, Michie had been so impressed by his audition that he'd personally contacted Hylton about him and now he was being invited down to London to try out for Hylton's West End show *Band Waggon*. Based on the hugely successful BBC radio comedy programme, *Band Waggon* featured

26

thirty-eight-year-old former concert party and seaside entertainer Arthur Askey, and its cheerful medley of music, comedy and dance was packing them in. Ernie thrust the letter into his father's hand. Harry sat down in the kitchen and read it aloud to Connie, while Ernie stood there pleased as punch.

On Friday 6 January 1939, Harry and Ernie travelled down to the big smoke, full of hope and excited anticipation. According to Jack Hylton Jnr, Bryan Michie called him asking if he didn't mind picking them up at the railway station. 'He told my dad that Ernest would be arriving by train at whatever time, presumably at Euston. When my dad asked how he would recognize Ernest, Bryan replied, 'Oh you can't miss him—he'll be wearing a dinner jacket and clogs!'

Quickly they made their way to the Princes Theatre, today the Shaftesbury, and were directed to Hylton's private office. Far from overawed, little Ernie performed the very same routine he'd done months earlier for Michie. Hylton leaned back in his chair, obviously impressed; he'd been in the business a long time and knew his stuff. In his late forties, Hylton was a down-to-earth individual, blessed with beguiling simplicity but a forceful nature given to fits of temper that evaporated as quickly as they materialized. Looking at father and son Hylton smiled, but what he said took both Ernie and Harry by complete surprise. He was putting Ernie into the show tonight!

So, there was Ernie, thirteen years old, totally untried in professional theatre, completely unknown to mainstream audiences, sharing the same stage with *Band Waggon*'s established star and

27

top of the bill, Arthur Askey. Even Ernie was to admit that this wonderful succession of events had 'a fairy-tale quality' about them. It was incredible and the newspapers weren't slow on seizing upon the story, creating headlines that Ernie never forgot: 'I had to pinch myself to make sure I wasn't dreaming,' he said. 'Fame in a night for thirteen-year-old', said one. 'Comedian, thirteen, hailed as great discovery', went another and, 'Railway porter's son star overnight', heralded a third.

The following day the *Daily Express* said: 'Ernest Wiseman—one quarter Max Miller, one quarter Sydney Howard, and the other half a mixture of all the comics who ever amused you. His timing and confidence are remarkable. At thirteen he is an old-time performer.' Certainly it was his supreme confidence that impressed most of the critics that night. 'He came on without a sign of nerves, full of Yorkshire cockiness, sang—in a voice that made microphones unnecessary—"I'm Knee Deep in Daisies" and "Let's Have a Tiddly at the Milk Bar", cracked a pair of north country jokes and did a whirlwind step dance with terrific aplomb and efficiency.'

Even forty years later, when asked, Arthur Askey could remember Ernie's West End debut, recalling him as, 'a fresh-faced, delightful kid, totally stage-struck. He had a good singing voice, and he was a very fair little dancer.' In fact the two later became good friends and often met up. Doreen recalls an evening in the early sixties when the three of them went to the cinema to see Alfred Hitchcock's *Psycho*. 'I have to say I'm not a fan of horror films, and this was no exception. The film was very scary so I really wasn't looking forward to it. Arthur was sitting directly behind us, and I think he knew I was a bit jumpy. When that infamous shower scene began I knew something awful was going to happen. I remember holding on to Ernie's hand very tightly, expecting the worst—and just at the moment when you saw the knife appear Arthur leant forward and put his hands around my neck. Well, I must have leapt at least six feet into the air. Ernie said I went white. God knows how much noise I made. He and Arthur absolutely wet themselves.'

It must have been a nerve-racking experience, taking to that vast stage for the first time, not only performing in front of a sophisticated West End audience, a world apart from the punters in the working-class clubs he was used to, but backed up by a full orchestra, where before a bored pianist usually provided his accompaniment. The reason the critics saw not a shred of nerves was probably because he was in total shock. Ernie later admitted that the whole thing passed by in a blur. Harry was perhaps the best judge, sitting in the auditorium. After the show he came backstage and, full of pride, sought out his son, tears welling up in his eyes.

With such great reviews coming in for little Ernie, Hylton knew he was on to a good thing and immediately signed him up to a five-year contract, after obtaining permission from Harry. From picking up pennies onstage, Ernie was now on six pounds a week, three times the wage his father earned at his latest job in the parcel depot at Leeds Central Station. It's hard to believe that deep down Harry didn't feel humiliated by this, his young son financially out-muscling him, but he was pleased to see Ernie settling down and being well looked after. There was even an offer from Hylton to stay on in London and be a sort of paid personal assistant to Ernie. Harry was sorely tempted but ultimately forces back home in Leeds made up his mind for him. 'Harry desperately wanted to stay to look after Ernie,' says Doreen. 'It was his mum, Connie, who said no and forced him to come back. You can understand why, of course, but it really upset him to have to leave his boy.'

One wonders what gamut of emotions Harry must have been feeling on that long train journey back to Leeds. Of course he was delighted that Ernie had been taken on by one of the most prominent men in show business, but at the same time he knew it marked the end of their double act. Not only was he losing his partner, Harry felt like he was losing his son, too. Ernie had always been the closest of his children. It wasn't until years later, after Harry died, that Connie mustered enough courage to tell Ernie that his father returned home after that London trip a broken man. He tried to interest the other children in taking Ernie's place in the act but they didn't have the talent for it. Harry's own heart wasn't in the enterprise any more and he soon gave up performing altogether. Then his health began to steadily grow worse with rheumatoid arthritis. Connie always used to say it had been brought on by the malnutrition he suffered as a boy. 'He came from the poorer end of Leeds,' said Ernie, 'and there never was enough food.' Soon Harry had to virtually give up working, so the whole family now relied on the money Ernie was sending home. Of course, living in London Ernie was oblivious to all this, so it must have come as an awful shock to find out that his father never truly got over the break up of their partnership.

THREE

ON THE BAND WAGGON

Mrs Rodway was a plain-looking woman, a nanny of a kind, hired by Hylton to keep a matronly eye on the young cast members of *Band Waggon*. Ernie didn't think he needed such mollycoddling though, as he boasted to a reporter the morning after his West End debut when asked who would be looking after him in London. 'Nobody,' he announced. 'Why should they?' He was plenty cocky. Another reporter enquired where he came from and when Ernie told him a place between Leeds and Wakefield the scribe replied, 'Isn't Wakefield the prison where they play cricket?'

'Aye,' said Ernie, feeling confident. 'But the warders always win!'

Contrary to Ernie's desire for independence Mrs Rodway took firm charge of him, especially his finances, arranging for three pounds out of his wages to be sent home to his parents every week, then paying his meals and accommodation out of the rest and giving him five shillings regular spending money. She also opened a bank account to deposit whatever remained from his wages; Ernie, though, took charge of the savings book.

He was also installed in a small flat above an Italian restaurant on St Martin's Lane, just off Trafalgar Square, nice and close to the theatre, with three other cast juveniles and Mrs Rodway, whose beady eye was never off them. After a couple of weeks Ernie began to feel pangs of homesickness, not helped by the fact that he never received a single letter from his parents. 'And if Connie was bothered about him staying on his own in London she never let on,' says Doreen. 'Ernie was very hurt and lonely initially.' Most of all he missed his dad, the camaraderie they'd shared on the road, those late-night bus journeys when he'd fall asleep huddled up tight to him.

However, as he settled into his new life those feelings eventually dissipated, helped considerably by two women in the show's band who took him under their wing. One was Doreen Stephens and the other was Pat Marlowe. Doreen Stephens was the singer with Jack Hylton's Band and was famous for performing 'Wish Me Luck as you Wave me Goodbye'. Later on she sang with Billy Cotton. 'Ernie also got on well with Arthur Askey's daughter, Anthea,' recalls Doreen. 'She was only about five or six at the time but he enjoyed looking out for her. It was like having a family again, except that everyone was in the same boat.'

Most importantly, though, Jack Hylton filled the space left behind by Harry and became a surrogate father to Ernie. It began with little acts of kindness. Meals served up to him from the Italian restaurant below didn't suit Ernie at all, the dishes were far too exotic for a simple Yorkshire lad; what the hell was lasagne anyway? Sensing this, Hylton often invited Ernie into his office after a show to share his dinner, sometimes a large pork pie he'd arranged to be specially sent down to London from a butcher he knew in Bolton, or maybe a plate of cold tripe. There were also little extra bits of cash for Ernie and when Hylton noticed him shivering outside the theatre in a cheap raincoat, the next day in his dressing room a thick brand-new overcoat was hanging in his wardrobe. On another occasion, Hylton instructed his manager to take Ernie to a department store and kit him out in a new set of clothes; he ended up with underwear, socks, shirts, ties, suits, and as a bonus two suitcases to put it all in.

Why did Hylton take so warmly to Ernie? Perhaps the answer is that well-worn cliché: that he saw something of himself in the little performer. Hylton hailed from Bolton and working-class parents, his own father had been an amateur singer working in northern clubs, while little Jack began by playing the piano in pubs. As Arthur Askey would later observe, 'Ernie was rather like a young Hylton then and I think that is one reason Jack liked him so much. He looked on him almost as a son.'

As for Ernie, Hylton wasn't just his boss but an inspirational figure, proof that someone from a similar background to his own could rise to the very top, and that class and where you came from didn't matter in the theatre as much as it did in other walks of life.

Hylton was important in other ways, too. It was he who suggested that Ernie change his name from Wiseman to the much snappier Wise. He also helped shape his act, straight-away getting rid of the clogs and replacing them with far more stylish tap shoes. Out went his bowler hat in favour of a straw boater; gone were all the shabby, comic clothes and he was put into a smart suit. Ernie now looked more like Maurice Chevalier, a sophisticated song-and-dance man rather than a music-hall comic like Max Miller. In essence, what Hylton was doing was changing Ernie's whole image: 'He knocked the raw edges off my act.'

Out went the twee and rather infantile songs, too, like 'Let's Have a Tiddly at the Milk Bar', replaced by more modern, sophisticated tunes. Ernie appreciated Hylton's input but with hindsight perhaps felt that his transformation into a slicker performer made him an adult before he was ready, 'a child without a childhood', as he described it. Confident onstage, like a seasoned pro, offstage Ernie was still immature and naive; many children his own age knew far more about the important things in life like girls, swearing and smoking. Performing and living in the adult world of the theatre, Ernie was to a large extent cosseted and sheltered from outside forces, existing in a cocoon. Although he did get a taste of normal work when he was installed as an office boy running errands, making tea and such, not only for Arthur Askey but also Tommy Handley, a popular comedian of the period best known for the BBC radio series *It's That Man Again* (ITMA).

When *Band Waggon* closed in May 1939, due to sliding ticket sales, Hylton took the show out on tour around the country, with Ernie in tow. And a theatrical touring company is an even stranger environment to be brought up in. On their arrival in a new town the local education officer would turn up at the theatre to see that Ernie and the other young artists were off back to their digs after the curtain came down no later than 10 p.m.; a minute over and they were not permitted to perform the following evening. By law they also had to attend a school wherever the tour pitched up in. That made things even more difficult for Ernie, as he felt a total outsider with nothing in common with the other pupils, and afraid to form friendships, none of which would last beyond a few weeks anyway. Being picked up at the school gates by Hylton's chauffeur-driven Buick hardly endeared him to the other kids, either. It was certainly an odd existence, picked up at break, taken to the theatre for rehearsals, and then driven back for afternoon classes.

If Ernie was lonely at this time, all that was about to change. Very shortly he was about to meet the boy who would provide not only friendship but also a professional relationship that would last for decades.

FOUR

ENTER ERIC

That spring Ernie was on tour in Manchester. The procedure was always the same: at each new venue, usually a large cinema that could seat over a thousand people, talented youngsters from the surrounding area were invited to come along and audition for Hylton. The turnover of little sprogs was sometimes fierce. As Hylton's child prodigy it was usual for Ernie to be in attendance, sitting quite prominently in the front stalls, within earshot of Hylton should he wish to offer an opinion.

One afternoon in Manchester, Ernie's attention was caught by a tall, gangly boy wearing glasses and a dopey expression on his face. He'd walked nervously onto the stage, followed by a rather stern-looking woman that Ernie guessed was the young lad's mother. What struck Ernie the most was the costume he was wearing, a beret perched comically on the side of his head with a kiss-curl on his forehead, and a large evening suit held together with a comedy safety pin; it was exactly the same gag Ernie had used years before. Ernie must have smiled and thought to himself: OK, show me what you've got.

The boy began with a song and then quickly went into an impression of Flanagan and Allen, which impressed Ernie no end, especially the way he'd managed to make the audience believe those two famous comics were right there on that stage. Just then, one of the members of the band sitting nearby nudged him and said, 'Bye then, Ernie. Things won't be the same with this new lad around. What are you going to do now?' It was meant in jest but got Ernie feeling, if not jealous, then certainly under pressure that his exulted position in the eyes of Hylton might be under threat. 'I have to admit my self-esteem took a bit of a knock.'

Although the two boys were never introduced, nor said a single word to each other, Ernie had just met Eric. It was an encounter that left an indelible impression on them both; Eric later recalling the 'smug mug' of Ernie sat in the stalls, his 'beady eyes' watching as he walked off the stage.

While Ernie had gone from success to success with Hylton, Eric was struggling to make his mark, pushed on all the time by his mother Sadie. From an early age Sadie recognized in her son a talent for performing, or perhaps it was the realization that he wasn't good at anything else! Just a year younger than Ernie and an only child, Eric came from similar working-class stock, his father George was a labourer at the Morecambe Corporation, his meagre income supplemented by Sadie's work as a cleaner. Forced to take dance lessons that he despised and a regular entrant in local talent contests, all these efforts paid off when Eric won the local leg of a nationwide competition organized by music magazine *Melody Maker*. First prize was the chance to audition for Hylton. Sadie had travelled down with him by train all the way from his hometown of Morecambe to Manchester, 'and drummed into me that this just might be the most important day of my life,' Eric recalled. 'And she was right, of course.'

It was a tinpot dictator named Adolf Hitler who put the knackers on the *Band Waggon* tour. When war was declared in September 1939 theatres and cinemas were closed down, re-opening a few weeks later when the government realized the public needed morale-boosting entertainment. Ultimately, many of Hylton's musicians were to receive their call-up papers so he had no choice but to disband the show. That left Ernie with a dilemma, return home or, at Hylton's invitation, stay with him and his Austrian wife Fifi and their children at their home on the Sussex coast. Hylton had already been so kind to him that Ernie felt he couldn't refuse this latest offer.

Just to make sure everything was above board, Hylton wrote to Ernie's dad:

ASTORIA HOUSE
62 Shaftesbury Avenue
London W1

6th September 1939

H. Wiseman, Esq.
17 Oxley Street
Pontefract Lane
Leeds

Dear Mr Wiseman,

Ernest is staying with me at my house at the seaside. He is very welcome to stay down there with me and I shall be glad if you will let me know if this is OK or if you would prefer that he is back home with you. We have six other children there, and his being with us does not inconvenience us at all, but it is entirely up to you.

Perhaps you will reply to me to my house address—'Villa Daheim', Kingston Gorse, Sussex.

Kind regards
Yours sincerely
(Signed) Jack Hylton

Situated near Worthing, the Hylton residence was a little slice of decadence, with a chauffeur, a cook, a maid and a nanny. During the several months Ernie stayed he was given pocket money and royally fed; it was as if the Hyltons had unofficially adopted him. They wanted him to stay even longer but by January 1940 Ernie had begun to miss his real parents and wanted to go back home. Over the past year he'd only seen his mother and father fleetingly, whenever the *Band Waggon* tour had passed near Leeds. Hylton understood and even paid for his rail ticket back up to the north.

By this time the Wisemans had moved from East Ardsley and now resided at 17 Oxley Street, Pontefract Lane in Leeds. Ernie hadn't informed his parents of his decision to return, intent on making his arrival a surprise, and when he walked in he found his dad in the small living room. Harry looked up, his face registering not one flicker of warmth or happiness. 'Why did you come home?' was all he asked. 'You had it made.' Ernie was crushed.

Back home now, Ernie had no intention of restarting the double act with his father, it seemed pointless to try and recapture the magic they had before: it had gone. Nor did he have any desire to perform as a solo artist in local clubs. Even though he was only fourteen Ernie considered himself a professional entertainer now, someone who'd moved on from those kinds of venues. That left the problem of how he was going to pay his way, so he decided to go out and find a job. One of the neighbours happened to be a coalman looking for someone to help out with the heavy loads and sometimes drive the horse and cart along the cobbled streets of Leeds. The wage was well below the six pounds a week Hylton gave him, but Ernie never felt humbled or demeaned by having to lug coal around, for him the most important thing was to earn a living. And when he looked back upon his life Ernie took great pride in the fact that he never once signed on as unemployed or took any sick pay. 'I have a need to be self-sufficient, independent,' he once said. 'My early experiences schooled me in that.'

The fact that he was the eldest child also meant his brothers and sisters looked up to him, especially when he got his break in London. They knew he was the breadwinner; in fact they used to call him 'Ernie the provider'. He would always buy them sweets and comics. His sister Annie never forgot the day Ernie came into the house and said to her, 'How would you like to go to Leeds College of Music to learn the piano?' The fee was three guineas a term, a lot of money in those days, but Ernie waved that away and Annie enrolled, which in turn led to teacher training and a long and happy career, culminating in her most rewarding job, teaching physically handicapped children in London.

When Ernie was the star guest of *This Is Your Life* in 1990 his brother Gordon made this heartfelt tribute: 'We have the kindest, most considerate, generous, caring and protective brother that anyone could wish for.' There was one proviso, however, the time an eleven-year-old Ernie shot him with an air gun. Gordon was seven years old at the time, 'and Ernie managed to get hold of dad's air gun, and I don't think he knew it was loaded, at least I hope he didn't, and he managed to shoot me in the leg.' Jumping up and down with blood oozing through his sock, Gordon yelled, 'What am I going to do?'

'Limp,' Ernie said.

Back home now for three months and just at the point when he started wondering how long he could take this back-breaking work as a coalman's labourer, salvation arrived in the form of a telegram from Bryan Michie. He wanted Ernie to get up to Swansea fast to join a touring revue called *Youth Takes a Bow*. It was a show of Hylton's own devising that featured young performers who he believed had the potential to become the stars of tomorrow. Ernie packed his bag and set off. It would prove a momentous trip and his life would never be the same again..

FIVE

ERN TAKES A BOW

Ernie's arrival to take over as top of the bill on *Youth Takes a Bow* was met with great anticipation by the rest of the cast. Here was someone who had already achieved the kind of fame they all aspired to, and merited critical salutes labelling him, 'the Jack Buchanan of tomorrow' and 'Britain's own Mickey Rooney'. It wouldn't be too strong a supposition to say that the youngsters on the tour looked upon Ernie with a degree of reverence. 'I was already something of a child prodigy,' he'd say. 'A star, albeit in a limited way.'

Catching up with the tour at Crewe railway station en route to Swansea, it was here on a busy platform amidst the clamour of screaming kids chaperoned by their brassy mothers that Ernie bumped into Eric again. Ernie recognized him immediately as the gangly youth who'd done such a devastating audition back in Manchester. Hylton had obviously been impressed by him too and rewarded Eric with a place on the tour. After a month on the road Eric had become quite well established; now here was Ernie Wise about to prise away any chance he might have had of the spotlight. As they passed on the platform both managed a meek hello as they sized up the other like gladiators about to enter the Colosseum, before going off to separate compartments.

For the next few weeks they were equally stand-offish with each other. From the wings Eric would watch Ernie perform. Yeah, he did a passable tap dance, but was it enough to merit the young tyke's self-confidence, which bordered on arrogance? Eric didn't think so. 'I thought he was a big-head.' It was jealousy, too. Although only six months his senior Ernie was considerably taller (yes, taller) than Eric, as fellow *Youth Takes a Bow* performer Mary Naylor affirms: 'At the time he was a giant next to little Eric.' Ernie even began to cheekily refer to Eric as 'Sonny', which narked him considerably.

In attitude and bearing Ernie also came across as vastly more sophisticated, not least because of his stylish wardrobe. Eric still wore baggy shorts at his mother's insistence and looked like someone Richmal Crompton's Just William might bully. As Hylton's 'golden boy' Ernie also got paid more than Eric, seven pounds a week. He was totally independent now, and sent money home of his own accord. It's no surprise then that in one candid moment Eric confessed to his mum that he didn't care for Ernie Wise at all.

But Sadie saw through Ernie easily enough, and realized all that cockiness hid a desperate homesickness and a basic insecurity. The fact he was footloose and fancy free, in other words he didn't travel with a mother breathing down his neck all the time, was looked upon with awe by everyone else who felt as if they might as well have been in Stalag Luft. Yes, the theatrical mum was a formidable breed, 'as tenacious as fox terriers with a bone,' said Ernie. Travelling for years with their offspring, these women knew the business inside out and would fight tooth and nail on their behalf. Ernie, then fifteen, didn't have any of that backup, no shoulder to cry on when things got rough.

Feeling sorry for him, Sadie took to keeping her eye on Ernie, just to see he was OK, a natural consequence of which was that the boys came into contact with each other on a much more regular basis. 'I think I like Ernie Wise after all, Mum,' Eric said to Sadie one day. 'He bought me a bar of chocolate today!' On such small things are great foundations built.

In spite of the worry of the early war years *Youth Takes a Bow* managed to find an appreciative audience. The first half consisted of adult professional variety acts, while the second half was the turn of the youngsters to shine. Ernie's act was strictly song and dance; Eric was the comic. Other acts included an acrobat, a couple of singers, an impressionist and Arthur Tolcher, who played the harmonica and who years later became a running gag on the Morecambe and Wise show, rushing onstage to play a tune only to

43

be told—'Not now, Arthur!'

Undoubtedly the star of the young talent section was Mary Naylor, a very pretty singer who also played the piano. Because she was still only fourteen, Mary had to attend school and years later recalled that in both Middlesbrough and West Hartlepool she got lost walking back to the theatre. 'So little Ernie Wise, being the gallant kid that he was, until I left school a month or so later, was always at the schoolyard half an hour before I came out, to see me home, so I wouldn't get lost!'

Just in case Ernie forgot to turn up and Mary did get lost again her father gave her a sixpence piece that would pay for a taxi, which she kept in a handkerchief with a knot in it stuffed down her navy blue gym knickers. Mary fondly recalled how in towns up and down the country Eric and Ernie always insisted that she went with them to the movie houses in the afternoon. 'There was a thing they called "on the card", which meant that we'd give our card to the cashier and when she saw that we were "pros" and we were playing the theatre of that town, they would let us in. But just in case they didn't, the two boys always knew that I had a sixpence, enough to get the three of us in to the movie house! So, I always wondered, did they really insist that I went with them because they loved me or . . . because of the lousy sixpence I had in my gym knickers?'

Mary and the boys grew very close. When her father got his call-up papers both Eric and Ernie organized a photograph to be taken of them along with Mary, as they said, 'Every soldier needs to have his beloved children's picture in his pocket when he is ordered to go over the top.' They also chipped in to buy him a farewell gift of the best cigar in the local newsagent's. Although when they heard that Mary's dad was rejected by the army owing to ill health, both grabbed the cigar and sped over to the shop as fast as they could to get their money back.

There were other very attractive young ladies involved in the show during its long run, but Ernie was no gallivanting Romeo, far from it. 'I was too keen to get on in show business to devote much ardour to the chase.' Besides, Connie had always warned her son against the opposite sex. 'Keep those scheming hussies at a distance,' was her mantra. 'They're either after your body or your money.'

Even with Sadie keeping an eye on him Ernie still had huge responsibilities. He was expected to make his own travel arrangements to and from each venue and find his own accommodation. Usually it wasn't too much of a strain finding rooms, but when *Youth Takes a Bow* landed in Oxford Ernie had, for the first time, failed to book ahead and with the city practically overrun by troops, vacant rooms were at a premium. In a blackout he trudged from one B&B to the next, knocking on doors, only to be turned away by successive landladies. Come ten o'clock Ernie was desperate. Wondering if he might be forced to camp out on the street, he tried another boarding house but got the same response. The sound of his pleading was carried up the stairs and overheard by none other than Sadie, a guest there with Eric. 'Is that our Ernie?' she said, coming down in her nightie. 'We can't let her turn the lad away.' The boys could both share the double bed, Sadie told the landlady, she was happy with the single. It was agreed.

The next morning at breakfast Sadie suggested that to avoid a similar occurrence Ernie might wish to travel with them from gig to gig and she'd look after all the arrangements. 'So, would you like to come with us? You can sleep with Eric. It will be a saving.' Ernie happily agreed. And Sadie smiled; she could sense the little kid was aching to be mothered.

From that moment on, Ernie, Eric and Sadie became almost inseparable. And being so much in each other's pockets Eric and Ernie grew even closer, bonded in fact; they'd laugh and joke together, impersonate their beloved Abbott and Costello and try out their solo spots in the show for the other to critique.

According to Ernie's old school pal Geoffrey Bell, Ernie took Eric back to his old haunts in Leeds a couple of times during this period, meeting up in the back room of a grocer's shop belonging to their friend Eddie Ward. 'There were five of us usually,' Bell recalls. 'And this included a lad called Eric Bartholomew. He was a friend of Ernest's who used to come and visit and they were always gagging and working out routines. They were just friends at the time and not working together. There was a piano at the shop and Ernie used to start off with a dance while I played.' Years later Bell joined ENSA and, abroad in places like Naples, was in army shows as a pianist for Gracie Fields. 'But back in those early days I would play the piano and Eric and Ernie would dance and do funny routines. I suppose it was the start of what would become Morecambe and Wise, although I knew them as Wiseman and Bartholomew.'

Soon it became clear that not only did Eric and

Ernie share a natural rapport and understanding, often finishing off each other's sentences, but a genuine talent. However, the thought of pooling their separate abilities into a double act never entered anyone's head and came about purely by accident.

In November 1940 the tour moved from Birmingham to Coventry, but the small digs Sadie had pre-booked had been damaged in an air raid, so she thought it best to remain in their digs in Birmingham and simply commute the twenty-one miles by train each day, a journey made longer by incessant delays because of the blackout. As usual the boys were supercharged with adrenalin after a show, cracking jokes, shrieking, jumping about, the works. Poor Sadie, who'd ask them to quieten down but got a fistful of cheeky comebacks for her trouble, had suffered this barrage for weeks. At least back in their rooms she could always walk out, here in a railway compartment there was no escape and she was tired, cold and wanted to sleep. Finally, in despair, she made an off-the-cuff suggestion. 'Look, instead of all this malarkey, why don't you put your brains to some use? Try and do a double act of your own. All you need are a few jokes and a song.'

The idea wasn't as outrageous as it sounded and the boys responded with immediate enthusiasm. There and then they decided, with a maturity belying their fifteen years, to split everything they might earn in this grand venture straight down the middle. Incredibly this would be the one and only agreement Eric and Ernie ever drew up between themselves in the entire course of their career; and it was settled on a handshake.

The next step was a little trickier: to come up with a funny and suitable routine.

Almost unconsciously Ernie had taken on the role of the straight man because, as Sadie saw it, 'he was the good-looking personality boy.' Eric had always been the comedian, so why change? Although, according to Ernie he was reluctant at first to take on that role in the new act. 'There was a part of Eric that longed to be a sort of Cary Grant figure, and part of him that resented being the comic while the straight man had the style.' Such reservations soon fell away when he started getting the majority of the laughs.

For weeks the boys worked flat out cobbling together material, mostly old jokes they'd heard from other acts, and painstakingly rehearsing a soft-shoe dance to 'By the Light of the Silvery Moon' until they'd got all the moves down pat. From the very beginning Sadie believed that the two boys had a chance of making it because they were both prepared to sweat blood and were utterly professional in their approach. 'They always worked very hard. It was perfection or nothing.'

Their act, fine-tuned to within an inch of its life and lasting four minutes, was finally unveiled before Bryan Michie, in the hope he might put it in the show, but his reaction was somewhat muted. He didn't quite know where it could fit since it would mean dropping one of the other acts, and Michie visualized being chased around the stalls by an irate theatrical mum wielding a handbag. The final decision didn't rest with him either, only Hylton had authority over such matters and the next time he was catching up with the tour was in Liverpool that summer. The boys would just have to wait till then. 'Leave it to me,' said Ernie, turning to face Eric. 'I'll tackle Mr Hylton.'

As the tour slowly wound its way to Liverpool, Eric and Ernie simply had to make do with performing their contracted solo spots, even though both felt their future now lay as a double act. All the time Sadie was in the background, pushing them on. She even invested in a tape recorder, a bulky thing it was, for the boys to record their routines and play them back in order to methodically analyse and perfect things. It was a clever idea and indicative of the kind of thorough woman Sadie was, leading Ernie to call her 'the key element' in the growth of the act.

Described by Ernie as a small, but indomitable woman 'with a tungsten carbide core of solid ambition', who chain-smoked roll-ups made out of tobacco she took out of other people's old fags, Sadie has passed into the mythology of Morecambe and Wise.

Far from your average showbiz mum, Sadie was intelligent, reassuringly down to earth and blessed with a sharp tongue. You always knew where you were with Sadie; she called a spade a spade.

Her relationship with Ernie was certainly an interesting one. Taking the youngster under her wing on the road she virtually became a second mother to him. If she could have adopted him one gets the sense she would have, so close did they become. According to Eric's widow Joan, Sadie loved Ernie almost as much as she loved her own son. She'd never do something for Eric unless she could also do it for Ernie. She treated them both exactly the same, there was no favouritism.

This must have grated a little with Eric, especially his mother's assertion that Ernie was always the more eager and helpful. At train stations

Sadie would look and there'd be Eric helping out one of the pretty girls and her mother with their luggage. Exasperated, Sadie would then see Ernie by her side, holding her cases. 'It's all right, Sadie, I'm helping you.' It's no surprise that one of Eric's early nicknames for Ernie was Lilywhite, because he was so spotless in his character. 'Ernie never did wrong,' said Sadie. 'Not that he was prim or prissy, or goody-goody, which is a person who just acts good but is really not good inside. Ernie was just naturally good, naturally truthful, fair and honest.'

At last the moment of truth arrived when *Youth Takes a Bow* rolled up at the Liverpool Empire. Coming in early, the boys watched as Hylton's car drove up to the theatre and he got out and strode into the lobby. Racing in through the stage door, Eric and Ernie were just in time to see Hylton walk into Michie's dressing room. Ernie tapped Eric reassuringly on the elbow, straightened his tie and entered. Hylton looked up and his face immediately broke into a warm, welcoming smile. 'Hello, Ernie, how are you getting on?'

'Fine, Mr Hylton. Yes, fine. By the way, we've got a little double act together; Eric Bartholomew and I. Would you like to see it?'

'Certainly. Come along during the interval.'

Hylton was true to his word and watched the boys go through their routine. It was nerve-racking to say the least; their entire future could be decided in the next few minutes. When they'd finished Hylton looked intently at them. There was a pause. It seemed to hang in the air for an eternity. 'That was great, boys,' he finally said. 'But take out that bloody awful song.' Then, turning to Michie, 'Put them on this Friday night.'

28 August 1941 at the Liverpool Empire marked the professional debut of Bartholomew and Wise. Hylton and Sadie both stood in the wings watching, Sadie bursting with pride. 'I can see the two of them there on the stage in the full glare of the lights,' she recalled in 1973. 'So very young but already such ardent and hard-working little troupers. The audience loved them. I was in tears.'

The audience did indeed warm to the boys, but it wasn't so much the material they responded to, rather the performers themselves. Even in their earliest flowering Eric and Ernie seemed perfectly matched. Hylton, too, saw enough to warrant them continuing at the tour's next port of call, a week-long residency in Edinburgh.

Ernie himself later admitted that their act was far from perfect, which is understandable, but what it lacked in finesse the boys made up for in sheer enthusiasm and energy. Some of their very early material was almost naïve in its content. Eric would appear holding a fishing rod with an apple on the end. 'You can't catch fish with an apple,' said Ernie, 'you need a worm.' To which Eric replied, 'Ah, the worm's in the apple.' Cue spontaneous eruption of laughter, hopefully. 'It was terrible stuff, really,' said Ernie.

Here's another example, this time a military skit.

Ernie: You're advancing towards the enemy and suddenly you get an ear shot off. What would you do?

Eric: I'd carry on, sir.

Ernie: You advance a little further and you get the other ear shot off. What then?

Eric: I'd stop.

Ernie: Why?

Eric: I'd have to. The tin hat would be over my eyes!

As 1941 turned into 1942 the boys continued to feature as solo performers in *Youth Takes a Bow* but whenever Michie could he'd ask them to roll out the double act, which by now could last some, 'seven minutes of pure rubbish,' Eric later mocked. 'Or ten if we worked slowly.' Ernie even managed to get Hylton to up their salary by a pound a week.

Although huge fans of Laurel and Hardy, the boys took as their main inspiration the current top American double act of Abbott and Costello, even to the point of delivering some of their patter with a mock American accent. Both would later admit to plain thievery of material from the US duo, which they'd simply adapt to suit their style; a not unnatural deceit since most acts emulate somebody else in the beginning until they start to get an angle of their own. Indeed, in their early days both regularly stole other people's gags, not caring a jot where the material came from just so long as it got a big laugh.

Strangely, the war didn't really impact on Eric and Ernie as they continued to travel round the country with *Youth Takes a Bow*. Of course, it was ever present, through the bomb damage they saw inflicted upon towns, and Doreen recalls Ernie telling her that the bombing was at its worst when they were staying in Swansea one time. In digs during a stay in Sheffield their bedroom had a dirty great hole in the roof and they were forced to sleep huddled together to keep warm. Perhaps they saw their entertaining as a form of duty to cheer up the masses in so uncertain a time. They contributed to the war effort in other ways, too, such as fire watching. Some of the older male members of the cast were required to stay behind at the theatre all night in case of an air raid and to raise the alarm should the building be hit. A few didn't want to do it and paid the boys to take their place, even though you had to be at least eighteen years old by law. Eric and Ernie didn't mind and happily pocketed the loot, staying up into the wee small hours playing cards.

Another milestone in the Morecambe and Wise story occurred when the tour hit Nottingham. Michie had always been a supporter of the boys and thought they really had something, but never liked their name much, Bartholomew and Wise just wasn't catchy enough. During a conversation with one of the musicians in the show this problem of a new name for Eric came up. Back came a story of an American entertainer who simply called himself after his hometown. 'Where do you come from?' asked the musician.

'Morecambe,' Eric replied.

'That's a good name. Call yourself Morecambe.'

And so Morecambe and Wise were born. Though it's a good job Eric didn't come from Berwick-upon-Tweed. Bizarrely, Ernie thought this naming yourself after a place of birth an inspired notion and for a while actually toyed with changing his name to Ernie Leeds and calling the act Morecambe and Leeds. 'But in the end it sounded too much like an invitation to go on a coach tour.'

SIX

STRIKE A NEW JOB

By early 1942 audiences had began to dry up for *Youth Takes a Bow*, while backstage tensions had reached boiling point, resulting in Sadie having to pack her suitcase and leave. Pop Naylor, Mary Naylor's father, was very keen to get Mary and Ernie together at the time, but Sadie wanted Ernie to remain teamed up with Eric.

The inevitable result was quite a bit of friction. 'Although they were both vying for Ernie's attentions Ernie always knew what he wanted, and if he didn't want to do it he didn't do it,' confirms Doreen. 'That went for Pop Naylor, Sadie, everyone. He was a very determined young man. His relationship with the Naylors was more sociable, though, really. Mary was far more confident as a solo performer and already quite established. I don't think that partnership would have gone very far. Either way, Ernie obviously decided that he and Eric were the future.'

Throw Arthur Tolcher's mother into this mix, and one or two other very ambitious parents wanting the best for their children, and the backstage machinations and politics rivalled those of the Roman Senate. Inevitably something had to give. 'And I think Jack Hylton saw Sadie as the most disruptive element, so sent her home,' according to Doreen.

By this time the tour was on its last legs anyway and eventually folded, leaving the boys facing unemployment. Undeterred they set their sights on London and getting an agent. 'We'll be snapped up,' said a positive Eric.

'Yes,' concurred Ernie. 'The agents will jump at us.'

Sadie didn't think so and baulked at the idea. They'd been fine as child discoveries in shows that focused on youthful talent but she feared they weren't capable of surviving down in London in the dog-eat-dog world of professional variety. They were still too young and wet behind the ears. 'Get yourselves jobs till you're both older,' she advised.

'Jobs!' The very idea sent shockwaves through their combined nervous systems. As always, though, Eric took up his mum's advice and found a job back home, working a demoralizing ten-hour stretch in a razor blade factory. It was Ernie who was determined to test the water down in London, seeing how familiar he already was with the capital. Sharing theatrical digs with a family of acrobats from Japan, he looked desperately for work but in the end was forced to admit defeat and returned to his parents in Leeds, taking up his old job as a coal labourer.

Throughout this period, which lasted all of three months, the pair behaved like estranged sweethearts as they sent letters back and forth to each other. It was touching proof of the fondness that had been created and how dependent they'd become on one another. 'The great thing about a double act is you're never alone in the cold, cold world. Problems are things you share,' said Ernie, who finally took the initiative and visited Eric in Morecambe. Together they tried their luck around nearby coastal towns but the theatres were either closed because of the war or there were no jobs.

Seeing the boys miserable and understanding how ill-equipped they were, especially Eric, for life in the 'ordinary' world, Sadie arranged for them all to travel down to London and just go for it. She found a small flat in Mornington Crescent and even managed to get them an interview with an agent who had offices on the Charing Cross Road. The agent wasn't interested in taking them on as clients but did mention an audition that was taking place at the Hippodrome in a few days' time where impresario George Black who ran a number of theatres, including the London Palladium, was hiring for his latest variety revue, *Strike a New Note*. Black was an associate and near neighbour of Hylton's and Ernie recalled meeting him there several times during his stay. But there'd be no favouritism. They would stand or fall on their own talent.

At the Hippodrome, which years later would become one of London's great cabaret venues The Talk of the Town, Eric and Ernie watched from the wings as act after act got the classic, 'Thank you, next.' The tension slowly built up, and then it was their turn. Walking on with as much outward bravado as they could muster, the boys did their seven-minute spot as Black watched intently, sitting in the stalls surrounded by his minions. 'And I'll say this for him,' Ernie said. 'He politely endured the agony.'

About to leave they were approached by an assistant. 'Black wants to see you,' they were told, and were directed to a doorway that led straight into the auditorium.

'Hello, Ernie, you all right?' said Black before

turning to face them both. 'How much are you earning these days then, boys?'

'Not much, Mr Black, about twenty pounds between the two of us.' By pleading relative poverty Ernie hoped the impresario might feel sorry for them and offer a bit more. It was stupendous naïvety.

'Right,' said Black. 'I'll give you that.'

'You idiot,' blasted the agent on their return. 'I could have got you another fiver.' Realizing too late that he should have started at a much higher price, it was Ernie's first lesson in the wheeler-dealer world of financial negotiation in showbiz and one that still rankled with him decades later.

At least a top London impresario wanted them in his show, which was due to open at the Prince of Wales Theatre near Leicester Square in March 1943. Then came the killer punch. When Ernie asked where their double act would fit in Black replied, 'Well actually, I don't want the double act, boys. I just want you in the show doing bits and pieces.'

Eric and Ernie were shell-shocked. Ernie particularly felt incensed. 'Look here, Mr Black,' he said, lifting himself up to his full height of five feet four inches. 'If you don't want our act I'm not at all sure we can accept the offer.'

'Tell you what, then, lads,' said Black, admiring the youngster's guts. 'Alex Pleon is our second comic. If he ever goes off sick you can go on as your double act and replace him.'

'OK, Mr Black,' said Ernie. 'That seems very fair.'

Unfortunately, as Ernie would enjoy later testifying, 'In the whole history of stand-up comedy

Alex Pleon was its healthiest representative.' And no amount of praying on the boys' parts during the fourteen-month long run of *Strike a New Note* made the slightest difference. 'He'd arrive at the theatre with the most depressing regularity,' said Ernie. On the two occasions Pleon was sick and the boys came on in his place the act went down like the proverbial lead balloon. 'The audience simply stared at us, open-mouthed, aghast,' recalled Ernie. 'Wondering what was being inflicted on them and why.'

So, in spite of their lowly position in the show, little more than chorus boys with only a few individual moments in which to shine, Eric and Ernie decided to just enjoy the experience of being in a hit show. *Strike a New Note* really was *the* revue to see. Ernie would recall stars like Clark Gable, James Stewart, George Raft, Deborah Kerr and Alfred Hitchcock being in the audience and visiting everyone backstage afterwards. One evening the actor Adolphe Menjou, who'd played Louis XIII in the Douglas Fairbanks silent version of *The Three Musketeers* and starred with Rudolph Valentino in *The Sheik*, sought out Ernie to compliment him on his impression of Jimmy Cagney singing 'Yankee Doodle Dandy'.

It was a giddy time; one almost forgot there was a war on. Yes, there were still bombing raids, but not with the same sustained potency as the Blitz, which came to an end in May 1941, when at its peak London was bombed every day and night for three solid months. Now the capital put on a brave front and carried on as normal. The war had given everyone a licence to live now and pay later when it came to enjoying themselves, because tomorrow may find you in a crater left by a Jerry bomb. And the boys were, it has to be said, rather innocently caught up in this shallow, hedonistic pleasure-seeking with invites from chorus girls to weekend parties at stately homes, evenings at Mayfair's Bagatelle restaurant, London's top night-spot where Princess Elizabeth came to dance and mingle with West End stars at cocktail parties.

With not much to do in the show itself, the boys used the spare time to polish their act. They also didn't miss the priceless opportunity of watching from the wings the incomparable Sid Field do his stuff along with Jerry Desmonde, whose easy nonchalance and sophisticated demeanour made him the ideal straight man to Field's clowning, and years later for Norman Wisdom in the cinema. Their classic sketch involves the pair of them on a putting green with Desmonde as the golf pro attempting to teach the novice Field the rudiments of the sport. 'Address the ball,' says Desmonde, to which Field replies, 'Dear Ball . . .' It was like a university course. *Strike a New Note*'s sensation was Field; it made his name at the age of thirty-nine after slogging away for years in provincial variety. He certainly made an impression on one fifteen-year-old boy in the audience who returned a dozen times to watch him—Bob Monkhouse.

Field's act might also have left a lasting mark on Morecambe and Wise. Alan Curtis, a friend who appeared years later with the boys in panto and on television, recalls that the comic Jimmy James once made the suggestion to him that Eric needed a taller partner and named Curtis as the ideal replacement! 'You see Jimmy,' says Curtis, 'represented the old-fashioned face of variety where the straight man was always taller: Sid Field and Jerry Desmonde for example, or Arthur Haynes and Nicholas Parsons. Jimmy was a great comic, and very well respected in the business. He was very wrong about Ernie though, because Ernie wasn't just a straight man. Morecambe and Wise were far more than just a comedy duo. They were a rock-solid partnership.'

Luckily the idea was never even considered.

Another thrill for the male performers in *Strike a New Note* was the mature attitude the showgirls displayed when it came to nudity; their own that is. When the boys were required to enter their dressing room to attend to something the girls never bothered to cover up, which meant Eric and Ernie grew up extremely fast. Back in their own tiny dressing room, which they shared with Billy Dainty, another aspiring young comic, there was a pokey window directly outside in the corridor that just happened to overlook the Mapleton hotel next door—specifically one room where it was well known that the American GIs used to take their conquests. 'During *Strike a New Note* Ernie had become good friends with George Black's daughters,' reveals Doreen. 'And Eric, Ernie and the Black sisters used to stand on each other's shoulders to look through that window at the Mapleton and catch a glimpse of what was going on. That was their sex education!'

SEVEN

HMS *ERNIE*

Strike a New Note was still packing them in when Ernie, who'd just turned eighteen that November, received his call-up papers. Having only performed their double act a couple of times in the show, some friends and colleagues believed they'd never make it in the profession together. Of course Eric and Ernie wore blinkers and when anyone pulled them aside privately to say, 'You'd be much better off on your own, you know,' neither listened. Ernie had more reason to take heed of the doubters, after all he'd been by far the bigger solo star, but his loyalty to Eric was ironclad. But leaving to do his bit for King and Country changed things. Would the fledgling partnership survive what was bound to be a long separation?

Ernie was presented with a stark choice: going into the army, the merchant navy or down the mines. In truth, he didn't much fancy any of them and asked the management of *Strike a New Note* to see if they could pull a few ministerial strings and get him off. Alas their influence did not extend to the mandarins of Whitehall. While Eric stayed behind to see out the show's run, Ernie went into the merchant navy, where he was engaged in the vital task of bringing coal down from Newcastle to be unloaded at Battersea power station.

In the early days of the war this had been hazardous work, with the Germans out to dive-bomb or torpedo the ships as they made their way south hugging the coastline, and many seamen had lost their lives. By the time Ernie joined the worst of it was over, but it was still a sweat-inducing run, especially along a certain stretch of the east coast dubbed, for good reason, 'E-boat alley'. The metal blighters could pop up at any moment and the crew could only truly relax upon entering the Thames estuary, though at the back of their minds was always the thought that they'd soon be making the return trip. In the end Ernie saw no action, only witnessing a few daylight raids on London while on leave.

Aboard ship Ernie trained as a steward, laying and waiting on tables. Imagine then his surprise, nay shock, when, on being posted to another ship, the *Firelighter*, he was taken to the galley and told to prepare meals for the engineering crew. Before him stood a vast cooking range that he hadn't the first notion how to work, let alone cook on, but after a few days he'd just about got the knack of preparing soup, using old bones he boiled up with some vegetables. The engineers ate it without complaint. Nor did they grumble when served underdone potatoes or meat you could poleaxe a polar bear with it was so tough and overcooked. It made Ernie think, golly, if they like this stuff, God knows what muck they were eating before!

If anything, the odd dive-bombing Stuka might have relieved the dreary monotony of these trips. The sole bit of action involved two shipmates having a knife fight: one had come on-board late at night drunk and urinated in front of his fellow mate's bunk. Another crew hand made a habit of feeding mustard sandwiches to the seagulls and watching them vomit and crash into the sea.

It was unrelievedly depressing, not least the conditions in which everyone worked. The coal dust got everywhere, and mixed with human sweat and axle grease, it covered every inch of the ship in an unpleasant gunk. It got in your hair, on your clothes, on your bed sheets and, worse, in your food, although in Ernie's case that probably made it taste better. After a couple of hours at sea you looked like the chorus line of *The Black and White Minstrel Show*. What made it even more depressing for Ernie was the total lack of opportunity for him to entertain the crew a little with portions of his act, a few gags, a song and dance maybe; the oppressive atmosphere made such light relief totally out of place. He missed his family, too, and on leave would return to Leeds in his role as Ernie the provider, bringing with him a sack full of food purloined from the ship. This at a time when everything was rationed—big bars of chocolate for his brothers and sisters and corned beef for Connie.

After his experiences on the *Firelighter* Ernie went into something called 'the pool', a permanent reserve of seamen that could be brought into service at short notice. One job was aboard a fuel tanker, delivering highly inflammable aviation fuel to Southampton. This was the SS *Ben Read,* a small coastal tanker built in 1923 that had four tanks and was able to carry some five hundred tons of refined products as cargo. To all intents and purposes the thing was a floating bomb, any spark or naked flame would send its occupants in a vertical direction very fast. So it was probably not a good idea for Ernie the cook to go down to the galley in the bowels of the ship and heat up the engineers' soup using a blowlamp. It was an awful risk he was taking and a highly illegal one.

As gaps between work in the reserves grew longer Ernie took to contacting agents with a view to getting his career up and running again. It was Bryan Michie he'd usually call first, and he was put into another touring discoveries show billed as, 'the star comedian of the forces'. Michie would lay it on thick into the microphone as the curtain twitched and swayed: 'Ladies and gentlemen, tonight we bring you a boy from the brave merchant navy, that fearless convoy bringing supplies of food and fuel to the ports of our land.' After working the audience up into a patriotic fervour, Ernie would walk onstage dressed in full naval regalia to a round of applause. 'They were totally oblivious of the fact that when not onstage I was singlehandedly threatening to incinerate the country's dockyards or poison essential personnel.'

It was perhaps these solo performances, going back to his old song-and-dance routines, that made Ernie put pen to paper some time in 1944 and write a letter to Eric essentially breaking up the act; whatever act that was since the boys hadn't as yet established themselves anywhere as a performing duo. The letter read as follows:

SS *Ben Read*
c/o Petroleum Pool
Shell Mex House
Strand
London wc2

Dear Eric,

Thanks for your letter. Well Eric I want to get straight to the point. I want us to break up the act. I'm afraid it won't work.

I have such a terrific amount of animosity to put up with at home. I feel it would be better if we parted.

I know this will be quite a shock to you but I had to come to some decision, I can't go on the way things are.

I am not satisfied with my work, I have lost a lot of zip and it will take time to regain it.

I can't keep you waiting around for me; I don't know definitely when I will be out. I feel it's a great pity after we planned so much, but my mind's made up.

I have no idea what to do in the future, all I know is that I want us to remain friends.

Hoping to hear from you.

Your Best Pal

Ernie

This letter reveals some interesting things. The 'animosity at home', according to Doreen, refers to his father, 'a real slave driver, who had forced Ernie into showbiz in the first place and who never wanted him to stop his regular work because he was afraid it would affect him being the main breadwinner.' With his brother and sisters still at home and below proper working age, the Wiseman family relied heavily upon the earning power of their firstborn. Harry in particular must have looked upon Ernie's career with a mix of pride and greed, believing the best option for his son was to build on his previous successes and carry on as a solo artist rather than gamble on this new double act he'd formed.

The general gloomy tone is largely down to the fact Ernie felt depressed and isolated in the merchant navy. It was a particular low point for him. But what's most telling is the personal nature of the letter; almost as if it was written by a lover dissolving a romance, and it's indicative of just how close both men were to each other so early in their relationship.

When Eric received the letter he wrote back almost immediately, dismissing Ernie's concerns, saying he'd never heard such rubbish in his whole life and that his partner ought to take a few days to reconsider. But Ernie was still very much undecided.

His contribution towards the war effort may have been small but Ernie felt he'd done his duty, although such toil also made him realize that 'ordinary' work was something he neither enjoyed nor felt he was particularly suited to. So when his two years in the merchant navy was nearing an end, and with the war finished, he was looking forward to returning to Civvy Street and resurrecting his career, crucially without Eric. 'I felt happier relying on my solo routine for my professional survival,' he admitted.

It's obvious that he kept in touch with Bryan Michie and wrote to him offering his services again, hoping for more solo work. In June 1946 Michie wrote back:

Jack Hylton Ltd
His Majesty's Theatre Offices
Haymarket
London sw1
28 June 1946

My dear Ernie,

It was so nice to get your letter. Please forgive me for being so long in answering it.

We missed you very much when you left the show and I can only hope that you will let me know the moment you are demobbed and if there is anything going you shall certainly be in it.

Hope you are having not too bad a time and that the family are well. Do let me know when you are next in London.

Yours sincerely
(Signed) Bryan Michie

It was now that fate played a remarkable hand. Was it coincidence that shortly after his return to London, Ernie was taking a stroll down Regent Street and who should he see walking down on the opposite side of the road but Eric and Sadie. Eric's papers had arrived not long after Ernie's and he'd become a Bevin Boy, one of a cohort of young British men conscripted to work down the mines, literally digging for victory. Eric found himself in Accrington, Lancashire in a mine that he later discovered had been condemned twenty years earlier. The conditions were appalling. Up at the ungodly hour of 5.30 in the morning, Eric pushed huge loads of coal down tracks in near pitch black. 'I lived for the weekends at Morecambe when Ernie might turn up with a lump of boiling bacon or silverside.' Pilfered, of course, from the ship's stores.

Though passed fit, eleven months of hard slog underground placed a huge physical burden on Eric and he was eventually discharged citing heart trouble. From being deemed originally A1, Eric was now classified C3. Returning home Sadie nursed him back to health, but the shadow of those awful working conditions and the heavy toll it may have placed on his overall health would make dramatic reappearances throughout his life.

Sadie and Eric had arrived in London looking for work and were lodging in Chiswick. Since Ernie was staying at rather less appetizing digs in Brixton, the idea was broached that perhaps he could stay with them, 'and since resisting one of Sadie's suggestions was like fighting against fate,' said Ernie. 'I found myself once again bound up with the Bartholomew family.'

EIGHT

IN THE SOUP

It was a hare-brained scheme doomed to failure, but then the entertainment profession is littered with the corpses of ideas that looked good on paper but in practice proved monumentally impractical or just plain stupid. Step forward *Lord John Sanger's Circus and Variety Show*. Lord John Sanger was a circus impresario who originated the three-ring circus. Lord by reputation rather than entitlement, and long dead, now his descendants were carrying on the family business but facing a bleak future. Their idea was to tour round small towns and villages with a combination of the best elements of a big top circus and a variety revue, but so dumbed down was it that it ended up a poor relation of both. 'It was killed by the belief that country people were so starved of entertainment that they would accept any rubbish,' said Ernie. It was a disaster and poor Eric and Ernie found themselves right bang in the middle of it.

For six months the boys travelled with the show, getting more and more miserable as they, like everyone else, had to pitch in with erecting the vast marquee, big enough to cover a football pitch, and set out the seven-hundred-odd seats. Both also had to sell programmes and drum up business outside wearing evening dress and wellies. The public's apathy to the venture was thunderous as it often played to half empty houses; once the audience consisted of just six spotty adolescent boys who'd paid half price.

As for the artistes' accommodation, it made Colditz look like the Ritz. Eric and Ernie were forced to share a tumble-down trailer with the show's pianist. Washing facilities consisted of a bucket of cold water and the toilet was an evil-smelling pit outside covered for modesty's sake by a canvas screen.

For Ernie the endurance test that the tour quickly became was lightened considerably by the fact he'd fallen head over heels in love with one of the dancers. Alas, his ardour was not reciprocated; indeed it was positively discouraged. Her name was Doreen Blythe, a pretty fifteen-year-old from Peterborough who'd trained as a ballet dancer and performed mostly in and around her home town in shows and pantomimes. One she recalls was with Dan Leno Junior, son of the famous Victorian music hall entertainer, when Doreen was just thirteen. 'He was wonderful. I used to stand beside the stage in the wings looking at him. He was gorgeous. I remember he had this long black cape which he wore on his entrance and sometimes small beads used to fall off and I would pick them up and keep them as souvenirs. He was a very well-known actor and a bit of an idol of the time.'

At the age of fifteen Doreen met some girls in panto in Torquay. They were going to do a summer season and asked if she'd like to join their act. Ultimately the summer season fell through but jobs were going in some sort of variety circus that would be touring the South of England. 'I asked my parents if I could go and they said it would be fine, so long as these girls were going too. They were all a bit older than me so Mum and Dad thought I'd be

OK. So anyway, we all turned up at the start of this tour, and that's when I met Ernie and Eric. Ernie was a comic at the time, and Eric was the stooge.' Indeed, Ernie had been hired by the promoters as the comic, billed on the posters as 'England's Mickey Rooney' with Eric as his straight man, earning two pounds a week less. Doreen didn't think much of their act. 'Comics were comics to me. If they weren't Fred Astaire or Gene Kelly I wasn't really bothered. Comics were always considered old and a bit scruffy by other acts, so Ernie didn't really register with me at first.'

Eric and Doreen met for the first time in Horley, Surrey, during a cafe lunch get together for the whole troupe prior to going out on the road. Ernie sat directly opposite her, and was 'being my usual forward cheeky self to cover up the nervousness I felt inside.' While everyone tucked into their soup Ernie made some wisecrack about how some people could be noisy with their slurping just as Doreen took an audible mouthful and elicited a ripple of laugher. A shy and reserved girl, Doreen turned quite beetroot with embarrassment, 'and looked supercilious daggers at me. I think I fancied her from that second.' Doreen, though, wanted as little as possible to do with Ernie. 'She treated me with a very proper disdain.' The trauma of it also put Doreen off eating soup for years.

From then on Doreen avoided Ernie at all costs, Eric too, since the boys were invariably always together. She might spy them walking down the high street and dash into a doorway to avoid any contact whatsoever. Undaunted by the aftermath of 'soupgate', Ernie continued the offensive as Doreen remembers. 'I was very nervous in those days and

71

used to have a slight stutter, which still comes out even today, and Eric and Ernie suddenly said, "We want a girl to do one of the sketches, you'll do," and I went bright red and started stammering and squealing and they said, "Yep, you're the one." But I think it must've been because Ernie fancied me. It was just an excuse to come up and speak to me, but it worked. I was obviously very flattered.'

All the artistes were sustained by food cooked on a gas stove. Ernie had the task of getting supplies, riding into town on a bike armed with everyone's ration books. One day he invited Doreen along. 'Will you come with me to the grocer's and talk to the man and smile while he's cutting the coupons out of the books,' he asked. 'Yes, I don't mind.' Ernie had a butcher's bike with a large basket on the front so Doreen hopped in and they rode into the local village. On the way back Ernie turned to Doreen and said, 'Here, have this,' and handed over a huge slab of chocolate. 'Where did you get that from?' Ernie smiled. 'Well, because you distracted him, there were two books he counted for but didn't cut.' They kept the chocolate, a rare treat in those days of rationing and doing without.

Ernie next asked Doreen out to the pictures. 'I thought his hands would be all over the place but they weren't. He was very good mannered.' At this stage it was purely platonic. 'He had another girlfriend he was always talking about and I had other boyfriends.' That girl was Dorothy Ward. She lived in East Ardsley and was the sister of Ernie's other best friend, Eddie Ward. Their dad owned the grocer's shop where they all used to play around. Dorothy and Eddie also performed in an act, and because their dad had a car Harry made sure his family were in with them. It meant he and Ernie would sometimes get a lift to and from talent contests!

After a few more tentative dates Doreen was soon doing Ernie's laundry. 'Do you think you could wash this shirt for me?' he'd say and some sweets would sail through the window of her caravan. True love, if ever there was, thought Ernie, 'to tackle my underwear on that tour.'

Finally, on another date, Ernie plucked up the courage to say to Doreen, 'Would you mind if I kissed you goodnight?'

'Yes please!' she said.

Meanwhile attendances to the shows had barely improved and everyone had to make the unpalatable sacrifice of halving their wages to keep the whole thing afloat. Lord John Sanger's theatrical hybrid limped on for another month before coming to its inevitable demise in October 1947. It was a mighty relief, although the boys had welcomed the opportunity to try out their double act a few times, and Ernie and Doreen had agreed to keep in touch. Before she left, Ernie gave her the first of what would be many presents, a cookery book with the inscription: 'I hope you will read this book and I can digest it.'

So it was back to London and an uncertain future, but a future that would have to be navigated without the encouraging and often dominating presence of Sadie.

NINE

ON THEIR OWN

Back in Chiswick in their old digs, Eric and Ernie took stock. Sadie had reluctantly packed her bags and returned to her husband, having seen the boys start to become more and more independent over the last year or so. They were relying on each other now and didn't need Sadie any more. Having mutually reached the decision that it was time for her to go, they both literally frogmarched her to the railway station and put her on the train. It must have been tough for Sadie to face up to the truth that her fledglings, for want of a better word, had flown the nest and she was of no further use.

At least in Ernie she had found that special person to take her place and look after Eric. 'Until Ernie came along, Sadie had always cared for Eric,' says Doreen. 'But she must have thought: "Oh, this is a good, reliable sort of fellow. I can have a bit of peace finally." So Ernie got the job of looking after him.'

This raises several interesting questions, namely why Sadie took Ernie so willingly into her family in the first place and why she got the boys together. As Eric himself put it, Sadie pushed him into show business, 'and kept me there until she knew I was safely in Ernie's hands; he's been doing the pushing ever since.' Spoken in jest perhaps, but there's real truth behind that statement. 'Until Eric and I teamed up, his mother was the driving force in his life,' said Ernie. 'I took over from her.'

Sadie must have sensed very early on that Ernie was the perfect replacement. Eric's daughter Gail Morecambe recalls that her grandmother had a strong belief that she had one more duty to perform before letting go of Eric's career completely. 'I think Sadie handed him over to Ernie, like she was saying—here you are, now he's your responsibility.'

Without Sadie getting them jobs any more the boys realized they needed a proper agent, but here they fell into a classic catch-22 situation: no agency would take them on unless they had bookings, but to get bookings they needed an agent. Dispiriting trips to every agency in town, from Oxford Street to Soho, resulted in no takers; it was an experience that left a sour taste in their mouths. Even though they would be well represented in later years, the boys always exhibited a playful antipathy towards the agents' profession. 'They're forever on the phone when you're on a good run,' observed Ernie, 'but hit a bad patch and they're strangely unavailable.'

In the end they resorted to approaching theatres directly, trying to persuade the booking manager to take them on; a ploy that was hard work, demoralizing and only intermittently successful. Ernie recalled one gig at the Palace Theatre in Walthamstow as going down 'stupendously badly' and their services were not required again. It was a lean period, perhaps their worst. 'Frightening', Eric called it, because even though they were supremely confident in their own talents, they weren't being given opportunities to show it and maybe for the first time the terrible thought entered their mind that they might not make it. And if they didn't make it the 'real' world of 9-to-5 jobs beckoned and that didn't bear thinking about.

For Ernie it must have felt doubly depressing: having been a child star with a seemingly bright future ahead of him, here he was in a dingy bedsit scrabbling around for morsels of work. They even resorted to playing dates in pubs and Masonicdances; there was the odd date with ENSA and a short tour of US army camps in Germany, but nothing very secure. And there were bouts of unemployment stretching on for months, with Ernie surviving on his savings and Eric getting by on money sent from home. When things got really bad they'd both catch the overnight coach and go back to Morecambe to stay with Sadie for a week and recharge. Indeed, so attached to Sadie had Ernie become that he wouldn't think twice about booking a visit to Sadie ahead of going to Leeds to see his own parents. It was a second home to him—for now.

It also helped that the boys' landlady in Chiswick, a Mrs Duer, was painfully familiar with theatricals and so quite obliging when it came to the rent. 'Pay me when you're back in funds, boys,' she'd say. Had it not been for her kindness, Eric and Ernie might have faced life out on the streets. Mrs Duer had two young boys, both of whom were mad about planes and flying and wanted to be pilots. Years later Ernie and Doreen were flying by private charter to stay at their holiday home in Malta, and who should the pilot be but Mrs Duer's son.

In spite of the hardships, Eric and Ernie were determined to stick it out, come what may. Neither of them even considered taking a normal job just to tide them over, a bit of dishwashing in a restaurant, say, or factory work. 'No, we were variety artists, we were pros,' said Ernie, proudly. 'To consider anything else would have been heresy.'

Things perked up a little bit in 1949 when the boys landed a job at the Windmill Theatre in Soho, famous for its tableaux of nude glamour models. The girls were required to stand stock still onstage in a series of pleasing poses; according to the censorship laws of the day even one involuntarily muscle reflex was deemed illegal. However, if they had strategically placed fans or feather boas they were allowed to move modestly about. All totally harmless today, if not wistfully nostalgic, but back then it was enough to bring down the Empire.

The man who ran the Windmill was Vivian Van Damm, known affectionately to his friends as VD. His motto, 'there are no pockets in shrouds', was framed and hung on his office wall. Van Damm did everything at the Windmill, from opening the mail to hiring the girls, and firing them when their assets dropped enough to require the assistance of a bra. As the shows ran continuously all day, these poor models needed some respite and so variety acts, mostly comics, were brought in to fill the gaps. These were tolerated rather than enjoyed by the audience, which consisted largely of men in raincoats, who were there to see nubile bosoms rather than a stream of hackneyed one-liners, and so, in Ernie's words, 'They took to the entertainers as ducks do to orange sauce.'

This didn't deter the boys from auditioning for Van Damm in his tiny office. 'It was the smallest room I've been in outside a loo,' said Eric. Hired for the week at twenty-five pounds for six daily performances, with an option for a further five weeks, they began on a Monday and very quickly wished they hadn't. They took to the stage in utter silence, and the situation did not improve. Each punchline fell on stony ground, getting about as many laughs as a funeral cortège passing an orphanage. They left having raised not a titter or even a semblance of a guffaw. But the shock of their performance was as nothing compared to the realization that they had to go through it all over again another five times that day. Even the sight of near naked women in the wings failed to cheer the boys up.

Tuesday continued in much the same vein. The only time the audience sprang to life was when one of the seats at the front became vacant and there was an almighty stampede for it, known as the 'Windmill steeplechase'. Men, some of them pensionable age, would leapfrog over rows of chairs to claim the prize, an unobstructed view of the lustily anticipated meat market. The more refined gentlemen didn't bother, having secreted about their person a pair of opera glasses; though perverts were not tolerated. Anyone seen to be, shall we say, taking too much interest in the contents of their trousers, was identified, usually by one of the girls coming offstage yelling, 'Row three, seat twenty-six—dirty bastard!' and he'd be hauled out.

It was soul-destroying stuff for the boys who didn't really stand much of a chance. Once they came on just after an act where a bare-chested man in leather strode round the stage cracking whips at naked women; would you want to see two comics after that?

By Wednesday it was all over for Morecambe and Wise: Van Damm fired them on the spot. The boys weren't expecting it; invited up to his office they believed it was to be told the option was being taken up. 'Get your pen out for that contract, Ernie,' said Eric. Instead Van Damm relayed the news they were being let go at the end of the week, 'with all the charm of a surgeon telling you the worst,' recalled Ernie. They were to be replaced by another eager young comic who was getting more laughs than them, which wasn't difficult; his name was Tony Hancock.

Years later, when Van Damm was organizing a plaque to be mounted outside the Windmill, comprising of a list of the now famous names that got their early breaks at the club, he approached Morecambe and Wise. Ernie took great delight in reminding their former boss that he'd in fact fired them. 'His reaction to my suggestion as to what he might do with his roll-call of honour must sadly go unrecorded.' For Ernie some things were never forgotten, or forgiven.

The sacking from the Windmill wasn't merely a further blow to their fortitude it put a dampener on further chances of work, if word ever got out that is. Astutely, Ernie managed to persuade Van Damm to allow them to place an ad in *The Stage* saying they were leaving the Windmill due to prior commitments. That still left them with a major problem. With its growing reputation as a nursery for budding comedians, agents were attending Windmill shows all the time and the boys had rather hoped a long run would get them spotted; now they'd only a few days left. Pooling their resources, complimentary tickets were paid for and hurriedly sent out to a host of agencies but by late on Friday no one had showed. Then in walked Gordon Norval, a middling agent who took bookings for the Grand,

Clapham and the Empire, Kilburn, hardly premier venues but sweet enough for two soon-to-be-out-of-work entertainers.

'Can you do the Clapham Grand on Monday?' Norval asked as the boys came offstage.

As usual Eric stood aside, happy for Ernie to conduct the negotiations, a policy that began very early in the partnership, as Eric once explained: 'Every act has to have one bastard who can say no and I thought it might just as well be him.' Joking aside, Ernie very quickly became the business brains behind the outfit, agreeing payment terms for both of them and dealing with contracts. 'And, believe me, Ernie did that very well,' says Michael Grade, who later worked as the boys' agent. 'He was a very good negotiator. What do I mean by a good negotiator? Well, first and formost he always thought about it before he went into the meeting. You always knew, and this was crucial, that he never went into a negotiation without being able to do the deal. He would never get to the end and say, "I've got to run this by Eric first." He and Eric would work out what they wanted beforehand, and then it was Ernie's job to go in and do the deal. You knew when you were negotiating with Ernie that whatever was agreed it would stick. The deal would be done there and then and that would be that. No reason to worry about second thoughts etc. He was extremely honourable—but tough!'

Joe McGrath, who directed the boys last ever piece of television, *Night Train to Murder*, remembers asking Eric one day where Ernie was. 'Ah, he's over there on the phone talking to our agent. They're talking telephone numbers. I leave all that to him. That's nothing to do with me. I do the clearing up in the studio. That's my job.'

Ernie was also the prime organizer and motivator out of the pair of them, having quickly sussed that he was the one with the most drive. 'I was always the one with the push and Eric was happy to have it that way. I negotiated our fees, planned our seasons, worked out our dates. He was content to go along with the arrangements.'

So, ever the businessman, Ernie took out his diary and diligently thumbed through an alarming succession of blank pages with a thoughtful expression on his face. 'Ummm, I think we might just be free that night, Mr Norval.'

'Good, I'll give you twenty-five pounds a week. Can you do two spots either side of the interval?'

The boys agreed, perhaps prematurely—it was only later that it dawned on them what they'd done. For years they'd been honing their act until it was as good as they could make it. The problem was it lasted around seven minutes, and that was it, they didn't have anything else. What were they going to do for the second spot they'd promised Norval? Panic took over: they had to find seven minutes' worth of brand-new material, literally out of thin air, and in just a matter of a few days.

Back at their digs the boys began frantically working out a new routine, running through in their minds every Abbott and Costello film they'd ever seen, dredging up memories of some of the acts they'd watched from the wings and the jokes that had made them laugh, old gags they'd scribbled down in notebooks—anything! It got so desperate they were putting in hoary old stuff like this exchange: Eric walks onstage in a very mincing fashion and declares himself to be a businessman.

81

'But a businessman doesn't walk like that?' Ernie would say.

'You don't know my business.'

It had been years since they'd first heard that one, and being rather young not got it. Now it raised a knowing smile and a minor titter—so in it went. This was desperation time. Then, after a day or so of solid work, they came up with an inspired idea that today can be seen as one of the turning points in the duo's history. It was to lampoon a popular tune of the period sung by Danny Kaye called 'The Woody Woodpecker Song'. Ernie would take the vocal lead but manage to convince Eric that his role in the rendition was in fact the main part, while in reality it was just the silly little woodpecker trill at the end of each phrase. Hopefully the audience would twig Eric was getting conned and thus be in on the joke. It was simple but effective and their first truly original sketch, born not so much out of their usual fast repartee but interplay between their personalities. After running through it plenty of times they had their second spot—well, at least something they felt they could just about get away with—and in the nick of time, too.

On the Monday evening the boys went onstage at the Grand and performed their old regular routine to an absolute stonewall, or what was affectionately called, 'the Clapham silence'. It was bad. They walked off terrified. If their well-honed material had flopped, what chance did their new stuff have? They were to find out shortly after the interval when they were back on again. Fearing the worst they launched into 'The Woody Woodpecker Song' routine. Slowly but surely the audience twigged what was going on and little ripples of laughter began to echo round the auditorium, they got louder and more frequent until the whole audience seemed to be on Eric and Ernie's side. They had them; they'd won. The boys came off beaming; it was one of the biggest successes of their career so far.

Asked to play the Kilburn Empire the following week, the boys cleverly opted to run with the Woody Woodpecker routine first. Again it was an unqualified hit and the goodwill they'd built up with the audience carried over into the second half and gave their old material a new lease of life. Soon managers and promoters were after the boys with offers of work and Gordon Norval stepped into the breach and became their first agent. It was back to the Clapham Grand first and then a return to the Kilburn Empire—this time as top of the bill. Pretty soon they were able to pay off their debts, especially those suffered by their poor landlady. Ernie would define this period as 'the moment when the tide turned for Morecambe and Wise'.

TEN

THANK YOU, I SHALL TELL MY FRIENDS

Since meeting during that circus debacle Ernie and Doreen had kept in touch. 'But our relationship didn't become serious until I was about seventeen.' Doreen explains. 'I'd had other boyfriends, and it got to a stage when Ernie started to become very interested in when or if I was seeing them again. That's when I knew he wanted to make the next step. I suppose we really became a couple when we attended a Water Rats Ball at The Dorchester. That's when we went "public", if you get my drift. After that he started writing me love letters all the time; usually in the style of telegrams which was romantic but also very funny.'

With both Ernie and Doreen in the business they were always on the road playing in different theatres up and down the country and often the only time they could get to see each other was a snatched hour at a railway station. 'We had coffee at Preston when our trains passed,' Doreen related on Ernie's *This Is Your Life*. 'Or we would have a kiss at Crewe.' To which Ernie interjected: 'You should have seen what happened in Manchester!'

The problem with these precious and fleeting meetings was that Ernie and Doreen were never alone. 'I'd be waiting on a platform and suddenly see Ernie coming, with that big smile,' Doreen recalls. 'But then, beside him, would be Eric. We could never get rid of him. Later, I used to joke that we'd have to find a girl for Eric because otherwise we'd be lumbered with him for ever.'

That day almost came not long afterwards when the boys were staying at Doreen's parents' house in Peterborough. 'Eric got up early one morning and caught the train to London,' Doreen recalls. 'Eric never usually got up early so we all asked what he was up to, and Ernie said he was going down to London to propose to a girl he'd met. Ernie had lent him money for the fare and to buy a ring, and off he'd gone. When Eric eventually came back he

84

went straight to his and Ernie's room and wouldn't come out for a day and a half. It turned out that the girl had refused him and had gone back to America. Her name was Veronica Martell and she became quite famous in the States.'

Doreen had found work as a dancer in a revue run by Reggie Dennis and managed to persuade the impresario to book Eric and Ernie for another of his tours entitled *Front Page Personalities*. On the bill was a real motley collection of artistes, from plain singers and dancers to a mind-reading act and a trampolinist. Bizarrely one girl was introduced to audiences as having been a spy during the war behind enemy lines who'd then begin a striptease; perhaps that's what variety's all about.

Being with the tour for just under a year turned out to be a major learning curve, presenting the boys with plenty of time to polish their act and grow more relaxed in front of live audiences. With this new-found confidence their performances grew sharper and more clinical, the repartee smoother, and as a result their own personalities, perhaps for the first time, really shone through. They discovered gags that had flopped in the past worked well if delivered with panache and proper stagecraft. Take this exchange:

Eric: I came home last night and my wife was sitting up in bed crying.

Ernie: What had happened?

Eric. We'd had a burglar. So I said, 'Did he get much?'

Ernie: What did she say?

Eric: She said, 'Yes, I thought it was you.'

Neither did they feel the need to rely on other comics' material any more and began formulating their own ideas and jokes. It was a natural progression but on some nights they took a battering and their act performed in complete silence, a horrendous experience, especially in a large barn of a theatre. If anything these bad nights served to keep their egos in check.

If things were going particularly badly the boys simply raced through the act in order to get off as quickly as possible, which could sometimes cause problems. The close of their act was usually accompanied by a rousing blast from the orchestra, but, musicians being musicians, drink was never too far from their thoughts. Aware that the boys' act lasted twelve minutes, they felt that was twelve minutes better employed propping up the bar, so on a bad night Eric and Ernie would look for their finale music and see the orchestra pit barren save for an embarrassed conductor. Sometimes the musical director, sensing what was happening, would race over to the bar to try and fetch back as many musicians as possible. 'But many a time,' recalled Ernie. 'We would do our big finish to the thin notes of a piano and one violin.'

If a performance had been a bit of a howler the boys always insisted on a post-mortem afterwards. More often than not they'd blame the audience. This wasn't selfishness on their part, since they'd calculated that the worst nights tended to fall on a Monday when the house was full of people who had a week of work ahead of them and so weren't much in the mood for laughing. This bizarre logic actually made some kind of sense since on Friday nights, the beginning of the weekend, laughs were much easier to come by.

As the tour wound its way round the country the boys found themselves staying in B&Bs run by theatrical landladies who ranged in quality from your favourite maiden aunt to the wicked queen from Snow White. Some of these places were passed on to them by fellow pros and there was a secret code that everyone followed. Sylvan Mason, who befriended Ernie and Doreen in the seventies, remembers Ernie signing the guestbook at her house in Esher and telling her that during those early days on tour when he and Eric stayed at a guest house that was a bit rough they wrote in the book, 'Thank you—I shall tell all my friends!!!' That was code for 'It's a dump, get out while you still can'.

The boys were never to forget some of the downright hovels they were forced to stay in, or their favourite landladies like Mrs McKay of Manchester who owned two semi-detached houses which she'd knocked together, one side for variety, the other for 'legitimate' theatre, and her policy was that never the twain should meet. Then there was Mrs Coomes in Bimingham, whose pride and joy was a private dining room that was reserved for stars only. One evening that theatrical knight Sir Donald Wolfit was eating alone when part of the ceiling plaster collapsed and landed in his soup.

Just as *Front Page Personalities* was nearing its end in the autumn of 1950 Eric and Ernie were spotted by one of London's top agents Frank Pope, who handled bookings for the Moss Empires circuit, which owned some of the premier variety venues in the country, including their flagship theatre the London Palladium. Reluctantly, because he'd become a close friend, the boys had no choice but to sever links with Norval, feeling that Pope was better placed to take them to the next level, nearing what Ernie called, 'the apex of our ambition', to top the bill at places like the Palladium. Pope acted quickly and got the boys a gig at the Empire, Swansea, with the Irish tenor singer Josef Locke topping the bill.

Out of all the Moss Empire venues the one that struck the fear of God into entertainers, especially those of an English disposition, was the Glasgow Empire. Such was its reputation that you'd get paid extra for appearing there, like danger money. The unadulterated antipathy audiences had for English comics in particular is legendary. Perhaps the classic story is the one that befell poor old Des O'Connor (or Desperate O'Connor, as the boys would later call him), in his pre-singing days, when he faced an audience that wasn't just apathetic but positively antagonistic. His nerve went and he dried, not a good thing to happen on the stage of the Glasgow Empire where you're utterly alone. Des did the only thing he could do in the circumstances, he fainted, preferring the indignity of his carcass being dragged off under the curtain than any more bear baiting.

Another story has Jimmy Edwards not doing very well when a punter right down the front offered some words of advice: 'Why don't you just fuck off?' Edwards was nonplussed. 'I beg your pardon.' A voice shrieked from the back of the circle, 'You heard what my friend said. Why don't you just fuck off?' By comparison the Christians in the Colosseum got off lightly.

Eric and Ernie were up there for a week—and

lived to tell the tale. Their last night was a classic, no scriptwriter could have written a better scene. The boys finished their act and walked off to not one solitary clap from the three thousand-strong audience. In the wings a stagehand smiled benignly and said, 'They're beginning to like you.'

The Glasgow Empire was a beautiful old theatre, so aesthetically at least it was always a pleasure going up there. A lot of those old variety theatres were charming, certainly better than the multi-storey car parks and soulless supermarkets that ultimately replaced them. Not all of them were fleapits. Some of the Scottish ones even had en suite dressing rooms, as did the Liverpool Empire. In fact, Doreen remembers visiting the boys in Liverpool and seeing they had showers in their dressing room, a rare luxury. 'Don't get me wrong, though, a lot of those variety theatres were pretty awful. I remember the one at Sunderland used to smell of coke, because as you went through the stage door you had to pass the boiler house and the coke fumes were unbelievable. Audiences varied a lot. Not all of the audiences were hard like Glasgow. I remember that Nottingham, Manchester and Leeds were always good, always up for a laugh.'

Failures like Glasgow, though, Ernie particularly saw value in. 'We needed to have experienced the knocks working in variety. It chipped the rough edges off us.' Like an actor learning his craft in repertory theatre, the variety halls the boys played in up and down the land were their comedy university and they met an array of fascinating people and often encountered the downright unusual. Take the occasion when their act was near its end and two old dears in the front row got up

89

and began to walk out.

'Have we upset you, ladies?' asked Eric.

'Oh no, we've just got to leave for the last bus home. We've told our friends here to tell us tomorrow what we've missed. Goodnight.'

Eric looked at Ernie and then back again out front to the audience and said, 'There's no answer to that!' and bang, a Morecambe and Wise catchphrase was born.

Ernie also remembered appearing at Watford Town Hall in 1948 on the same bill as the legendary Max Miller, who Ernie reckoned was the greatest music-hall comic of them all. He took a shine to the boys and, about to go onstage one night, he turned to Ernie and said, 'Don't forget, lad, in this business when one door shuts, they all bloody shut!'

Glasgow notwithstanding, the boys were working well on the variety circuit, confident with their act and the kind of material their audiences liked. It's interesting to note that during this period they much preferred working in the North than down in London, one supposes they related more to northern audiences.

The early fifties was the fag end of variety, with its crumbling theatres and outdated acts that had more than a whiff of faded Edwardian music hall about them. It's a world that exists now only in memory and creaky black and white film. But for years, and before the advent of television, it was one of the few sources of entertainment for the masses, where on the same bill they could laugh at a comic, be mesmerized by magicians or ventriloquists, ogle at shapely dancers and stare in wonder at speciality acts, people who might balance a fish tank on their nostril or some such idiocy.

Variety was a tough world in which to survive. Not only could the public be demanding but there was also an adjudicator who would sit in on performances once a week and take notes. If an act was dying on its arse the management would be told and they'd have by midweek to sort it out. If by the time the adjudicator returned the problems were persisting, the act was let go.

Obviously some acts proved more successful than others. Eric and Ernie were once performing at the Metropolitan Theatre on the Edgware Road on the same bill as Anton Karas, the Viennese zither player made famous by the 1949 film *The Third Man*. It soon became obvious to the management that Karas's repertoire consisted chiefly of different variations of the same *Third Man* theme and audiences were getting fed up. Hurriedly the boys were asked to do a second spot. 'So we rushed off to a cafe on the Edgware Road and tried to work out how they were going to do another two or three minutes,' Doreen recalls. 'I sat there with a watch and I timed them. Towards the end they were still a few seconds short and we couldn't for the life of us work out how to fill it. Then Ernie suddenly piped up and said, "Hang on, what if people laugh?" And so that filled in the time, if they got the laughs, of course, which they did. It was funny that two comics had forgotten to take into account laughter!'

Many of these variety acts were truly mindboggling, so much so that after sixty years Doreen hasn't forgotten them. One that springs to mind is 'Vogelbein's Bear', a gentleman who would travel around working the theatres with an enormous bear. 'It could be slightly disconcerting for some of the other acts but it was very tame—

and very entertaining. How on earth he got into digs I'll never know.'

Another act had a troupe of chimpanzees and the chorus girls were told by the management not to stand too close to the stage when they were on, since once a chimpanzee reaches five years old it has a pretty clear idea of the difference between the sexes! This act always used to travel around in a caravan as no landlady was stupid enough to allow them to stay in their boarding house. It was always parked close to the stage door and one afternoon Eric, Ernie and Doreen were leaving to go back to their digs when Billy Dainty mentioned that the owners of the chimps, a man and his wife, were about to have lunch. 'They're having soup,' he whispered. Surreptitiously, Dainty led them all right past the caravan, and in full view of the chimps looking out of the window. 'Well, of course, the moment the chimps caught sight of us they all started leaping around and getting excited,' recalls Doreen. 'The caravan started to rock and there was a fiesta of soup and screams. Absolute chaos!'

Talking of animals, when the boys were working the variety halls they used to do a routine using crisps and the speciality dog acts would complain if they didn't sweep the stage before they went on. Most of the time all the dogs would be interested in was hoovering up the crisps! This happened on more than one occasion. 'The boys probably did it on purpose in the end,' thinks Doreen.

Whenever the boys were appearing in variety near to where Doreen was working, say in Manchester or somewhere, she'd always try and stay with them at the weekends and have some fun. When Doreen was seventeen she was doing a summer season in Blackpool and it was suggested by Sadie that she could spend the weekends with her in Morecambe. 'Not something I was overly keen on, to be honest,' admits Doreen.'Looking back, it was nothing more than a pretty poor attempt to garner some influence over the boys via me. She was very good at that during previous times I'd stayed with her, constantly dropping in the odd, "wouldn't it be better if the boys did this" or "why don't you suggest this to the boys". I was now closer to them than she was, so she wanted to get her claws in and put me to work on her behalf.'

The fact that Sadie had come to have less and less influence over Eric and Ernie caused her deep distress. In her mind, it was as if nothing had changed, that the boys were still wholly dependent on her, couldn't make a move without her and needed her encouragement and guidance. During long train journeys to different venues Doreen used to pass the time knitting. 'I once knitted Ernie a Fair Isle pullover which took me absolutely ages. I showed it to Sadie before I gave it to Ernie and she said, "You can't give it to Ernie unless you knit one for Eric." So I had to knit another one. I was very young and shy at the time, so did as I was told. I was halfway through doing some argyle socks at the time, so I kept them quiet!'

It got to the point where Eric and Ernie rarely told Sadie when they were appearing close to Morecambe so they didn't have to go and visit because they knew what would happen, she'd sit them both down and quiz them on how the act was going and then offer her two-penneth worth on how to improve things. It was one of the reasons why she started trying to use Doreen as a way to get her points across to the boys. 'But I refused. She'd used me in the past and I wasn't going to let it happen again. After me she had nobody left to nobble.'

Perhaps sensing that variety was about to be read its last rites, Eric and Ernie urged Pope to chase the two most important dates in the entertainer's calendar: summer season and panto. Each gave you twelve weeks of solid work that set you up nicely for the whole year. For summer season the boys found their variety act worked perfectly, while for panto they devised new bits of business, like playing a comedy captain and his mate, which could be incorporated easily into, say, *Sinbad the Sailor*, or a comedy robbers routine that could win them a place in a production somewhere of *Babes in the Wood*.

With summer and panto booked, Eric and Ernie could cast their net further afield and it was now that they began to make inroads on BBC radio. That was where the mass audiences were, a successful radio series could turn an unknown comic into a household name within weeks. In January 1952 the boys landed a spot on *Workers' Playtime*, which famously broadcast live each week from a factory canteen, 'somewhere in Britain'. Their appearance went down so well they were regularly invited onto another popular radio show *Variety Fanfare*, which though only broadcast in the northern regions from studios in Manchester, still marked just how far they'd come in a relatively short space of time.

With their professional lives on a sound footing at last, the focus shifted to their private lives, which were about to radically change. As friends and partners Morecambe and Wise were never to be quite the same again.

ELEVEN

THIS HAD BETTER BE GOOD!

For some time now Eric had hankered after a leggy chorus girl by the name of Joan Bartlett, indeed upon first meeting her at the Empire Theatre, Edinburgh that June he had declared his undying love for her and that she was the girl he intended to marry. When they tied the knot in December 1952 after a whirlwind romance Ernie was best man. 'I felt like a mother with an unmarriageable daughter that's miraculously swept off her hands by an unsuspecting sailor,' he joked. Secretly, though, Ernie was nervous about the impact it might have on their professional career. 'He was upset in a way that Eric had got married and probably worried about how it would affect the act,' Joan revealed. 'It would mean that Eric had a family and his attentions might be turned to that.'

Joan tried to put Ernie's mind at rest, telling him that she had not the slightest intention of interfering, but the doubts remained. 'It was like having three people in the act now,' recalled Joan. 'And I think that gave Ernie the push to get married himself.' Even though by this time Ernie was already engaged!

Doreen had waited long enough for Ernie to pop the question, but he always seemed more focused on his work. For a brief period she considered working in a dance act in Canada with an ex-boyfriend. Perhaps spurred on by this Ernie did the decent thing and, on Valentine's Day 1952, proposed. 'The engagement ring cost him two weeks' salary, which was eighty pounds,' Doreen remembers. 'It had three diamonds set, which stood for "I love you". He proposed in my mother's front room. There was no carpet, only vinyl, so he was making a big sacrifice!'

Just weeks after Eric and Joan walked down the aisle, on 18 January 1953 Ernie and Doreen were married. Eric was best man and when he arrived at the chapel took Doreen by the hands, smiled warmly and said, 'This had better be good, Sunshine. We've turned down a spot on radio for you!'

Connie travelled down from Leeds to Peterborough for the occasion, as did Ernie's brother Gordon. Harry couldn't make it due to illness. But both parents were delighted at the union, although they never had a say in it. 'And as far as I know Ernie never asked their opinion,' Doreen recalls. 'I don't think he could have cared less if they'd liked it or not. In fact, they were very welcoming and we all got on very well.'

By this time Doreen had left show business and was running a dance school. 'And my girls came to the wedding and formed a guard of honour for us, outside the chapel. I think they used tap shoes.'

As with Eric and Joan's nuptials, there would be no honeymoon for Ernie and Doreen due to work commitments: the boys were appearing in panto in Sheffield. They also needed a special licence in order to get married on the Sunday, Ernie's day off, and the next afternoon Doreen recalled sitting in a theatre box watching the boys perform onstage. 'We had the honeymoon nine months after we got married,' reveals Doreen. 'It was a week in Paris.'

And there was certainly nothing romantic about their first few weeks together as a married couple. Fed up of using trains to get to gigs, the boys had invested in transport of their own. First a two-seater ex-army truck which usually broke down. Next they bought a thirty-five-seater Bedford bus that had been converted into a caravan. And this is where the Wises lived until *Dick Whittington* finished its run. Eric and Joan meanwhile took the more conventional route of renting a house.

There was just one problem; the bus-caravan was parked outside Doreen's parents' house in Peterborough. After the Saturday show Ernie and Doreen went off to fetch it and then drove back to Sheffield. All went well until they reached the outskirts of the city and the engine stopped. Braving the cold Ernie tried his best to budge the thing but it was dead. Just then a smartly dressed young man on his way to some function offered to help, but after an hour the engine still refused to start. All through their exertions Ernie had kept reminding the man that he was going to be late, until he finally decided not to bother to go at all. Ernie broke down in tears, overcome by the stranger's generosity. 'I think the engine felt sorry for us after that,' recalls Doreen, 'because it burst into life.'

Feeling slightly guilty about the situation Ernie begged the man to accept some form of payment, this he refused. Ernie burst into tears again. Eventually they managed to get the caravan to a garage but it would go no further, so that's where the couple stayed, on the forecourt. It had begun to snow heavily in Sheffield and after performances

Ernie and Doreen made their way back to the garage, sometimes walking on piled-up snow that took them above the roofs of cars, the blizzards were that bad. Inside the only source of warmth came from a cook stove and each other, of course. It was surprisingly cosy, though once a policeman shone his torch inside expecting to see two frozen corpses.

For the following few months Ernie and Doreen lived in the spare room of her parents' house before managing to invest in a home of their own which provided, in Ernie's words, 'a feeling of domestic and financial security'. Before they married Ernie and Doreen had often walked around the streets of Peterborough, looking at the nondescript suburban houses, with Ernie promising, 'When I get married I will take the woman I marry to a house like this and it will all be paid for.' He insisted that he was not going to get married until he had a sound bank account.

The thing was, they were hardly ever at their new home as they were on the road so much. From that point of view Peterborough turned out to be conveniently positioned, pretty much slap bang in the centre of England, perfect for driving to venues in the north or south in a new Triumph Mayflower Ernie had invested £600 in.

Now married, the dynamics of the boys' personal relationship changed dramatically, not least because early in their marriage Eric and Joan began producing children, a son and a daughter, which impacted on the couple travelling everywhere together. Doreen and Ernie, on the other hand, hardly ever spent a night apart. It must have been difficult sometimes for Eric in hotels or digs without Joan. Doreen recalls one night when Eric swore he saw a ghost in Blackpool. 'He came into our room in terror and threw a mattress at the foot of our bed. He was frightened to sleep on his own. "Oh yeah," I said. "Any excuse."'

*   *   *

Very early on in their relationship Ernie and Doreen made a conscious decision not to have a family. 'Ernie always said that as soon as children are involved the wife stays at home, and that's where trouble lies,' says Doreen. 'He knew about the temptations of being on the road. And I knew that I could never have tolerated infidelity.' Indeed, Doreen admits that one of the secrets to their long and happy marriage was an active sex life. 'I never said no and never had a headache. We used to have a "Sunshine Breakfast" if it was morning or a "Marvellous Matinee" in the afternoon. Evenings were usually quite quiet as he was always working!'

Unwilling to suffer the strain of long separations, the sacrifice both of them made was not to have a child. They'd seen so many show-business couples spending so much of their lives away from each other when children came along that they didn't want that to happen to them. Travelling, sharing digs, stuck for hours in stuffy dressing rooms and living in caravans during summer season was no life for a child. And endlessly placing them in the care of other people like grandparents would have been equally unfair. 'People didn't understand our desire not to have children,' says Doreen. 'We used to get letters saying: "If you are having trouble, here is the name of a good doctor." But we never regretted it.'

Indeed, for a while Doreen didn't just travel with Ernie, she was an active part of the act. 'I used to drive them around. I also used to give the lighting cues and the sound effects offstage, as well as answer the phones and the fan mail. That was from the early 1950s and lasted a few years. I think it was the unions who put a stop to most of it.' Few, if anyone, spent more time with the boys than Doreen and saw how close they were and how much fun they had together and how each made the other one laugh. 'They invented a special language which only the three of us understood. For instance, if they saw anyone with really terrible dress sense— you know, yellow check flares with a purple-and-green striped jacket—they'd say, "I'll have a second violin copy of that." Then they'd dissolve into uncontrollable laughter.' Even after a hectic show, if you were passing the boys' dressing room you always heard them laughing inside.

It was also Doreen's job to go out and find a Christmas card with either two monks or two choirboys on the front and when she found one buy up the shop's entire stock of them. 'Even back then they used to send Christmas cards and things like that from the two of them, never from just one.'

TWELVE

RUNNING WILD

The success of the boys' radio appearances on the BBC prompted producer Ronnie Taylor to gamble on giving the pair a show of their own. It was called *You're Only Young Once* and began in November 1953 and went out live from Manchester on Sunday evening, the boys' only day off since they were hard at work playing in variety the rest of the week. And for the first time the boys had the services of a professional writer, Frank Roscoe. However, it's fair to say that a lot of the ideas and jokes stemmed from Eric and Ernie themselves.

This radio success had not happened by accident, rather by design. For years Ernie had launched a furious one-man letter-writing campaign to BBC producers offering their services. And now that they'd shown they were more than capable radio personalities (Taylor had given them a second series), Ernie turned his sights on the new medium of television and began bombarding BBC executives over at Lime Grove.

Whether that led directly to the boys being hired for a spot on a live televised broadcast from the Tower Ballroom in Blackpool is unknown, but that appearance convinced Ronnie Waldman to offer them their own series. 'You boys are natural TV material,' he said. And they believed him, after all Waldman was Head of Light Entertainment at the BBC so obviously knew his onions, and had also given early breaks to the likes of Julie Andrews and

Benny Hill.

This was a monumental opportunity, the vehicle that could propel them to national fame. Far from overawed by it, the boys saw no reason why they couldn't adapt to television in the same way they'd taken to radio. But things started to go wrong almost immediately. *Running Wild* was to be the title of the show and it was strictly bread-and-butter stuff, comedy sketches and a musical guest star, a format that even by mid-fifties standards was corny and old-fashioned. Then they met their producer Bryan Sears who failed dismally to hide his disappointment that Eric and Ernie were 'Northerners'.

Back then there really was a perceived North-South divide when it came to comedy. What worked in London, went the argument, didn't work up North where the likes of Sears imagined people watched TV wearing cloth caps, snacking on black puddings with a ferret down their trousers. It was an arrogant point of view, but then the BBC in those days was, as some would argue it is today, a very middle-class, London-centric organization. As far as Sears was concerned, the boys simply came from the 'wrong' part of the country—he was mindful of the fact that the majority of television sets were then being bought in the South—so they would have to compromise their style to fit in with a general audience. The boys bit their tongue, after all Sears was the 'expert'.

As for material, Eric and Ernie made suggestions, came up with some new ideas and things that had worked well for them in the past. Sears blocked the lot, didn't want to know; he was bringing in a team of writers, six in all, to come up with routines for them. Again the boys went along with it but secretly they were growing extremely nervous, even more so when it became patently clear that none of the writers were capable, or willing, to write to their particular strengths. As transmission of the first show drew near, Eric and Ernie were fully aware of the unsuitability of what they were being asked to perform, that it wasn't showing them at their best, and yet they had no choice but to grin and bear it. After all, they were the novices with not a shred of power or control.

Running Wild went out live on 21 April 1954 at 9.40 p.m. This at a time when there were no other competing channels and the BBC had a total monopoly on the airwaves. Ernie had invested in his first television set so Doreen could watch the show at home. Up in Morecambe Sadie and Eric's dad sat round the box with friends anticipating great things. As did the corporation around Lime Grove as Eric and Ernie were seen very much as Ronnie Waldman's protégés. Much was expected of them. Those hopes were to be dashed in the cruellest fashion imaginable.

After the show finished both of them knew it hadn't quite worked, but nothing prepared them for the critical onslaught the next morning. The reviews were catastrophic, almost career-wrecking. 'This was one of the most embarrassingly unfunny evenings I have spent in front of the home screen for some time,' said one. 'How dare they put such mediocre talent on television?' said another. One critic pointed out that their musical guest Alma Cogan, 'stood out like a sunflower on a rubbish tip'. Most famous of all was the critic of the *People* newspaper who came up with a new definition of television as, 'The box they buried Morecambe and Wise in.' That more than any other notice touched a nerve with Eric who carried that clipping around with him in his wallet until the day he died.

It took a while for the initial shock to subside and when it did it led only to 'depression and a serious reconsideration of our future', said Ernie, who broke out in nervous boils, large angry red lumps all down the back of his neck.

Worse was to come when the boys received a broadside from Sadie when she phoned them up. 'What the devil are you two playing at? Everybody's talking about it round here. I daren't show my face outside the house, and I can't go shopping for fear of who might see me. We'll have to move. We'll have to change our name.'

Predictably, Sadie's words hit Eric badly. 'He became terribly morose,' remembered Ernie. 'Losing all his sparkle for days and threatening to pack in TV for good.' Ernie tried to snap him out of it but when he went round to see his partner the dejection, 'hung over him like an actual, physical presence'.

Whenever the boys hit a setback it was always Eric who took it more personally than Ernie. It stressed him out, as did much in life. Unquestionably Ernie was better suited to the often tough world of show business where a thick skin was mandatory if you were going to survive—and stay sane. Critical bullets, while having an emotional effect, usually bounced off Ernie, with Eric they always drew blood and it was left to his partner to cheer him up, to act as a source of encouragement and not let anything stall them. 'Ernie, from a very early age, had to wear armour plating,' says Doreen. 'He didn't really have much of a childhood and was left alone in London at thirteen. So things like the critical mauling *Running Wild* got used to wash over him. He used to say, "Well they don't know what they're talking about. We'll make it better." He was a tough little Yorkshire lad. If he'd reacted like Eric, Morecambe and Wise would never have got past *Running Wild*. Ernie was definitely the pusher.'

Paradoxically, when the boys were indeed boys, it was Morecambe rather than Wise who would be called upon to act as counsellor. By the time of Ernie's now infamous letter to Eric asking to end the partnership he had already been an 'adult' for some years and had the emotional scars to prove it. Eric then was exactly what Ernie needed at the time, a happy-go-lucky teenager whose only emotional scars came from going a few rounds with a pushy mother. Now though, with timing worthy of a Morecambe and Wise sketch, the roles had been reversed. Ernie had matured, was conditioned to criticism and ready to return the favour, while Eric had finally begun to experience the emotional turmoil of 'professional opinion'.

Ernie revealed his true emotions only ever behind closed doors: personal criticism affected him but he never allowed that to be seen. Instead he had to remain detached from this TV disaster, get his partner back on his feet and work out a plan to survive it and keep going. His great idea was to get the BBC to pull the plug.

When the second show was broadcast with little sign of improvement, both Eric and Ernie went to see Waldman, voicing their deep concerns about continuing. 'We're scared to death,' said Ernie.

'If it's all the same to you we'd like to pull out.'
Beyond the public embarrassment there was real
fear the bad publicity could severely damage their
reputation. 'Not on your life,' said Waldman. 'Look,
I'm not doing this because I'm bloody-minded. I'm
doing it because I believe you two are first-rate TV
comedy material. Stick it out. I have faith in you.'
Besides, they'd signed a contract, so really the boys
had no choice.

After another couple of episodes Eric and Ernie
really couldn't take any more and urged their
agent to get them out of it. Going back in front of
those BBC cameras was like walking out in front
of a firing squad. Waldman again refused. Finally
the last show was broadcast and Eric and Ernie
breathed a huge sigh of relief. Unsurprisingly,
producer Bryan Sears felt *Running Wild* failed
because of the boys' Northern roots. Ernie put
it down to inadequate material and their lack of
experience on television. 'But Ronnie Waldman
thought we were great,' he said. 'Unfortunately, he
was the only one.'

THIRTEEN

IT'S BEHIND YOU

Not long after the final episode of *Running Wild* the
boys took a phone call from a top booking agent:
'Hello, is that Morecambe and Wise?' The reply
went something like this: 'That depends. Have you
got a television set?'
    'No.'

'Yes, then it is . . .'

It wasn't so much the pasting from the critics that kept the boys awake at night, rather what effect it was going to have on their variety careers. Would their loyal audiences accept them back after such an inglorious failure? Would they be laughed and heckled off the stage? The poor reception to *Running Wild* had certainly knocked them back a few pegs and if proof were needed their first booking at the Ardwick Hippodrome in Manchester saw them slip to fourth on the bill.

In a bid to come back stronger the boys decided to freshen things up a bit, their act needed yet another overhaul. Just like the time they had to produce a new second spot within days, Eric and Ernie shut themselves away and experimented with new styles and new material. What they'd found had always worked best in the past was how an audience reacted to them as individuals rather than the routine itself. The decision was reached that from now on their own personalities would be at the forefront of the act: 'To be more ourselves rather than just two comics telling jokes,' said Ernie. Or rather slightly exaggerated versions of themselves. 'I'm an idiot, Eric is a bigger one.' In this respect they were now emulating Laurel and Hardy, a partnership comprised of two funny men, rather than Abbot and Costello, where one was the clear comedian.

Like Laurel and Hardy, Eric and Ernie became two characters, each imagining he is the brains of the outfit and the other one is the fool. It was a formula on which much of their humour would now be based. Of course, both had idolized Laurel and Hardy since their youth. Ernie saw their films at the local fleapit as a boy and managed to see them perform live at the Embassy Theatre, Peterborough in 1952 during their British tour. Even though this was at the end of their career and they were past their prime, it was still a thrill.

Interestingly, the man who brought Laurel and Hardy over to the UK was Bernard Delfont, the brother of Lew and Leslie Grade and a leading theatrical impresario, and it was Billy Marsh, Eric and Ernie's future agent, who looked after them while they were here. Oliver Hardy regarded himself as an actor first and foremost who'd enjoyed a successful career before being teamed up with Stan Laurel, who had only ever been a comedian. Billy Marsh and Oliver Hardy were on Regent Street one afternoon and Billy had to stop to get the papers, so Ollie was left standing waiting for him and the newspaper vendor did a triple take, he couldn't believe who was standing there. Plucking up courage the vendor said, 'Hello, Ollie,' and Ollie replied, 'Hello.' Then the vendor asked the worst possible question: 'Where's Stan?' To which Ollie replied, 'In my fucking pocket.'

Nervous about the reaction they were going to get at the Hippodrome, Eric and Ernie were pleasantly surprised when they walked out onto the stage. Alan Curtis, who appeared with the boys a year or so later in panto, remembers Ernie telling him that they got a huge round of applause from the audience. 'Although their TV series wasn't a hit in the business or with the critics, the public loved them because they'd actually *been* on television, and television was something new and exciting. I remember Ernie said it had given them both such a boost because they weren't top of the bill and were obviously feeling a bit unsure of everything.'

It was a vindication of sorts, and a much needed lift after weeks of deep depression. One reviewer commented, 'These can't be the same two I saw on television the other night because these guys were brilliant and are going places.'

Unlike today, if a comic died a dog's death on TV back in those early days few people either knew about it or cared. In the industrial North where the boys tended to gig few people actually owned a television set because they were far too expensive. So while the boys' failure was well known within the industry itself, in the outside world people had enough problems to cope with to even give it a second thought. In fact, promoters happily exploited their TV status to help boost the box office, advertising them outside their theatres as 'Those inimitable TV comedians'. In return, the boys received a warm reception and some much-needed adulation. Everyone was happy. Those nasty reviews, it seemed, had been forgotten by everyone. For a while, anyway.

And they remained popular enough to still be in demand for panto and summer season. Panto was great and the boys loved doing it but they did play in some theatres well past their sell-by date with dressing rooms full of cracked mirrors, moth-eaten carpets and wardrobes that looked on the brink of suicide. Doreen would do her best to spruce them up to make them look a bit more homely for their twelve-week stay. Another drag was the producer's habit of rehearsing not in the theatre itself but in an old drill hall somewhere sans any central heating with the inevitable result that come opening night everyone had the flu. Ernie himself suffered a lot from sinus troubles, 'and I would go on the stage drugged up to the eyeballs.'

In 1954 the boys appeared in panto at the Derby Playhouse with Alan Curtis, one of the great pantomime villains of his day. Curtis was The Baron, while Eric and Ernie played the two robbers he'd hired for his own devilish ends. Curtis remembers it all well. 'There was one scene based on a ship where Ernie and I walked up and down smoking cigars and swapping dialogue, with Eric interrupting and us telling him to shut up. There were other bits and pieces to it as well, but that was essentially it and the scene went on for about four minutes, and Ernie in particular worked extremely hard to make it work. When the first night came we did the sketch, but it only got a few laughs, it just didn't work. Anyway, the sketch was out straight away. They were totally ruthless like that. If it didn't work for them, it was out.'

Curtis next appeared with the boys in panto in Swansea where he thought they very cleverly solved the problem of their exits during the show. The idea was to have a song instead of always going for the big laugh. So when their exit was due either Eric or Ernie would say to Curtis or the Dame, 'We've got one more thing to say to you,' cue the line, 'What's that?' and they would break into song, perhaps 'You Can't Tell a Waltz from a Tango', which was a hit for their old friend Alma Cogan. 'Actually, we often used to go to the cinema in the afternoons during panto,' says Curtis. 'One day Ernie, Eric, Doreen and I went to see *The Tender Trap* with Frank Sinatra. The boys were quite taken with the theme tune as I remember, sung by Sinatra, and used it that night as their get-off music.

Their favourite though was "Dear Old Donegal", which was a big hit for Bing Crosby. I think they chose that because it had lots of quick patter in the chorus. It saved them the problem of having to think of a good laugh, you see.'

The last panto Curtis appeared in with Eric and Ernie was *Dick Whittington* in Dudley, where he played Alderman Fitzwarren and the boys played the captain and his mate. Every night the show closed with the full cast singing "See You Later Alligator", with the lyrics changed to fit with the story and accompanied by a twenty-one-piece orchestra! 'When we were rehearsing this song, I remember Ernie saying, "This music is going to take over the world, you just wait and see." He was the first person I'd heard who'd made such a prognostication about rock and roll. Everyone else had been quite negative. Not a bad forecast really!'

When it got to Christmas Day, Ernie and Doreen invited Curtis back to their home in Peterborough. 'However, coming back for the Boxing Day matinee almost saw the three of us killed. We were driving up a hill and a huge bus driving in front of us lost its grip on the ice and headed straight towards us—backwards! Ernie was driving a beautiful Triumph Mayflower at the time and was fortunately an excellent driver. He got us out of trouble, but only just!'

There were more celebrations on New Year's Eve. The whole cast of the pantomime had been given caravans to stay in and Ernie and Doreen invited Eric and Joan and Alan Curtis back to theirs to see in the New Year. Ernie was by no means a big drinker, in fact Doreen only recalls ever seeing him drunk once, and that was in this caravan in

Dudley. 'He'd drunk far too much. I remember him looking at me and saying, "I'm going to have to sit up all night," and when I asked why he said, "Because whenever I lie down I feel sick." He got through about five Alka-Seltzers the next day. Not very glamorous was it, a caravan in Dudley!'

FOURTEEN

ROCKING IN BLACKPOOL

With panto finished every entertainer worth his salt looked to get Blackpool for their summer season. Quite simply, if you were top of the bill there, 'you'd reached the Mecca in show business,' said Ernie. 'It dispelled all the memories of cramped railway compartments, unreliable motor cars and grim digs at a stroke. It was twelve or fourteen weeks of sheer joy and not a little glamour.'

Packed with theatres, cinemas, nightclubs and plush restaurants, the Lancashire seaside resort was at its zenith in the 1950s. At any given time of the day, if the sun was out, not an inch of sand could be seen on the beaches, so crammed were they with holidaymakers. Eric and Ernie always loved coming to Blackpool, it was weeks of hard work, yes, but also fun, with a great sense of community among the artists, who'd meet up each morning at the Winter Garden restaurant for coffee and a gossip.

There was also plenty of opportunity for practical jokes, like the time they got hold of a life-size ventriloquist's dummy and put it in their theatre's only backstage toilet. Several chorus girls bursting for a pee opened the door and, thinking it occupied, ran out screaming.

Being booked for an entire summer season also meant the boys could live a normal married life since they rented a house and could furnish it with knick-knacks from home. Sometimes Harry, Ernie's dad, would pop over and stay with them in Blackpool. Doreen liked the old fella well enough, 'but he could be very embarrassing (in a nice way) and was awful with money. Ernie would give him money and it'd be gone in no time. You know those shirts you used to get that had a spare collar, well he used to try and glue them onto other shirts and things like that. It was his slightly bizarre way of being thrifty I suppose!'

One skit the boys tried out in Blackpool involved a paddling pool onstage. Eric would be standing in the middle of it splashing about and holding an inflatable donkey under his arm. After a while Ernie would wander up playing the responsible adult and order, 'Come on you, out!' to which Eric would reply, 'Awww no, I haven't even got my dobbin wet!' For some reason the gag never seemed to go down particularly well with audiences, 'but I absolutely loved it,' Doreen confesses. 'Eric did too, so he kept it in especially for me. Nobody else seemed to enjoy it so I suppose it was our gag.'

It was during these summer seasons that the boys struck up a friendship with comic and musician Stan Stennett who often topped the bill at the shows Eric and Ernie appeared in. 'We got on very well,' recalls Stennett. 'They really were very funny. The great thing about them was that they were always

113

concerned about what they were doing. Although a lot of the things they did onstage seemed off the cuff, or looked as if they came easy to them, they worked very hard at it and were extremely dedicated about everything they did.'

Stennett would also sometimes appear with Eric and Ernie in panto. 'And there was one scene we always insisted on doing whatever pantomime it was and that was the "schoolroom" scene.' The trio had made it quite famous in previous pantos. It was one of their first big successes and was admired throughout the industry. It went like this, Eric and Ernie were Stan's two buddies in the classroom and they'd sit on opposite sides of the stage, Stan on one side, the boys on the other. 'And we'd have banter between the three of us and I used to throw buns at them. Actually, Little Ern became known as "Buns Wise" because he used to catch them and start eating them! Yes, that became quite a thing, the "schoolroom" scene, it's a classic pantomime routine and after doing it for something like four years, for ten weeks a time, twice nightly and so on, we made that our own, we really did.'

One afternoon Alan Curtis had to take over from one of the actors who was ill and without any rehearsal whatsoever appear in the 'schoolroom' scene. 'I was very nervous. The sketch went well, but when it finished Ernie stood up and started applauding me as I left to go back to the dressing room. Eric followed, as did the crowd. It was a very sweet and generous thing to do. Very Ernie.'

Working as closely as he did with Eric and Ernie, Stennett couldn't fail to notice the obvious affection both men had for each other, especially Eric towards Ernie. 'He had a great concern

114

about Ernie. He loved Ernie. Well, they were like brothers obviously. We used to always have fun with Little Ern, especially in pantomime. I'll tell you what Little Ern used to love. If I got my guitar and started playing a little rhythmic piece he would do a tap dance. He was a great tap dancer was Little Ernie. And Eric became a dancer as well, because of some of the routines they did. But Little Ern was a real pro. He really was. I loved working with them. And it was obvious, to people like myself anyway, that it wasn't a question of "Would they hit the top?" but "When?"'

At the time Stennett was a keen flier and owned his own small plane. 'I formed the Welsh air force. I called it the BERKS air force because anyone who flew with me was a berk!' After a few trips in his plane Stennett tried to persuade Ernie to buy his own. Ernie couldn't really afford such an extravagant luxury back then but he did take a number of flying lessons in Blackpool, much to Doreen's constant worry. 'He once took me out on a lesson, and the instructor was teaching him something called "stalling", which is where they start and stop the engine in mid-flight; probably not the best lesson for me to be asked on, if you think about it. And I thought, "Oh Christ, we're all going to die." It was so tiny this plane. I mean, if you leant to the right the whole plane leant to the right.'

While Ernie never continued his flying lessons, his love of aeroplanes continued for the rest of his life. So fixated was he by them that he'd literally fly in anything given the chance. Invited once to an event near Glasgow he flew back home overnight in the mail plane, which he was thrilled about. 'He also went to Germany with the Hampshire

Regiment once,' says Doreen. 'And they took him in a helicopter on the Dambuster's route over the Mohne and Eder dams. He talked about that for days. He also once talked the MOD into letting him go in one of those spy planes.' Ernie thought that was hilarious as you had to have a pipe attached to your 'bits and pieces' in case you had to spend a penny.

Naturally, when Concorde began flying in the early seventies Ernie was a regular passenger, even on one occasion sitting in the cockpit during landing, which was highly illegal, but somehow he managed to arrange it. 'And I remember we were in Australia once,' says Doreen. 'And the army had given him one of those hats that are raised on one side, a slouch hat. Anyway, the next time we were on Concorde he pulled it out of his bag. "This hat's the perfect shape for flying Concorde," he said, and he was right! Because of Concorde's slanted and very tight interior it looked like the cap had been moulded to fit!'

You can just see Little Ern sitting amidst the champagne-quaffing businessmen flyers with a smile on his face and that hat on!

116

FIFTEEN

SUNDAY *NOT* AT THE LONDON PALLADIUM

Although the pain of *Running Wild*'s failure was still vivid, the boys had no choice but to embrace television again. The fallout of their first foray into this new all-conquering medium was never going to be truly neutralized until they'd made it their own. Variety was on its knees and radio was already beginning to lose its audience to the wonders of the small screen. It was obvious that little box in the corner was the future and they had to master it or face extinction.

Ernie certainly recognized they couldn't rest on their laurels and needed to push on and develop further. 'That was where Eric and I differed. Of the two of us I think he was more interested in having a good time and enjoying himself, whereas I was constantly working towards a goal.' Ernie appreciated and fully recognized Eric's dedication and work ethic when it came to the act, 'but his ambition had its boundaries.' Eric wouldn't have minded never reaching the top of the bill, just so long as they had a successful career and were well respected, 'earning good money,' he said, 'but without carrying the whole responsibility for the show.' That was never going to be enough for Ernie who'd been one of life's go-getters ever since he was in short trousers. 'He was always terribly ambitious,' says Doreen. 'Rather like a donkey with a carrot in front of his nose.'

As the driving force behind the act in terms of naked ambition, 'Ernie was the one concerned with their long-term career and Eric was the one concerned with their next sketch,' is how friend Francis Matthews puts it.

Ernie was the polar opposite of Eric, whose self-motivational skills were practically non-existent. Professionally, Eric had rarely had to think for himself; Sadie had done all that for him. She wasn't just his mother and mentor; she was his ego and vital to his frame of mind and his ambition. Unfortunately for Ernie she never thought of telling Eric that this was only a temporary arrangement and that one day he might actually have to think and act for himself. While Eric was an instinctive comic, a complete natural, when it came to organizing and planning things, well, that wasn't for him, and it wasn't what he'd been accustomed to with Sadie pushing him on during those early years. With Sadie's drive and verve gone, often Ernie found himself urging Eric to think bigger, to push the act as far as it could go in terms of playing bigger venues and making it on TV.

A few guest spots in 1956 on *The Winifred Atwell Show* was a nice easy way back into television. Atwell was a hugely popular Trinidad-born pianist and her show was the usual light blend of music and comedy. And as it didn't revolve around the boys there was no responsibility or pressure on them, they could simply be themselves and perform with a confident freedom. The show's resident writer was a young Johnny Speight, who was a couple of years away from creating one of British sitcom's greatest characters in Alf Garnett. He liked the boys immediately, noting they were 'natural for television'. Speight became possibly the first professional writer to tailor his material to their strengths.

Incredibly, according to Alan Curtis, the boys rejected an offer around this time to appear on television's most popular entertainment show *Sunday Night at the London Palladium*. During panto season Stan Stennett was asked to do it and Alan Curtis went up with him. Bob Hope was top of the bill. A little over two weeks later Eric and Ernie were asked to appear but they decided to turn the prestigious gig down. Why? Curtis explains: 'You see, at the time they didn't feel that they had an act ready. It was very much Ernie's reasoning and sensibility. They weren't going to risk appearing with an act that they didn't feel was rehearsed or right for the show. It was an extraordinarily brave move, but ultimately correct. After *Running Wild* they were going to make sure that any future TV opportunities were given the best possible chance of being a success for them. *Sunday Night at the Palladium* was a very big new show and a huge opportunity for anyone. Far too big an opportunity to waste with the wrong act though! Val Parnell quite understood, but I'm pretty sure it niggled him a bit.'

When Curtis first heard the boys had turned the offer down he drew a little memorial cross on their dressing-room door. 'Underneath the cross I wrote: "In Memoriam of Morecambe and Wise— who turned down *Sunday Night at the London Palladium*." Fortunately they took it in very good spirits!'

The prank did come back to bite him, though. Eric and Ernie used to be huge fans of Robert

Orben, an American comic who'd been around since the late 1940s and wrote a multitude of joke books. The boys made frequent use of these books when they were working out their own routines in the early days and they used to keep some of them in their dressing room. 'These books were sacred to them really,' says Curtis. 'Almost bible-like! Well, not long after I'd put the memorial cross on their door I asked if I could borrow the books as I was about to start directing a show and thought they might come in useful. The boys wouldn't play ball though and said no. Anyway, I thought they were joking so I took the books and started to walk out. Before I reached the door a kerfuffle ensued and the boys tried to take the books back. Just then, Doreen turned out the lights—I was completely overpowered—lost the books, and they ended up tickling me almost to the point of wetting myself. Then Ernie said, "That'll teach you to put up a cross regretting the demise of Morecambe and Wise!"'

On a more personal note, Ernie and Doreen had been presented with the opportunity to build their dream home. The businessman who rented them the caravans they stayed in during summer season suggested they buy a large plot of land near his own property in Peterborough. It was too good an offer to refuse and, after some difficulty getting planning permission, construction began and they eventually moved in. Features included an open-plan lounge with stairs that came down into the room, a Cotswold stone fireplace, under-floor heating and a bar nestled discreetly at the back. The house also had three bedrooms and an extensive garden.

The whole place was designed from magazines

and built from scratch while Ernie and Doreen were overseas, so every now and then they would receive the odd tile or bit of sample wallpaper when the builders needed a decision from them. 'The house that we originally wanted to build was going to cost about £6,000,' says Doreen. 'But we couldn't afford anything over about £5,200, so in the end they made it two inches smaller all the way round and that saved the money.'

It would be their home for many years and Ernie became so synonymous with Peterborough that people imagined that's where he came from. He was even invited to become chairman of Peterborough United, although he wasn't much of a football fan. Eric took him along to one particular home match against Oldham and as the match progressed had a go at explaining the rudiments of the game. When Peterborough won Ernie turned to Eric saying, 'I'm going to congratulate our boys,' and went into the dressing room. 'Great game, lads,' he said.

'No, it wasn't,' the players replied.

'Yes it was,' said Ernie.

'No it wasn't. How could it be?'

'You won. What more do you want?' said Ernie.

'No, we lost.'

Ernie had walked into the wrong dressing room and was addressing the opposing team.

SIXTEEN

DOWN UNDER

In the autumn of 1958 Frank Pope managed to book the boys on a six-month tour in Australia with a revue starring Winifred Atwell. Sadie offered to look after her grandchildren so Joan could accompany Eric, and Doreen, naturally, was by Ernie's side. It was a huge commitment, taking a full week to get there with all the stopovers, including everyone's first trip to New York. Ernie was in paradise and did the whole tourist bit, walking in Central Park, going up the Statue of Liberty and travelling by bus and subway, even crossing the Hudson River by ferry. In fact, he made a list of all the things he wanted to try. 'He was America-mad and couldn't wait to get there,' remembers Doreen. 'There was a milkshake, a hamburger, a martini and eggs over easy. Not all at the same time, of course. He also wanted to go to all the jazz clubs. We saw Woody Herman, Miles Davis—loads of people. Ernie would have made a very good American. When he and Eric started out they used to do their act using American accents, of course. Not very good ones, mind you.'

In New York everyone stayed at the Sheraton Hotel and every morning Joan and Doreen had morning tea in the lobby while the boys always had coffee, 'because they'd gone all American!' says Doreen, who recalls that one morning the waiter got the order wrong. 'He had a very strange accent and was horribly loud, shouting all the orders through to

122

the kitchen. He walked over to us and said, "OK, you all have coffee," and before we had a chance to put him right he shouted at the top of his voice, "Hey, Fuck-off-ee!" which was obviously supposed to be "four coffees". People looked round in shock but we were in hysterics. The waiter had no idea what was going on.'

When it came time to leave and pay the bill the two couples were in for a shock: the Sheraton Hotel wouldn't accept Barclays' traveller's cheques, they'd never heard of them, and no one had any cash on them. It was a New York cabbie who came to the rescue. He'd picked them up at the airport—'Hello, kids, where're you going?'—and after depositing them at the Sheraton arranged to pick them up again when it was time to leave. 'So when he arrived we had to tell him we couldn't go because we couldn't pay the bill,' says Doreen. 'He asked us how much it was (I think it was about fifty dollars) and he said, "Oh, I'll pay the bill." We told him we'd pay him back later when we were able to cash the traveller's cheques and he said, "We'll see about that when we get to the airport, and if they don't do it you can send it to me. You've got honest faces." So when we got to the airport the driver parked outside the departure lounge and we were immediately accosted by the police. "You can't park there!" they said. "But these kids have gotta catch a plane," argued the driver. We eventually got into the departure lounge, managed to change the traveller's cheques and paid the chap back, with a very big tip, of course. And that story was printed in the *New York Times* and in the papers back home, saying that not all New York taxi drivers were miserable.'

Next stop was San Francisco, followed by Honolulu. In their live act the boys used to do a gag regarding Honolulu. It went something like, 'Where does the hair grow darkest and thickest on a woman?' And the answer was, 'Honolulu' or 'On-her-lulu'. Doreen remembers everyone standing in the sea in Hawaii and Eric and Ernie shouting, 'Where does the hair grow darkest and thickest on a woman?' and Joan and Doreen shouting back, 'HERE!' and pointed to their Honolulus!

After a few days they caught a flight to Melbourne. Or rather that was the plan. Soon after take off the boys noticed flames and sparks cascading out of one of the engines followed by sudden jerks and shudders as the plane dipped violently. The tannoy cracked on and the pilot, in a deep Australian drawl, announced they were turning back to the airport. If that wasn't enough, when they hit the air again the plane encountered an electrical storm that bashed it about like a pair of socks in a tumble drier. Eventually, upon landing, everyone quickly found themselves flats in a house that overlooked a delightful park. 'I remember we got soaking wet every night in Melbourne,' says Doreen. 'We used to get off the tram and walk through the Royal Botanic Gardens to look at the possums in the trees.'

The owner of the boarding house they stayed in lived there with his family on the top floor and like those old theatrical landladies back in Blighty rented the lower floor to showbiz people. Ernie and Doreen discovered that the tenant after them was going to be Sabrina, the British-born glamour model, cabaret star and Jayne Mansfield lookalike whose main claim to fame was her impossibly proportioned bust, which she'd just had insured for £100,000. It was a visit the landlord's twenty-year-old son was particularly looking forward to.

'Will she wear a bra?' he asked Doreen one day.

'Of course,' she replied.

'That's a swizz. If she wears a bra in her act I'll ask for my money back.'

One morning Ernie and Doreen lay in bed deciding whether to get up or not when a little piece of plaster fell on the sheets. They looked up and saw the top of a drill puncturing a hole in the ceiling, followed by a beady eye staring down on them. Later that same morning Doreen was in the bathroom when a face appeared upside down at the window. It was the son, suspended by his ankles. His obsession with Sabrina, thought Doreen and Ernie, was perhaps bordering on the psychotic.

In spite of the landlord's lunatic offspring, Ernie and Doreen enjoyed their three-month stay in Melbourne. With the boys second on the bill the shows went down a storm. Then it was off to Sydney where they stayed in a delightful flat overlooking the famous Bondi Beach.

The Australian tour had come at a good time for Eric and Ernie; it was a nice change of scenery and time to re-evaluate where they were going and what they wanted to achieve. Back home they'd grown a little disenchanted with the endless touring and theatres that were mere shadows of what they'd been in the glory days of variety. In truth, they needed shaking up themselves—understandable when you think they'd been a working double act now for seventeen years.

Heading back to Britain, they flew via New

Zealand and Fiji. 'And that was terrible,' Doreen recalls. 'Because it rained all the time and there were creepy crawlies everywhere, and I mean everywhere. I remember walking into the bathroom and there was a reddish furry thing in the bath. I was absolutely terrified and screamed at Ernie to go in and get rid of it. Tough Little Ern, nothing fazed him. Not even red furry monsters!'

After Fiji they landed in Los Angeles for a short break. Ernie had arrived in Hollywood at last and he was like a child wandering around looking at all the sights. Then it was off to Las Vegas where Eric, according to Ernie, 'hardly saw the light of day,' fixated as he was with the slot machines, while the girls and Ernie took in the sun by the hotel pool.

Back in Britain finally, it was indeed fortunate that their agent had already booked them a summer season in Blackpool because elsewhere there was no work to be had; their datebook was conspicuously empty. 'You've been away so long you're forgotten,' excused Frank Pope.

It wasn't quite as simple as that, there were other factors at play. 'What had happened during our absence was the beginning of a drastic change on the entertainment scene in Britain,' said Ernie. Those clapped-out old variety theatres the boys had been playing were now closing in their hundreds. The biggest casualty was the Butterworth circuit of theatres, for which, unfortunately, their agent Frank Pope had the sole booking, leaving him with virtually nothing of any merit to offer the boys. They had no choice now but to focus all their energies towards making it on television, and that meant finding a new agent. It was a hard decision because Pope had served them well and they both thought a lot of him, but this was business and he just didn't have the specialized contacts needed to push the boys towards more high-profile television work.

According to Doreen it was Ernie who eventually decided to get rid of Pope. The final nail in his coffin came one day when the boys were doing an audition for Bernard Delfont and Pope said to Ernie, 'Why don't you go and have a word with him and see if you can get a summer season.' Ernie thought, hang on, my agent should be doing that, not me. Ernie did ask him though! 'I think they'd almost made up their minds anyway regarding Frank,' says Doreen. 'But this made it a bit easier.'

Pope took his dismissal badly but it never affected their personal relationship and for years he'd occasionally drop in backstage to see the boys and indulge in nostalgic chats about the old days.

In late 1959 a prominent ad was placed in the *Stage* newspaper to the effect that Morecambe and Wise were looking for representation. Every leading theatrical agent got in touch save one— Billy Marsh. The boys wondered why, and the more they thought about it the more they came to the conclusion that Marsh was their man as he took bookings for summer seasons and for Bernard Delfont, the influential television impresario. Ernie sat down and wrote Marsh a letter asking if he'd like to take them on as clients. Within a day Marsh was on the phone inviting them to his office for a chat.

Once there the boys explained their current predicament. 'We're a standard act and have always had plenty of work, but things are tough now and work is difficult to come by.'

Billy Marsh looked at them through a cloud of

smoke. He was a compulsive smoker, yet he was far from the clichéd figure of the cigar-chomping, wheeler-dealing agent typified by the movies. Then in his early forties, Marsh was of slight build, wore glasses, dressed in a conservative manner and was quietly spoken. But he had an outstanding talent for spotting future stars and he was looking at two of them right now. 'An excellent standard act,' he said. 'In fact, a standard act that should really be top of the bill. But the only way to stardom these days is via television.'

'That's what we feel,' said the boys. 'We want to break into television and that's why we have come to you.'

Marsh picked up one of the phones on his desk and within minutes had booked the boys a spot on ATV's *Sunday Night at the Prince of Wales*. And that was it: Billy Marsh was their agent. They all stood up and shook hands and that was the agreement, no contract was ever drawn up.

Eric and Ernie adored Billy Marsh and stayed loyal to him for the rest of their careers. Jan Kennedy, who worked for the Billy Marsh agency from the mid-eighties and now runs the company, enjoys telling one story that perhaps more than any other encapsulates the relationship the three of them had. 'One day Billy rang up the boys and said, "Now look guys, we have a product placement going here, would you like a pair of Rolex watches? You've got to wear them on-screen." They used to do that in those days, they used to do a lot of product placement. And Eric and Ernie replied, "Yeah, that's great, absolutely great." So Billy said to Ernie, "Well, that's all right, Ernie, but what's in it for me?" There was a slight pause and then Ernie

128

said, "You can ring us every ten minutes and we'll tell you the time." So they all had a great sense of humour and Billy had a wonderful sense of humour as well.'

Although they were represented by the highly experienced and respected Billy Marsh, far from taking a back seat on negotiations Ernie often made sure he was with Billy when the big deals were going down. 'And they made a formidable team,' confirms Michael Grade. 'I remember popping in to see my father one day, Leslie Grade, and he'd just had Billy Marsh and Ernie in with him. It would have been 1965 and they were there to negotiate terms for Eric and Ernie's summer season at the ABC Theatre in Blackpool, which my father owned. So I asked my father how he was, and he just sat there dazed. I asked him what the matter was and he looked at me wide-eyed and said, "I can't believe I'm going to be paying Morecambe and Wise two thousand pounds a week." I asked if that was a lot of money, because I wasn't in the business at the time, and he said, "That is a lot of money. I've never paid anyone anything like that, ever!" My father was a very good negotiator, but he was reeling.'

However tough Ernie and Billy Marsh were as negotiators it was always done in a gentlemanly way, confirms Grade. 'There were never any tantrums. If you refused their terms they'd just say, "OK, we accept your decision, but that's what we think we're worth and we're not moving." There were no histrionics. I mean, if they had thrown their hands up in the air and started shouting it would have been easier, simply because you'd have had something to react to, but they never did. They simply shook your hand and got up to go. Nine times out of ten they'd be stopped before they reached the door, and would get what they wanted. Not many people were daft enough to turn them down.'

After their success on Bernard Delfont's *Sunday Night at the Prince of Wales* Billy Marsh got Eric and Ernie multiple spots on other hit shows like Val Parnell's *Sunday Night at the London Palladium*, *Saturday Spectacular* and *Star Time*, featuring a young Bob Monkhouse, in addition to the all-important summer season bookings. They ended up doing a dozen London Palladium shows, then a huge favourite with family audiences, once topping the bill; 'one of the great high spots of our career as a double act,' said Ernie, 'because we wowed the audience that night.' They got in trouble once, though, appearing a week after Rudolf Nureyev had performed in a pair of tights that left little to the imagination. In the middle of a ballet sketch Ernie ad-libbed, 'What about Rudolf Nureyev?'

'What about Rudolf Nureyev?' said Eric.

'Didn't you see it last week?'

'I'm sure everybody saw it last week.'

Smart innuendo was always a feature of Morecambe and Wise banter, but Delfont personally rapped them over the knuckles for that one. Yes, they could be blue on occasion but never coarse. Nor were they cruel. Ernie characterized their comedy as 'gentle, kind and innocent'. The watching public knew nothing was going to be offensive about them and that's why the whole family could watch. You could say the boys epitomized family entertainment. Once when they incorporated the word 'bloody' into their act

130

it drew an audible gasp from the audience. 'We were given a licence to perform by a public who knew we would keep our comedy within acceptable bounds and who trusted us,' said Ernie. 'We were not dangerous.' Ernie believes it was this innocence that allowed them to do the famous television sketches of them both in bed without anyone either complaining or even raising an eyebrow.

SEVENTEEN

TWO OF A KIND

Having done so well on television as guest artists, Billy Marsh and the boys agreed it was about time they had a show of their own again. Early in 1961 Marsh contacted Lew Grade, the power behind ATV, part of the ITV network, and pitched the idea. 'You must be joking,' Lew blasted back over the phone, his trademark cigar no doubt propelled out of his mouth with the speed of a V1 rocket over the channel. No matter how hard Marsh pressed Grade over the matter the tycoon simply would not budge. 'Maybe they are good, but they don't warrant a series of their own.'

A few days later Marsh took a call in his office, it was Lew. He wanted to give the boys their own series. It was an amazing turnaround and Marsh was never to learn the reason behind it. The offer was for thirteen half-hour shows to be broadcast live. Eric and Ernie were obviously delighted but still greeted the news with some trepidation, not to say nervousness. A second high-profile TV failure wouldn't just damage them it would almost certainly finish them off. But they also knew they had to take the plunge and hope that their experience of getting it so badly wrong before would help them this time. Even so, the boys sought the advice of their friends Jimmy Jewel and Ben Warriss, who in the late forties and early fifties had been the highest paid double act on the circuit with twelve Blackpool summer seasons and seven Royal Variety performances behind them: what these lads didn't know about the business wasn't worth knowing. Their advice to Eric and Ernie was simple: if they were to succeed on television they needed a top team of writers.

*　　　*　　　*

Back in the golden days of variety an artist could tour around the country for something like eighteen months and then merrily start all over again, singing the same songs, telling the same old hoary gags and audiences never clicked. Some people could survive on the one act their entire career. Television was different, it was a monster whose appetite was never sated, it could swallow your act up and spit it out again and it was gone, used, seen by millions, you could never do it again. Constant fresh material was the name of the game. It was an invaluable lesson, one Ernie mentioned years later to Lord Archer during a conversation: 'Ernie once said to me, "Our biggest problem with television is that once we've told one joke the whole world has seen it and every comedian in the world has stolen it."'

To fill thirteen half-hour shows, it wasn't just a huge raft of material they needed, it had to be the best, too. The writers they had in mind and had admired for a long time were Dick Hills and Sid Green, who'd worked for the likes of Harry Secombe, Bruce Forsyth, Sid James and Charlie Drake. No mugs then when it came to comedy but Lew Grade wasn't having it—they were too expensive or unavailable—and he told them to choose someone else. The boys refused to budge: it was stalemate until Grade finally gave in and got them.

The first episode of *Two of a Kind*, as the show came to be called, went out live from the Wood Green Empire at 8 p.m. on 12 October 1961. Favourably received, Eric and Ernie themselves believed the debut show was only partially successful. Their main angst was directed towards the writers' insistence on populating the sketches with a multitude of characters, with the result that too much was going on and it swamped the comedy; the boys always felt they came across best when it was just the two of them. Hills and Green were unrepentant and continued with their policy of multi-character-driven sketches for the second show.

Then, as luck would have it, the actor's union Equity called a strike. Eric and Ernie weren't affected, being members of the Variety Artists' Federation, but it meant the producers could no longer hire any actors for the sketches. The format of the show had to drastically change. Now the focus was completely on Eric and Ernie and it worked brilliantly. The reason was clear: after two decades together they had perfected the secret of their act, themselves. The relationship and rapport between them was the cornerstone of everything

133

they did. It had got to the stage where each knew what the other was thinking, it was almost a form of telepathy as Sadie herself pointed out. 'Eric and Ernie can practically read each other's thoughts. They have been together for so long and they are so much on the same wavelength and they know each other so intimately that each can, probably through instinct and habit, guess precisely how the other is going to react.'

It was a remarkable relationship that had transcended even friendship. 'I know Ern. I understand him,' said Eric. 'I know him better than his wife knows him, possibly better than he knows himself, and he understands me. It's good for the act. It's one of the reasons for our success.' Hills and Green eventually twigged and began tailoring their material to concentrate much more on the unique rapport that existed between the boys and the show went from strength to strength.

The friction, however, between Eric and Ernie and their writers never really dissipated. Yes, they worked well together but there were always tensions bubbling under the surface, and especially in Eric and Sid Green's relationship; their personalities just didn't mix and as usual Ernie was the peacemaker, getting everyone settled down and back to work although, as he later admitted, 'many great ideas sprang out of arguments.'

The work schedule was always the same. The writers arrived at the studio in the morning to meet with Eric and Ernie, bringing with them not completed scripts but a heap of ideas that would be bounced around by the four of them. The boys always offered ideas of their own, 'Twenty years' worth of stored material,' Ernie called it, in a bid to insert their own style. These sessions were often so fast and furious that a secretary was hired to take notes. All this disparate material was then put together into a script, rehearsed, and then performed on the live show.

Inevitably there was backbiting and recriminations if material didn't work, and arguments over who came up with what gag. It was important to the boys that they received fair credit for the success of the show. 'The makers of Morecambe and Wise were Eric and I,' said Ernie. 'We were indebted to our writers, but in the final analysis we had to shape the scripts to our own personalities.' Ultimately, they knew best. 'Whenever they put themselves completely in the hands of other people, it all went pear-shaped,' says Michael Grade. 'For example, look at *Running Wild* and their movies. In those situations they had very little say or input and all of them flopped. They knew what was best for Morecambe and Wise more than anybody else.'

In a 1967 interview for the *Stage* newspaper both Eric and Ernie perhaps went too far in glorifying their own contribution to the writing, to the detriment of Hills and Green, by inferring, whether in jest or not, that the writers provided something like six lines only and then everybody pitched in to complete the sketch. Hills in particular blew a gasket when he read this and wrote a heavily sarcastic letter to the paper's editor, which was published. With tongue firmly in cheek, but his annoyance all too evident, Hills insisted that he and Sid Green contributed at least eight lines, thus: 'Enter Ernie on his own . . . (one line). Smiles and acknowledges applause . . . (two lines). Adjusts tie, maybe blinks a couple of times . . . (three lines). Maybe dusts a speck off his suit . . . (four lines). Good evening ladies and gentlemen . . . (five lines). Our first guest is that popular singer Dusty . . . (six lines). Springfield . . . (seven lines.)'

Hills wasn't finished, since he recalled another line written on the inside of Sid's Benson and Hedges tin: 'The bit of paper which holds the fags in. But I can't trace it. I think it said—"Enter Eric."'

Years later, and after receiving an unusual number of suggestions for revisions, Eddie Braben, the boys' writer for the duration of the seventies at the BBC, showed his annoyance by sending Eric and Ernie a package containing forty sheets of blank paper along with a covering note that read: 'Fill these in—it's easy!'

Working closely with the writers though did allow the boys the freedom to deviate from the material, so they weren't tied down to a rigid pattern. 'Having worked together for so long,' observes comedy actor, writer and fan Kevin Eldon, 'they had gelled into this really tight little team that were technically superb yet they remained at ease enough to be able to riff with each other and do a bit of on-the-spot banter. You could always tell when something extra and unrehearsed was going on and it all added to the delight of them.'

It also tells you how uniquely close the pair of them were. 'Dealing with Morecambe and Wise was like dealing with one life form,' said their agent Billy Marsh. While Braben said they were so close there shouldn't have been 'and' in the way, it should simply have been: 'Morecambewise.' John Mortimer called their partnership akin to an English marriage, 'missing out the sex as many English marriages do.' Bill Cotton, their boss at the BBC, would recall that at meetings it was obvious both of them knew what the other one was thinking. 'They had been together for so long and when you saw them in the studio that is what came through.'

It also tells you how dependent Eric was on Ernie. The dynamics of the relationship in real life and on the screen were quite complex and quite sophisticated. Ernie wasn't a straight man in the conventional sense. After all, the people that make the best straight men are usually comics because they know where the laugh is. A lot of the humour depended on Eric bouncing jokes off Ernie and relying on him being sometimes equally as funny. 'Ernie was of course highly trained as a performer,' says the English actor, Francis Matthews. 'But could be extremely funny in his own right. He was a great comedian, but with Eric's extraordinary sense of fun and passionate front that aspect of Ernie's talent often got overlooked.'

This is the misnomer, Eric was the funny man, yes, but Ernie could also be very funny. Michael Grade offers this example. 'There was a famous flamenco dancing sketch they did back in the mid-sixties. It was written by Sid Green and Dick Hills and they did it on TV and onstage. When it came to rehearsing the sketch it seemed quite obvious that the guy doing the singing and the guitar playing was going to be the funny role, and that would go to Eric. But in rehearsal it didn't quite work, so they decided to switch it around and Ernie was absolutely hysterical.' The sketch depended entirely on Ernie's ability, or rather inability, to sing flamenco folk songs during a coughing fit. There he was, wailing and coughing and choking falteringly through some high screeched notes as the audience roared with laughter. 'He was hilarious. Eric was crying with laughter at Ernie. It was clowning of the highest order. And if you watch that sketch today it still stands up. Ernie has you crying with laughter. But you cannot define what they had. You can't measure it and you can't bottle it. It was the indefinable chemistry that made Morecambe and Wise, and Ernie was fifty per cent of that. There's no question about it. I've watched them at rehearsal, from the wings in theatres, in the studio and on TV. I've watched them over and over again and believe me Ernie is as integral to their greatness as Eric.'

Indeed, Eric was always quick to acknowledge Ernie's gifts; that he'd never have achieved the success he did without him. 'In a way Ernie was Eric's best audience,' is how Joan Morecambe sees it. 'Eric appreciated Ernie and his sense of humour and that always comes through. They didn't work against each other in any way.' More than once Eric described Ernie as the greatest straight man in the country. 'I remember when Eric used to get a particularly big laugh he would always say afterwards that if it wasn't for Ernie, none of that would have happened,' says actress, singer and comedienne Millicent Martin. 'They were always very generous to each other as performers. There was enormous appreciation, particularly from Eric to Ernie.'

Comedy writer and friend Barry Cryer, however, remembers Eric saying to him on more than one occasion, 'Ernie's not the best straight man in the world, but he's the best one I'll ever have.' It was a strange, almost subtle put-down. 'And yet they were so very close,' says Cryer. 'They really loved each other.'

Billy Marsh recalled once asking Eric who he believed was the greatest performer in show business. 'Ernie, of course,' he replied without hesitation.

EIGHTEEN

AMERICAN ODYSSEY

Any chance to perform at the London Palladium was rarely passed up by Morecambe and Wise and this particular eve-ning in late 1962 they knocked them dead, as they say. Sitting in the audience watching was arguably the most powerful man on American television—Ed Sullivan. He liked the boys; in fact, he liked them so much he booked them for his own variety show on CBS. When informed they'd be playing in front of a US home audience of 50 million, 'we were thrilled to bits,' said Ernie.

Flown out in grand style the boys made their debut on the show in March 1963. Ernie recalled that Sullivan was 'charm itself'. Though considering just how influential and famous he was Sullivan was not a natural performer, looking awkward on-screen, as if his mother had just been kidnapped and he was awaiting the ransom note. He really wasn't all there, first introducing Eric and Ernie as 'Morrey, Camby and Wise' as if they were a trio. On return visits he'd introduce them as, 'Morton and White,' and even, 'Bartholomew and Wisdom.'

Unquestionably their biggest gig to date, the

pressure understandably got to them and their debut performance on US television wasn't up to their usual high standard; in truth it was a little edgy.

'Good evening ladies and gentlemen,' Ernie started things off. 'It's very nice to be here. It really is wonderful to see all your happy, smiling faces.' They probably weren't smiling and the silence was palpable.

Things marginally picked up as the act carried on and they got a few laughs, emphasis on the word few, when Eric announced a sword swallower that was going to come on and swallow a four-foot sword.

'What's clever about swallowing a four-foot sword?' asked Ernie.

'He's only three feet tall.'

Afterwards Ernie was the more positive of the two, believing they could get better and make a real go of it. Eric was the complete opposite. 'He was unhappy with the reception we got,' Ernie recalled, particularly the fact that the scale of laughter and applause wasn't what they were used to back home. There were a number of reasons for that, the boys' routine lasted only eight minutes, not long enough to build up a rapport with the audience, and their accents and fast delivery might have proved a barrier, too. Asked by a journalist on their return how they got on Ernie said communication was the key problem.

'You mean they didn't know what on earth you were talking about?'

'Exactly,' Ernie replied.

The constant commercial breaks were a further irritant and made it difficult to sustain the charged

140

atmosphere the boys felt they needed for comedy. On their ATV show Eric and Ernie used to carry on joking and play-acting with the audience while the ad breaks were on to keep the vibe going. On the *Ed Sullivan Show* they noticed the audience just sat in hushed silence while the watching public were sold soap powder. However, even if it appeared the audience didn't exactly warm to Eric and Ernie, Ed remained a huge fan and invited them back a further eight times over the course of the next five years.

It didn't help that some of their familiar material was censored, deemed too rude for American families. As we know, innuendo made up a large part of their banter, 'naughty school-boy humour,' said Ernie, with plenty of double entendres but nothing too risqué. 'But yes we do have the occasional, shall we say, music-hall vulgarity,' confessed Ernie. Obviously music-hall vulgarity was beyond the pale for American TV producers. One musical comedy routine had Eric going 'rum-titty-tum-tum', well, that was out for a start, replaced by 'dum-diddy-dum-dum', but what do you expect from the halfwits who responded with horror to Elvis Presley's pelvic thrusts when he first appeared and ordered the cameraman to only film him from the waist up.

Other jokes went for a burton too, such as when Ernie put his arm around Eric and said, 'I've got a great idea.'

'I bet you have,' says Eric. 'I've heard about you.'

The producer shook his head. 'It won't work, guys. It's too sort of faggotty. You know what I mean.' Not really, this was all very innocent stuff, but out it went. No wonder Lenny Bruce never got a break on Ed's show.

Exasperated by having to change their act, Ernie gamely persevered, while Eric resented the intrusion and the effort of adapting to a new audience. It was a pattern that repeated itself throughout their American odyssey: Ernie hurdling all the obstacles put in their way, Eric bludgeoning through them not caring. Why did they have to conquer America anyway, was his thinking, wasn't adulation back home enough? Not for Ernie, he wanted this chance badly, much more than Eric who hated the whole experience, so much so that after every *Ed Sullivan Show* he insisted on getting the first available flight back to Britain, even if that meant flying at midnight. He just wanted to get out.

Ernie never truly understood his partner's antipathy towards making it in America. Maybe it was insecurity. Ernie noted in Eric a strange dichotomy. Performing onstage together he always had the utmost confidence in Eric that he could deal with any situation, yet offstage, principally during their American adventures, 'he seemed to go to pieces.' And try as Ernie might to encourage Eric to persevere in making a go of it in the States he wouldn't budge. Maybe it was an insecurity born out of being cosseted and mollycoddled by Sadie. Then again, maybe it was just Eric. 'It was probably the only time I became impatient with Eric,' Ernie later confessed. 'I was willing to give it a try. I was willing to work at it.'

There was something else that was strange. It wasn't just that audiences didn't find them hysterically funny in America; Eric didn't enjoy walking the streets there, because no one recognized him. In England they were household names. Put into any public situation Eric could crack a few jokes and everyone was putty in his hands. Not so in America, and he came to despise their anonymity. 'He needed the recognition,' said Ernie. 'He needed to be told he was funny.'

Eric didn't take to New York either; he never warmed to the city. Ernie and Doreen certainly got to know its sights and smells well, all the clichés, gun shots at night near their hotel, criminals being frisked in public with their hands up on car roofs, dead bodies on street corners; sometimes it was like being in an episode of *Kojak*. And there was one very unpleasant flight over when their plane was full of GIs retuning from Vietnam, 'all drunk and quite uncontrollable,' said Ernie.

Eric hated the flying, drunk soldiers or not. Ernie always tried to anesthetize him before take off with a generous slug of whisky but it never worked. As for Ernie, he had his own special take-off ritual according to Sylvan Mason, who befriended the Wises in the seventies. 'Ernie told me that when he went on a plane in those days he would order a brandy and put it upright to his lips. As the plane rose at an angle the drink poured into his mouth. You couldn't do that nowadays.'

The boys' last appearance for *Ed Sullivan* was in 1968, a special gala celebrating the eightieth birthday of Irving Berlin. They were in distinguished company that night, US President Lyndon B. Johnson introduced the event live from the White House, and Bob Hope and Bing Crosby numbered among the guests. During the show the boys were handed rather a large amount of money for their performance that evening and a previous show, all together it amounted to $14,000—in cash! Understandably the boys were nervous about

143

keeping it on them in the theatre. Not knowing what to do, they asked Doreen if she could look after it for them. 'Well, I wasn't going to keep it in my handbag as it could easily have been pinched, so I decided to keep it in my bra and then take it back to the hotel. There was only one person who was allowed to go in my bra (apart from me) and he'd just handed me half the money. It seemed like the safest place.'

When it came time to leave the boys were delayed so Doreen made her own way back the short distance to the hotel, feeling more than a bit vulnerable. 'There I was, walking down Fifth Avenue in New York, wearing a full-length mink coat with $14,000 stuffed inside my bra. And as I got to a pedestrian crossing a man approached me and started talking to me. 'Hello,' he said—and I think I muttered something back. "Hey, you're English, would you like to go for a coffee?"

'"No thank you," I said. "I don't know who you are for starters."

'"Oh, you don't want to worry about that, I work for the IRS, you can trust me."

'Well, I just froze. It was a natural reaction. My eyes must have been sticking out on stalks. I pulled my coat around myself as tight as I could, muttered some kind of garbled apology and ran off. Fortunately he didn't give chase!'

A review the next morning in the *New York Daily News Record* about Eric and Ernie's appearance said, 'There was one curiously out-of-place vaudeville team called Morecambe and Wise which should remain England's problem, not ours.' In spite of negativity such as this, there were times when the boys clicked on the *Ed Sullivan Show*

144

and did well. Ernie always took encouragement from those brief moments and was never to be dissuaded of his belief that they could have made it in America had they really gone all out for it. It was a disappointment that never left him. For much of his life Ernie harboured what some might say was an unrealistic notion of being a star in Hollywood. As Ernie was wont to say, 'You haven't made it to the top unless you've made it in America.' It was something Eric never understood, this yearning to be a Mickey Rooney type. 'But you became Ernie Wise,' he'd tell him. 'Isn't being the first Ernie Wise better than being another Mickey Rooney?' Not when it had been his ambition since he was a child performer.

For Ernie, Hollywood was much more than a fanciful dream, it kept him going sometimes and he'd always look back on that *'Ed Sullivan'* period as, 'the break that never was,' and brood about what it could have led to had they put more energy and commitment into it. 'The American episode ended without bitterness,' he said. 'But with the lurking feeling, on my part at least, that this was unfinished business.'

Eric always argued that to concentrate on America would be to the detriment of their British audience, which had taken so long to conquer. 'Ernie was always interested in cracking America,' says Barry Cryer. 'Eric once said to me, "We're as big as we could ever be over here, why would I want to start from scratch somewhere else?" But I think if Ernie had made it in America, he'd have liked it to be as a song-and-dance man like a Gene Kelly or a Fred Astaire. The thing was though, America had hundreds of them. I remember Bruce Forsyth used to have a similar ambition. He was a good dancer, could sing and do impressions etc., and he loved all the same people Ernie did. I remember Bruce saying to me once, "Barry, they've got hundreds over there. Why on earth would America want an English impersonator? I wouldn't stand a chance."'

Once asked what he thought of American audiences Eric replied, 'I like them. I like them because they're over there.' That sums it up, really. Ernie particularly had this Hollywood dream and would quite easily have upped sticks in Britain and lived over in the States to pursue it. You can visualize Ernie blending in at showbiz parties in LA or New York, sipping cocktails, while Eric waits at the airport in a raincoat waiting to get back to rainy England and fish and chips.

NINETEEN

TOM, DICK, (ERIC) & ERNIE

Their first appearance for *Ed Sullivan* might have been mixed at best, but back in Britain Eric and Ernie's ATV show had become so successful that in 1963 it was second only to *Coronation Street* in the ratings. Its anarchic humour was a hit with young audiences while the nostalgic echoes of variety pleased the older types. Their summer season in Blackpool broke box-office records and they were voted Britain's top TV light entertainment personalities of the year by BAFTA, an evening they'd never forget, not merely because it was their first major honour but as they were being presented with it there was a disturbance in the audience as

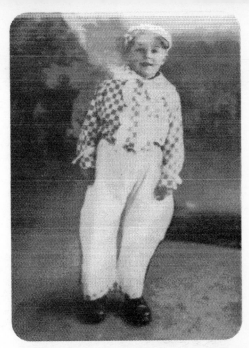

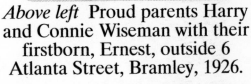

Above left Proud parents Harry and Connie Wiseman with their firstborn, Ernest, outside 6 Atlanta Street, Bramley, 1926.

Top A very early publicity shot of Bert Carson's Little Wonder, soon to become Ernie the Provider.

Above Ernie with his sister Annie and brother Gordon, circa 1935.

Left One of Ernie's first professional portraits. Although already a seasoned performer, he could hardly have imagined what he would go on to achieve.

To ERNEST

NOTTINGHAM EXPOSIT

JACK HYLTON A

Ernie duets with
Bryan Michie, th
man who discover
him in 1938.

ay 10-20 1939

IS BAND

Above Ernie (centre) together with friend and mentor Jack Hylton (in the dark suit) and his orchestra. This photo took pride of place on Ernie's study wall throughout his adult life.

Left 'The Jack Buchanan of tomorrow' (as young Ernie was sometimes known) now looking every inch a professional in *Youth Takes a Bow*, 1939. It was during this show that he met and became friends with a young hopeful called Eric Bartholomew.

Pretty dancer
Doreen Blythe
performing in
Blackpool aged
seventeen.

Doreen and Ernie share a moment
together in Harry and Connie's
kitchen, 1952.

Eric and Ernie visit Harry and Connie on a trip to Leeds in
the early 1950s. By now their careers had taken off and they
were becoming regulars on the radio.

A portrait of Ernie, obviously taken before he destroyed his pipes!

Doreen's dancers form a guard of honour for the newlyweds on Sunday 18 January 1953.

A very happy couple.

Ernie, Doreen and a rather pensive-looking Eric, on a night out in Blackpool during the mid 1950s. Others joining the party include singer Alma Cogan (far left) and comedian Billy Dainty (second right).

A 1950s Showbiz XI. Joining Ernie on the back row are comedians Stan Stennett (third from left), Tommy Cooper (in a fez) and Jimmy Jewel (fifth from left). On the front row with Eric are the team's captain, the great Stanley Matthews (third from left), and Ben Warriss (fourth from left).

Eric and Ernie in 1941. The boys were working as a duo at this point, despite Eric posing here as his solo 'I'm Not All There' character.

Conscription broke up the boys' fledgling double act. Ernie gets to taste some of his own cooking on board *Firelighter*, 1943.

Work was hard to find after the war, which is why the boys signed up for Sanger's Circus and Variety. *Left* Ernie struts his stuff on the stage and, *right*, posing on the steps of the trailer he and Eric had to share with the show's pianist.

Who's the lucky lady? If it is a lady! Eric and Ernie during one of their many forays into pantomime—this time in the late 1950s.

Behind a camera at the BBC in 1954, shortly before the launch of the much-maligned *Running Wild*. A wasted opportunity perhaps, but an invaluable experience that was to serve them well in their quest to conquer TV.

news broke that JFK had been assassinated.

If such a thing were possible 1964 was shaping up to be an even better year. *Two of a Kind* continued to draw huge audiences and the Variety Club of Great Britain awarded them show-business personalities of the year. 'It seemed that we could do no wrong,' said Ernie. And he was right. But with success came not a little sacrifice. Early in the year Eric moved to a splendid house in Harpenden but spent less than a month there that first year, such was his and Ernie's workload. At least Ernie had Doreen with him for company on the road. They, too, hardly ever saw their house in Peterborough, using it just for weekends. With the TV show based in London they decided to invest in a second home in Harrow.

Actually, it was while Ernie was shooting the first Morecambe and Wise film that the idea was broached. Not having a London pad, Ernie and Doreen stayed in hotels, and while Ernie worked at the studio Doreen used to drive around and look at properties for sale. Choosing the right area was easy, they got a map, put it on the floor and worked out which district was closest to where the boys worked most—Elstree, the BBC and Pinewood— and Harrow seemed to be the one.

It was hugely ironic that having reached the top, a position for which they had strived for so long, they would find wealth and recognition but also unbelievable stress. 'People were making demands on us constantly,' Ernie complained. And yet, every offer of work was snapped up. Like all entertainers, who are perversely insecure creatures at best, they were frightened that tomorrow the phone would stop ringing and the jobs would dry up. Working flat out, after a show they'd come offstage and collapse in their dressing room so exhausted they couldn't stand up again. They were gigging with such ferocity they weren't giving themselves time and space in between engagements to relax and build up their energy levels again. Sometimes Eric and Ernie would do two Sunday concerts, say in Norwich and Scarborough, and they'd always fly up in something like a Cessna. 'Whenever we arrived at the airport the engines were always running and propellers going,' remembers Doreen. 'Then we were rushed on-board and set off. We felt like refugees or criminals!'

This pressure was felt most keenly by Eric, who got through sixty to a hundred cigarettes a day. 'I think I was better adapted by nature to cope with the treadmill,' said Ernie. 'Eric is a worrier and a perfectionist. He puts a great deal into a performance. I do too but it takes more out of him emotionally than it does out of me.'

Ernie also found it easier to leave his professional persona in the dressing room and become Ernie Wise, husband at home with Doreen. Once work was done he'd take off his make-up and be away as soon as he could whereas Eric couldn't get changed, he'd hang around the studio or the theatre, mope and mull things over and always be the last to leave. Even at home with Joan he couldn't relax completely. Ernie wasn't the sort to crack jokes around the house. 'Thank God,' says Doreen. 'He had a very subtle sense of humour.' It was another fascinating difference between the two men. 'Eric was nervous; I am calm,' Ernie explained. 'Eric couldn't relax, whereas I could. He was always sensitive to criticism. He worried if people thought he wasn't funny all the time. He was insecure and needed constant praise to reassure him. I was none of those things.'

Ernie had it too, of course, this incredible need to perform in front of people; he'd had it since he was six years of age. 'This isn't a job—it's a way of life,' he'd say. Addicted to applause, oh yes, the roar of the crowd was just as essential to him as it was for Eric, but he could control that need and switch off. Eric couldn't, he always had to be 'on'. Doreen once summed this up brilliantly to a visiting journalist. 'If Ernie was in this room with us, and you were chatting to me, he'd go and make the tea and be prepared to fade into the background. If Eric was here, forget it! He'd be there, centre stage, entertaining you. He always had to be the centre of attention.'

In this regard Ernie was very different to his television persona. 'Ernie was a far more reflective character,' remembers Sir Michael Parkinson. 'And I suppose you would probably get to know Ernie better than you would Eric after spending time with the two of them simply because you got to speak to the real Ernie, whereas with Eric it was always Eric Morecambe comedian. I'm not sure if anybody actually did know the real Eric.' Perhaps Ernie was the only one.

Barry Cryer knew both of the boys for years and whenever he met up with Eric Morecambe what he got was Eric Morecambe television personality and comic, whatever he was doing. 'Whereas Ernie Wise was either Ernie Wise the performer, or Ernie Wise the husband, friend or businessman; the two didn't cross.'

Angela Rippon got a sense that Eric and Ernie's

public personas very much tallied with how they were in real life. 'Ernie was the straight man so when you met him, he was straight, he didn't try to crack jokes all the time, he didn't try to be funny, he was just lovely Ernie Wise. And that was how it always struck me, that in fact the partnership that they created as a comic partnership was a very accurate reflection of the two men that they really were in their private lives as well.'

This frenetic workload caught up with them at the London Palladium of all places in March 1965. Waiting to go on, feeling jaded and low, Eric casually remarked, 'Jesus, I hope they're a better audience than we had last time.' Only the radio microphone round his neck was already switched on and it played around the whole auditorium. The boys came onstage to, shall we say, polite rather than rapturous applause and by the time they left it wasn't any more enthusiastic. Behind the curtain Eric grumbled, 'That must be the worst bloody act we've ever done.' Again the mike was still on and the audience replied in unison—'Yes!'

1964 had ended with panto at the Palace Theatre, Manchester with the Canadian actor and singer Edmund Hockridge, who along with his wife Jackie knew the boys well. They first met up in summer season at the opening of the Princess Theatre in Torquay in 1961, where Tommy Cooper was top of the bill. 'We became great friends when we were down there,' recalls Jackie. 'We all rented houses and used to have parties after a Saturday night show and of course Tommy Cooper and the boys were great fans of each other. Tommy's dressing room, Edmund's dressing room and the boys' dressing room were all on one side of the stage and after the show they'd all get together and would have a tremendous amount of fun. I remember Tommy Cooper would always claim he was on a diet and when he arrived at a party would refuse any food. This went on for an hour or so and he would always eventually relent and end up eating everything in sight.'

Tommy Cooper remained friends with Eric and Ernie and made a bizarre guest appearance on one of their television shows. Alas it was not seen on camera. Tommy was at the bar at Teddington Studios having a quiet drink. The news had been full of stories that day of Dick Emery's marriage break-up. Looking at a clock Tommy saw the time was fast approaching eight o'clock. He knew Eric and Ernie were in that evening and about to start taping their show. His giant lumbering frame walked down the corridor towards the door to the studio where a red light was flashing, a warning that transmission had started and not to enter. Tommy barged in and made his way to the foot of the seating area as Eric and Ernie began their warm-up with the audience. It was now that Tommy made his move and his entrance onto the stage was met with uproar from the audience and bewilderment from the boys. Grabbing Eric by the arm Tommy collapsed onto one knee and began to cry inconsolably. It took several moments for the audience to calm down, by which stage Ernie moved in and asked, 'Tommy, what's the matter?' That mug, sorrowful at the best of times, looked up and bleated, 'Dick Emery has gone and left me.' He then stood up and walked off.

That summer season was full of glorious memories for Jackie. 'We had a turbo speedboat which was quite new at the time moored near to the dressing room at the back of the theatre and we used to take members of the cast out on the boat, including Eric and Ernie and Doreen, we used to go mackerel fishing. Lovely memories.'

During the '64 Manchester panto the Hockridges, who had a young son, were looking to buy a property. One weekend Ernie and Doreen invited the couple to spend a quiet Sunday with them at their home in Peterborough. It just so happened next door was up for sale and they all had a quick look round and chatted with the owners. 'We were having a meal at the pub that night,' recalls Jackie, 'and the chap from the house came in and said I accept your offer. Ted and I were flabbergasted. We'd talked with Ernie and Doreen about putting in an offer but hadn't actually done so. It appeared that Ernie had done the deal for us. Anyway, it seemed like a good idea and Ernie was a very good businessman so we knew he'd have got us a good deal.'

Come Monday morning the Hockridges drove back to Manchester faced with the reality that they'd just bought a house in a town they knew absolutely nothing about. 'It was all such a whirlwind,' says Jackie. 'We were neighbours with Ernie and Doreen for quite a long time. So we went from living in a flat in London to living in Peterborough, which was quite, quite different. I remember in Peterborough we used to have our milk delivered by horse-drawn cart, the horse used to come and rest on the green just outside our house and munch the grass while the milkman delivered the milk. We couldn't believe it was so quaint. And Ernie used to come round for a chat and he had such a cheeky face and was such an awful tease. Believe it or not, forty-four years later I'm still here in the same house!'

TWENTY

RANK OUTSIDERS

It must have had something to do with Ernie's long-cherished ambition to make it in Hollywood. Otherwise, why else did the boys put in an audacious bid in 1964 to buy British Lion, the production company whose stable of films included *In Which We Serve* and *The Third Man?* This prestigious icon of British moviemaking had hit troubled financial waters and was seeking a buyer. The bid, one suspects masterminded by Ernie more than Eric, involved the boys getting other entertainers to come in as partners to raise the necessary one and a half million pounds. It was all pie in the sky of course; besides, Little Ernie faced stiff competition from big industry hitters like Leslie Grade, Sir Michael Balcon, the American producer Sam Spiegel and Brian Epstein. Let's face it: this was never going to happen, but the waves it generated within the show-business fraternity certainly alerted people that Morecambe and Wise were looking to extend themselves beyond their comfort zone.

Way back in 1960 producer Hugh Stewart had been in Weymouth shooting the Norman Wisdom film *The Bulldog Breed* with director Robert Asher. Eric and Ernie were there in summer season and experiencing quite an eventful time. Laurie Holloway, the pianist and composer best known as the musical director for Michael Parkinson's TV chat show, was on the same bill and living in a caravan just off the beach. 'And my next-door neighbours were Ernie and Doreen, so I got to know Ernie quite well. After a few weeks I got appendicitis and I ignored it, which is obviously the wrong thing to do, and eventually I had to be taken to hospital but in those days very few people had cars. Luckily Ernie and Doreen had a car and Ernie took me to hospital and from that day onwards he always claimed that he saved my life. "I saved his life, you know," he'd say whenever we met at showbiz functions. "I stopped him from dying!"'

As usual, Eric and Ernie played to capacity crowds and one evening Hugh Stewart caught the show and enjoyed it immensely. When *Two of a Kind* became a hit Stewart thought it was time to make an approach, certain that Morecambe and Wise could become top film comedians like Wisdom. The deal was irresistible: three films over the course of three years for Rank, the country's top film production company. The boys signed up without hesitation, hoping to bring the same kind of originality to movies as they'd brought to their TV shows. With that in mind Hills and Green were hired as the writers, while everyone agreed a good subject for their debut movie would be a spy spoof. It couldn't miss, could it?

The Intelligence Men was shot at Pinewood Studios. For Ernie especially it was a dream fulfilled: here he was at last working at a proper film studio. Maybe it wasn't quite Hollywood but it was the closest thing to it since Pinewood was home to the massively popular James Bond movies, the Carry On series was filmed there too and the studio had been the hub of British film-making since it opened in the 1930s. Ernie would single out his first day there as, 'The greatest moment I remember in show business.' He walked around the place, soaking in the hustle and bustle of a large working movie studio, like a kid in a candy store. 'I was certain I was now going to become that international film star.'

Even better news was that they were each to have their own trailer. The boys had always been used to sharing a dressing room on variety tours, so this was luxury indeed. That was until they saw it; the thing resembled a van more than a trailer and inside was even worse, with no heating or running water. A disillusioned Ernie had just sat down when there was a loud rap on the window, he opened it and a member of the crew handed him his dinner on a paper plate. He was a long way from Hollywood, to be sure.

Such harsh realities also impinged upon the film itself. The boys hadn't wanted to make your formulaic British comedy picture, but as production moved forward it became obvious that Rank weren't on the same wavelength. Not prepared to gamble, they approached the venture as if it were another Norman Wisdom movie, to the extent of bringing in Wisdom's regular director Robert Asher.

The Intelligence Men opened in March 1965 to disappointing reviews. 'An unspeakable British farce,' said the critic of *The Times*, who believed poor Eric and Ernie had been fed through the Norman Wisdom sausage machine, 'and come out looking as though they could not make a hyena laugh.' The *Sun* said the film reminded them of Abbott and Costello at their worst, while the *Sunday Express* called it, 'the ruination of two excellent comics.'

The critical backlash to their first film hit them 'like bolts from the thunder god', Ernie confessed. But there were some mildly positive notices, too, and *The Intelligence Men* ended up performing adequately at the box office, enough to warrant the second film in their deal to go into production. Called *That Riviera Touch*, while Hills and Green returned as writers, things looked decidedly more promising with the installation of Cliff Owen, a new and more interesting director who'd made *The Wrong Arm of the Law* with Peter Sellers, and it would be shot on location in the South of France.

The summer of 1965 was memorable indeed with the whole cast and crew, thirty in all, packed into a BAE Trident jet for their flight to Nice. The principal players stayed in the famous Negresco Hotel and every day Doreen and Joan had lunch on the beach while the boys toiled in front of the cameras.

Edmund and Jackie Hockridge, Ernie and Doreen's neighbours in Peterborough, came out to visit. Jackie, then pregnant with her second child, has never forgotten it. 'We met them for dinner one night after they'd been filming. Lionel Jeffries, Warren Mitchell and the boys took us to this beautiful French restaurant where they had a guitarist going around all the tables serenading people.' At one point Eric and Ernie invited the musician over to play something and at the end of each verse shouted at the top of their voices, 'Boom Oo Yata ta ta', which was a famous musical sketch they'd performed on *Two of a Kind*. 'Everybody

156

found this hysterical, except the guitarist,' remembers Jackie. 'But they hadn't finished their fun yet, for the next God knows how long the boys followed the guitarist around and each time he stopped at a table to serenade somebody they would wait until the end of the verse and shout, "Boom Oo Yata ta ta." They certainly had a captive audience and an appreciative one. So with Warren Mitchell and Lionel Jeffries telling stories and the boys with their poor guitarist it all made for an absolutely wonderful evening. Lastly, and this is true, at one point during the evening I genuinely thought I was going to give birth I was laughing so much. This was quite alarming as I was only five months pregnant, fortunately nothing happened!'

That Riviera Touch was a much more fun and relaxed film to work on than *The Intelligence Men*; Cliff Owen was less stubborn than Asher and more conducive in allowing the boys to throw ideas around. Their leading lady Suzanne Lloyd recalled that Eric and Ernie were so funny that the crew had trouble not ruining a take by laughing out loud. The fun proved so infectious that the cast and crew of *Khartoum*, which was being shot on the next stage, came over to visit. 'They had to stop that, though,' said Suzanne. 'Because the set was getting too noisy and besides they were drinking all our tea and eating our biscuits.'

One sensed that Owen at least attempted to make a film that was less archetypal of British comedy and to show the boys at their most natural. As a result it's probably the most admired and fondly remembered of the three pictures Eric and Ernie made. Again, though, they were let down by another formulaic script. As the critic of the *Daily*

Mail observed, 'Morecambe and Wise have it in them to be a side-splitting film comedy team, but they need funnier material than this to prove their mettle.' Despite that, the picture played well at the domestic box office.

In February 1966, shortly before the release of *That Riviera Touch* Ernie's father died. Ernie knew Harry had been ill for some time but still the news came as a shock. He and Eric were performing onstage when the call came through and Doreen took it. Deeply upset by the news, Doreen was unsure quite what to do, so in the interval she spoke to Eric and together they decided it was probably best if they didn't tell Ernie until after the show. 'So we told him as soon as the curtain came down and it really hit him. He would always go very quiet if anything upset him. You see, he and his dad weren't just father and son, they were partners. He was the only other person Ernie ever went on a stage with, and he was the first, of course. He was the one who realized Ernie's talent.'

Unlike Sadie, the typical stage mother who didn't really give two hoots whether Eric was enjoying himself or not, Harry put Ernie on the stage because he saw a spark in his boy, a spark and a big smile. He was a chip off the old block. What started out as a bit of fun and a few extra bob did indeed turn into Ernie being used as the family meal ticket. That said, Harry would never have let it go on if he hadn't been sure Ernie was enjoying himself—and Ernie enjoyed just about every minute. Despite his parental failings and slight eccentricities, Harry was a good man and a loving father. Nobody was as proud of Ernie's success as his dad and there was of course a tremendous bond between them. A bond that Ernie was reminded of when Harry died.

Coping as best he could with his grief Ernie threw himself into his work, taking just a single day off to travel up to Leeds to say one last goodbye, with Doreen at his side for support. He'd always been close to his dad, much closer than he was to his mother, who Doreen recalls was a very cold woman. 'His dad's death upset him more than anything. Ernie was like a rubber ball though, and always bounced back. He'd had so many knocks in his life that he was used to having to get on with it.' Touchingly Ernie wrote of his father's passing: 'The guiding light of my life had gone out. But its afterglow still remains.'

The boys' third and final film for Rank, *The Magnificent Two*, was released in 1967 and again hailed from the overworked quills of Hills and Green, with the not very able support of two other writers Peter Blackmore, a veteran of Norman Wisdom comedies (Rank playing safe again), and Michael Pertwee. The plot was hackneyed to say the least, with Eric and Ernie playing inept travelling salesmen who get caught up in a South American revolution, and despite machine-gun-toting girls in bikinis it was another flawed effort. As with their misfiring turns on American television, Ernie looked back on their cinema outings as another missed opportunity. 'We were caught up in something that was bigger than us and that wasn't under our control.' Not slow in criticizing the 'penny-pinching budgets' (filming at Pinewood Ernie was dismayed to learn that one set from the new James Bond movie *You Only Live Twice* cost the same as their entire budget for *The Magnificent Two*) and inadequate scripts,

159

Ernie had to admit that both he and Eric weren't totally blameless either. 'Basically I think they felt confined,' is Doreen's take. 'They didn't like the restrictions of film-making and the length of time it used to take. They also had far less control over proceedings, which was important to them. After all, nobody knew Morecambe and Wise better than Morecambe and Wise.'

In truth, film didn't really suit their style, that was the problem. They'd always reacted and played better to a live audience, be it in a TV studio or on the stage of a theatre. On a film set all they had to feed off was a bored-looking crew. Repeated takes also wore them down and killed any comic spontaneity. Suzanne Lloyd, an experienced movie actress, felt that the boys were never comfortable with movies. 'They were improv specialists. They did it once on TV and that was it. In film they had to do it over and over and matching was a nightmare for them both. They were concerned that the spontaneity would not be there and how to keep the takes fresh.' Joe McGrath, who directed *Night Train to Murder*, the boys' much-heralded return to the movie format, recalls Ernie saying to him one day on the set that one of the reasons their Rank films never worked was because of the editing. 'They paid us a lot of money to do the films,' Ernie explained, 'then they handed them over to an editor who was earning fifty pounds a week, and they ruined them. You can't just edit that kind of timing and experience and certainly not without our involvement.' McGrath thought Ernie's assessment was absolutely spot-on.

TWENTY-ONE

CANADA CALLING

Two of a Kind's mixture of comedy sketches and music was still proving a winning formula with home audiences, plus the occasional star guest like Ray Ellington, Tom Jones and most famously the Beatles. By the mid-sixties, though, their initial contract had run out and Lew Grade was keen for the boys to sign a new one. Eric and Ernie weren't exactly bowled over by the terms on offer so a meeting was arranged and Grade, along with Billy Marsh, drove up from London to Great Yarmouth where the boys were performing in summer season.

Early that evening Doreen just happened to be picking up the mail from the stage door when she saw Marsh and Lew Grade drive up towards the theatre. Lew got out of the car all flustered and started to undo his tie. 'God, that was an awful journey, Billy. If I don't get this contract signed tonight it'll be your fault.' Doreen dashed off to see the boys and told them what she'd heard. 'Well, they didn't like this one little bit—especially Ernie. They weren't going to be pressured into signing with anybody. Not even Lew Grade! The terms had to be right and they had to be completely happy.'

More than anything, Morecambe and Wise was a democracy, especially when it came to negotiations and decision-making, according to Michael Grade. 'If ever an offer came through or something like that, they'd debate it between them and when they'd finished, if one of them said no, the other

161

would say, "Right, that's the decision." It was the same with ideas for the act. It didn't matter how the other one felt, if it wasn't unanimous, that was it—out. That was the end of it. I'm not saying they didn't have their moments of course, but they kept it all very private.'

So the boys went into the meeting 'informed', so to speak, and subsequently refused to sign. 'I think they wanted to make Lew realize that they weren't going to be strong-armed into anything,' says Doreen. 'I'd have hated to be Billy Marsh on the journey back!' It's unlikely, though, that Eric and Ernie didn't forewarn their agent about their intentions, considering how close they were, and in the end they did sign up again with ATV.

It was like a game almost, these negotiations with Lew. Another time the TV tycoon almost fell off his chair when he heard what the boys wanted for their next series. 'They want how much?!' he blasted down the phone to Billy Marsh. 'Let me talk to them.' Eric and Ernie duly arrived for the meeting and Ernie opened the batting by announcing, 'Lew, we bought you a present.' From his inside pocket he produced a tiny packet of supermarket-cheap Manikin cigars: they looked positively skid row compared to the humongous Havana cigar Lew was puffing merrily away on. Michael Grade was at that meeting and remembers Eric, Billy and himself bursting into laughter. 'But Lew had a rare sense-of-humour failure and Ernie never blinked. He got the deal.'

A regular guest on the ATV shows was Millicent Martin, famous for her skits on *That Was the Week That Was* and West End musicals; she fell instantly under the charm of Eric and Ernie. 'I was doing this routine to the song "Chim-Chim-Cheree" from *Mary Poppins* and during rehearsals somebody jumped on my ankle and I thought I'd broken it so the boys carried me to my dressing room and called an ambulance. So I sat there very depressed thinking it was the end of the series for me. And about ten minutes later there was a knock at the door and there was Eric and Ernie with the biggest silver tea service you've ever seen. They must've been down to the prop department and come back with a teapot and milk jug and cups and the tray was absolutely enormous, like a flying saucer. And they walked in and said, 'We didn't know how long the ambulance would be so we thought we'd come and keep you company.' They were kind enough to realize that I might have been upset and depressed about the accident and decided to help cheer me up. It was such a sweet thing to do.'

Millicent's effervescence and perky talent seemed to compliment Eric and Ernie well and so when the boys moved into the London Palladium for a show she joined them. It was a fun experience and Millicent recalls guest stars of the magnitude of Roy Orbison turning up. Significantly she also remembers a certain André Previn, who that very year began his tenure as principal conductor of the London Symphony Orchestra, making a guest appearance and Eric getting huge laughs from the audience by telling Previn how to conduct the orchestra. These were early seeds of what would become one of their most famous sketches.

There was another sketch that involved Eric and Ernie sat in a café and after a blazing row Ernie moves to another chair. 'I don't want to talk to you any more,' he says with that kind of hurt pride

163

few entertainers could play better. 'Then in comes muggins,' recalls Millicent. 'And I sit in the now vacant chair between them and order a Pimm's. And Eric and Ernie continue with this row but don't look at each other so I think they are talking to me and they start giving me this terrible going over so I get quite angry and throw my drink in Eric's face. Of course, during rehearsals this cup of Pimm's was empty, but at the performance I let him have it and when I looked at him he had a piece of cucumber stuck to the side of his glasses, some celery pieces inside his jacket and all this Pimm's dripping off and I started to lose it. After I cleaned him up he looked at me and said, "Thanks, that was lovely." I was losing it but Ernie was in absolute hysterics. It was the worst time of my life but also the funniest.'

In May 1968 Michael Grade, then an agent under the supreme tutelage of Billy Marsh, came up with an idea that the press dubbed, 'operation madcap'. This involved transferring the entire London Palladium show over to Canada for a two-week run in Toronto at the O'Keefe Centre, an enormous theatre as Millicent recalls. 'The place held about two and a half thousand people. That was a bit daunting for me but the boys absolutely loved it. They thrived on big audiences.'

The flight over was exhausting and long, very long, but everyone cheered up when they stepped onto the tarmac to see a red London bus! 'That was Billy Marsh's idea,' recalls Grade. 'He thought it would be a great PR story if a big London bus collected the cast from the airport and took them to the theatre. I don't know where they got it from but this bus was ancient, an awful old thing from the 1940s or '50s. Anyway, they covered it with posters for the show and it duly turned up at the airport. The cast were quite taken aback when they saw it—as was I, if I'm honest. We all got on and it eventually set off, *very* slowly. I honestly don't think it had ever got out of second gear. It certainly didn't that day. It took an absolute age. Everyone was in absolute hysterics and the press loved it. Well done, Billy.'

Although you never quite know what might happen when you go to another country, Eric and Ernie were confident in their material and wanted to broaden their horizons. 'We couldn't lose money because we were on a guarantee,' says Grade. 'And when the show opened the boys were sensational—absolutely sensational.'

Millicent remembers her stay in Toronto with nothing but fondness. 'Eric and Ernie used to start every show by promising the audience that they would give away a motorbike by the end of the evening. They used to absolutely love the gag. I don't know how they did it but it started with them leaving a bingo ticket on every single seat in the theatre and they worked it so that nobody ever won the motorbike. On the face of it that sounds like something that would have annoyed an audience but they did it in such a clever way that by the end the audience had forgotten about who was supposed to win the motorcycle and were simply in stitches. The boys always went down an absolute storm.'

Millicent recalls another sketch that went down so well when they did it on *Two of a Kind* it was revived for the stage show. It was called the 'over the wall' sketch. 'It started with Ernie saying that he was going to sing me a love song. He sat me up on this wall and I'm all dressed up in chiffon and high heels and he sat next to me and started singing "Moonlight Becomes You". Then suddenly Eric climbs over from the back of the wall, grabs Ernie and pulls him off and takes his place. Now, this wall was a good six feet high. So Eric starts singing, then Ernie pulls Eric off and they keep pulling each other off the wall until they get so confused they end up pushing me off and there's chiffon and high heels everywhere and it's absolute chaos as we're all trying to get back on the wall. And we got such a reaction from the audience. Once the audience got so excited that when they pushed me off I completely missed the mattress and ended up in the lights at the back of the stage and all I could hear was Eric and Ernie shouting, "Where are you, son? We're waiting for you!"'

TWENTY-TWO

BYE BYE LEW

Over at ATV the boys' contract was up for renewal. Lew Grade's offer was a reasonable one: £39,000 for thirteen shows a year for the next three years, a lot of money and Eric was keen to accept. Ernie, who once again took the lead when it came to business matters, didn't think it was enough. He also thought three years was too long a commitment, especially since they'd already been with the network for almost five years.

In their meetings with Grade Eric left much of

the negotiating to Ernie, sitting back to watch the sparks fly as discussions grew ever more heated. In his memoirs, Grade made special mention of how tough a negotiator Ernie was, which Ernie took as a huge compliment. It wasn't meant to be one, often Grade threw his hands in the air and shouted across the table, 'Why do you boys want all this money?' Ernie looked at it very matter of factly, everybody was in show business to make money, Grade more than most.

To be fair on Ernie it wasn't just a scramble for more cash; there was another major stumbling block. The new series was again planned to be made in black and white, but the boys wanted to move into colour. This was the future and they felt their type of show merited it. ATV at the time was starting to produce in colour but only selective shows and mainly for the American market. Grade stared at them both through a veil of smoke from his latest cigar. 'You'll have colour when I say you have colour.' According to Ernie, that started another 'furious row'. Backed by Eric, Ernie was of the belief that no one, not even Lew Grade, was going to bully them into making a deal. It was a stalemate.

Over at the BBC the head of variety, Bill Cotton Junior, got wind of the situation and began making discreet enquires about the boys' availability. By a strange coincidence Billy Marsh was over in the US on business so the discussions were handled by his younger partner, Lew's nephew Michael Grade. It was the height of irony.

Cotton wasn't the kind of pen pusher or bureaucrat that would later take over such creative positions of power at the BBC: he was a show-business person to the core, understood the theatrical world and knew talent when he saw it. His father had been Billy Cotton, the famous bandleader, and as a kid he'd be taken along to theatres where, from the wings, he watched the great performers of variety's heyday go through their paces. Cotton's empathy and showbiz knowledge worked for him when he took over as Head of Variety at the BBC, and not for anything is his tenure now seen as a golden age for the network with shows like *Monty Python*, *The Two Ronnies* and, of course, *Morecambe and Wise*.

Cotton was not so very different to Lew Grade: both were showmen and made decisions on gut instinct rather than focus groups and market research. So it was a remarkable show of stubbornness on Grade's part that he refused to budge on the colour issue and was prepared to risk losing two prime assets. Michael Grade believes Lew thought the boys were bluffing and would eventually cave in but when Lew approached Billy Marsh one last time the answer was still no. Michael Grade picked up the phone to Bill Cotton and the deal was made that afternoon. Morecambe and Wise were heading to the BBC.

Lew was furious when he found out and his final meeting with Eric and Ernie was acrimonious to say the least. A few weeks later, after things had calmed down a bit, he sent the boys a box of his favourite cigars each. But the hurt always rankled with him.

The decision to switch sides and go to the BBC made perfect sense, really. The money was good, their shows would go out in colour and they had the prestige of a huge and respected organization behind them. And also a great champion in John Ammonds, who was a very experienced producer of comedy. 'He was the perfect go-between between the writer and the stars,' Bill Cotton remembered. 'He could get the best from both and end up with a great show.' And in order to keep a semblance of continuity Eric and Ernie were insistent that their writers Hills and Green be part of any deal. The shows were also half hours and kept pretty close to the already established winning formula.

The first BBC series was seen as a great success and more offers of work flooded in placing them both into the super bracket of income tax, paying something like 83 per cent of their earnings to the exchequer. The boys were as busy as ever: summer season in Great Yarmouth that broke box-office records, a trip over to New York for a nightclub date, an appearance in that year's Royal Variety Performance, interviews, cutting an LP, theatre and club gigs, it was go, go, go. Both of them became compulsives about work to the virtual exclusion of everything else. Looking back years later Ernie believed, 'We were crazy to accept the sheer volume of engagements that were beginning to swamp us.' Both Joan and Ernie could see the physical and emotional strain it was placing on Eric, but no one could have predicted what was about to happen next. Eric's comment that they were now working at 'a killing pace' was almost to become horribly prophetic.

TWENTY-THREE

BUGGER BATLEY

It's not a nice place to live Batley; dying there must be even worse. The Batley Variety Club, situated in an industrial town in Yorkshire, was something of a phenomenon in the late sixties. The owner, Jimmy Corrigan, who hailed from a Leeds fairground family, lured top entertainers to the vast cabaret club by paying them top dollar—why else would the likes of Shirley Bassey, Tom Jones, Roy Orbison, Louis Armstrong, Neil Sedaka and Gene Pitney agree to play at a venue situated next door to a slagheap?

At the start of November 1968 Eric and Ernie were midway through a week-long engagement at Batley, playing to packed houses. For a couple of days Eric had been complaining of acute pain in his chest. One night, onstage, Eric whispered to Ernie that he didn't feel well and could they cut the act short. Ernie could see by his face something was wrong. What both of them didn't know was that Eric was actually having a heart attack there and then in front of a live audience. 'Looking back at it,' said Ernie. 'I can only gasp in admiration at him for keeping the act going for as long as he did.'

Driving the ten or so miles back to his hotel Eric almost collapsed at the wheel and stopped a member of the public about to cross the road. 'Could you possibly drive me to the nearest hospital?'

The man scratched his head and looked with

puzzlement at Eric's Jensen Interceptor. 'I'm in the Territorials. I've only driven a tank, never anything like this.'

Anyway he got in and soon had them parked outside the Leeds General Infirmary. Taken into casualty Eric almost passed out and was rushed through. He sensed he was about to pass out again when the man thrust a piece of paper and a pencil onto his chest as he was being wheeled away on a trolley. 'Do me a favour, Eric, before you go— could you sign this for me?'

A trouper to the last, Eric scrawled his name. He thought it was going to be the last autograph he would ever give. He was forty-two.

It was in the early hours of the morning when Ernie got the call from Joan that Eric was critically ill in hospital. At first he thought it might have been an accident of some kind, until the ward sister told him his partner had suffered a heart attack. As he neared the casualty ward Ernie felt a deadening sensation in the pit of his stomach. 'How is he?' he asked the matron hovering outside Eric's private room. She didn't mince her words about the severity of the situation. Ernie turned white. Composing himself he held tightly onto Doreen's hand for support and they both walked inside. Eric was sitting up in bed. He looked frail and tired. 'You'll do anything for a laugh,' said Ernie, trying to keep up his friend's spirits. 'Here's a bunch of flowers. I got them at half price.'

Eric smiled. 'Put them in water and they'll do for the wreath.'

Ernie and Doreen were only allowed to stay for a few minutes. When they said their farewells and left, outside the room Ernie broke down.

Getting to the nearest telephone Ernie phoned Sadie but was still so upset he could hardly speak. After that, he and Doreen drove to Eric's hotel room to pick up his things and pay the bill. All the time Ernie must have felt like he was wandering through someone else's dream, as if it wasn't really happening at all.

Ernie and Doreen's next port of call was Ernie's mum, who now lived in a flat in Leeds. Connie had always been fond of Eric and greeted the news with shock and sadness. 'But she couldn't help expressing a thought which I suppose is only natural for any mother—"I'm glad it wasn't you."'

Des O'Connor, soon to be the butt of endless jokes on *The Morecambe and Wise Show*, had been performing in late-night cabaret in Paignton on the evening of Eric's heart attack. It had been a great show with a hugely responsive audience. 'I took a bow and as I walked into the wings the stage manager grabbed me and said, "Eric Morecambe's had a heart attack and he may not last the night." So I went back onstage and said, "If you believe in such things would you remember Eric Morecambe in your prayers tonight as he is fighting for his life." Happily he recovered from that first attack and he was doing this press conference and someone said, "Did you know that Des O'Connor asked his entire audience to pray for you at the Festival Theatre Paignton?" and Eric said, "Well those six or seven people probably made all the difference."'

A few years later of course Eric would deliver the brilliant but almost perversely poignant line: 'If you want me to be a goner, get me an LP by Des O'Connor!'

Alan Curtis was in Mike and Bernie Winters'

172

theatre dressing room when news broke about Eric's heart attack. With the place full of comics it was inevitable that one joker would pop his head round the door and say, 'Good for you, boys. If Eric and Ernie are out of it, you'll be up top!' No one laughed. 'It was just a joke of course,' said Curtis. 'But Mike and Bernie were extremely concerned about Eric, as the four of them had been very good friends for a long time.'

Amusingly, Ernie had only recently cancelled an insurance policy that paid out when one or both of them couldn't work. His accountant talked him into it and then one night Doreen said, 'I don't know why you've got that policy, you know. You worked with a broken ankle once, and you worked with Asian flu.' That was in the Isle of Man and Doreen never forgot it. 'We used to come to his bed, dose him up with medicine, lift him out, put him in the car and take him to the theatre. He'd go on with Eric, do the show, then come off and almost collapse. We'd then carry him back to the car and take him back to bed. People were much more stoic in those days!' So Doreen wanted rid of the policy. 'If you're ill, you work anyway!' was her reasoning. And sod's law, of course, just a few weeks later Eric had his heart attack, 'with what can only be called superb comic timing,' said Ernie.

After a two-week stay in hospital Eric was allowed home but told by doctors he needed three months' complete rest, which he extended to six months to be on the safe side. Bill Cotton had told Eric that the BBC was prepared to stand by him and give him all the time he needed. Meanwhile, Ernie was in a difficult position, he could hardly go out and start working on his own, not that he wanted to, not at least until Eric's future was sorted out. If medical opinion was that he couldn't work again, well that would be different. 'Although I wouldn't have another partner,' he announced at the time. 'I wouldn't form another double act. I think I would have to carry on single and do the best I could. Whether one could make it on the same level is another matter. I'd be more of an all-round entertainer like Des O'Connor or Max Bygraves.' Until then Ernie loyally stood by Eric.

There had been offers of solo work like a spot at the Palladium but he never countenanced any of it. He was even asked to become Basil Brush's new partner, which he thought absolutely hilarious. 'I'm not standing there with my hand up a fox's arse!' he said.

Ernie managed to remain busy in his own way, doing interviews and making public appearances, keeping the Morecambe and Wise brand fresh in the public's mind. 'Ernie I always thought was the one who looked after the brand name of Morecambe and Wise,' says TV director Alan Bell. 'He always talked about Morecambe and Wise as though it was a single malt whisky or something.'

One radio appearance had been scheduled for the two of them, but instead Ernie went on and did the show by himself. 'He collected his fee and gave half of it to Eric,' says Bell. 'Ernie always saw it as a double act and if he was forced to do things on his own then half of his fee went to his partner.' TV producer John Ammonds confirms that this generosity wasn't a one-off. 'It was quite touching to see Ernie do all of this. He was absolutely devoted to Eric. And I know that what he did meant an awful lot to Eric.'

174

Facing an enforced six months off, Ernie decided to largely relax and take things easy. He and Doreen took a small holiday and visited friends, although everywhere Ernie went members of the public naturally came up to ask how Eric was. For the rest of the time Ernie just pottered around the house and initially came to enjoy the feeling of being at home for a length of time without having to go off and do a show. It didn't last long though, he soon got itchy feet. He wanted to get back to work.

But things were going to be very different from now on. Even though Eric had been just as determined to return to work as Ernie, his heart attack had been a warning and prompted a total rethink about their work schedule. The frenetic pace of the previous years was now no longer possible. In view of this, Eric and Ernie decided to focus their efforts primarily on their television show and reduce theatre work to an absolute minimum. Inevitably they'd miss the hurly burly of live performance, the feedback from a large audience, like a junkie needing a fix, so Ernie devised what he called 'bank raids', a couple of variety bookings in a big theatre over one weekend, 'and then take the money and run.' They were always careful not to repeat their television material onstage, their theatre act always reached back to their glory days of variety.

The procedure was, Eric and Ernie would pay for the theatre and let the management keep the bar money, or sometimes they'd go on a straight profit-share. The term by which these gigs became known, 'bank raids', sounds rather clinical and mercenary, which was far from the truth, as the boys really enjoyed doing them. 'There'd have been no point otherwise,' says Doreen. 'When they did them they weren't doing a great deal during the week usually, so doing a couple of shows at the weekend was fun.'

Because every theatre was slightly different, the boys sometimes had to adapt their show a bit. When they played the Fairfield Halls in Croydon in 1973, the theatre didn't have house curtains (or Tabs, as they're called), which they'd often use during their act, so they had to change things round and work out something else. The Fairfield Halls show turned out to be a piece of Morecambe and Wise history, being their only live performance to be fully captured on film. Originally intended as a present to their manager and not for broadcast, its archival importance today is invaluable.

Then there was the time when they played a theatre in Chichester, which was in the round. Eric and Ernie managed to turn that to their advantage by making a big thing about the audience being able to see them from all angles, like doing lots of twirls etc. 'I think those concerts probably helped to keep them on their toes really,' says Doreen. 'Helped to keep them sharp. Norman Vaughan [the comedian] once said to the boys that they only had to walk onstage and bend a finger in order for everyone to fall about laughing. So one day, when Norman came to one of these shows, the boys strode out to centre stage, lifted up one finger each, bent it slightly, and said, "You're right Norman, the audience do laugh when we do this." I know what Norman meant though. People used to start laughing in anticipation, because they knew they'd be made to laugh.'

TWENTY-FOUR

THE ERN WOT EDDIE INVENTED

While Eric had been recuperating, Ernie and Doreen flew to New York on business; Ernie was hoping to persuade Ed Sullivan to screen some of their BBC shows. Instead of flying straight back home the couple indulged in a short holiday in Barbados. On the plane over, relaxing with a drink, one of the stewards came over to Ernie wearing a perturbed expression; was there a problem with the plane? No, the steward wanted to know if it was true what he'd just read in the newspapers, that Hills and Green were no longer going to write for *The Morecambe and Wise Show*. This was news to Ernie. As soon as they landed in Barbados Ernie put a call through to Eric, who was equally perplexed. News soon filtered through that their writers had gone back to ATV. It was understandable really; Eric and Ernie didn't expect two in-demand writers to hang around for six months and besides they hadn't known for sure if Eric would ever make a full recovery. What upset the boys the most was that after seven years together they'd been in effect the last to know. And now they had a major problem facing them: who was going to write their second BBC series?

On the showbiz grapevine Cotton heard that Eddie Braben, Ken Dodd's gag writer for the last fifteen years, was leaving the comic due to a financial dispute. Wasting no time Cotton got in touch with Braben, putting to him the proposal that every comic writer in the country would have sold their granny for: the chance to write for Eric and Ernie. But Braben didn't want it, he felt his style wouldn't suit the boys, he was a gags man, pure and simple and wasn't used to the sketchshow format. Cotton wasn't convinced and urged Braben to come down to London to at least meet them. Braben agreed, provided the BBC foot the bill of the train fare from Liverpool.

Eric and Ernie, too, had misgivings about the choice of Braben, although they knew his work for Doddy and greatly admired this quiet, unassuming and benign Scouser. The son of a butcher, Braben had his own fruit and veg stall in Liverpool's St John's market but spent most of his time scribbling down jokes on the brown paper bags. He sold his first gag to Charlie Chester. It went like this: 'When Hopalong Cassidy was a baby, his mother knew that he was going to be a cowboy, because he always wore a ten-gallon nappy.'

Cotton had a real task on his hands then getting both parties to agree. That meeting was going to be make or break. It took place at his office at BBC Centre and lasted all of two hours. 'But I think it took about ten minutes, though, for me to realize that something magical had happened between the three of us,' said Braben. 'What it was I don't know, but there was something there, something inexplicable.' Maybe it was their shared love of music hall, or the simple fact they all hailed from the same kind of working-class Northern background.

At the start of the meeting Braben told the boys he'd seen them live many times, the first occasion at the Liverpool Empire in 1952, 'when they were so far down the bill that their names were smaller than the printers.' Braben didn't mince his words about what he thought of them. 'You were painful to watch, just awful.' Eric and Ernie took that one on the chin. 'Yes we were,' they agreed. Those were the days when they were still very much on a learning curve, something Braben fully appreciated. 'And every time they went onstage they learned something. They were building experience.'

After watching that Liverpool Empire debacle Braben confessed that he didn't think he, or the British public for that matter, would ever see them again. 'Then I heard you on the radio a couple of years later and noticed a stark difference,' he told them. 'I felt you came across very well on radio.' As for their move to television at ATV, Braben had another confession to make. 'I didn't like them.' However much he admired Hills and Green something was missing from those shows. Braben had never been able to put his finger on quite what it was until that meeting in Cotton's office, because there it was right in front of him, he couldn't miss it. It was the way the boys interacted together, the way they spoke and the way they behaved. He could feel the very real affection each had for the another. 'I knew then what was missing from the Eric and Ernie I had watched on television. I saw what was missing; it was warmth.'

Not content with just providing the boys with gags, Braben was determined to develop the on-screen relationship between the pair. In truth, there wasn't much he could do with Eric, his persona was pretty much already defined and highly popular, it was Ernie that Braben honed in on. 'Ernie was your typical straight man, but I always

179

felt, as I watched him, that there was something more there, that there was a lot more to Ernie than we had seen up to now. So I wanted to give him a character, the thing was what to do with him. So I pondered that one for quite a while, long days wondering what to do with Ern. Every time I wrote a line that was a straight-man line I was thinking that's not right, that isn't right, he is being wasted. And then it happened.'

What Braben came up with was a masterstroke and completely changed the dynamics of the partnership. 'I decided I would put a pen in Ernie's hand and make him a not very good author, an egotistical little author who had ideas well above his capabilities. And everybody knew this except Ern. Eric, of course, knew that Ernie wasn't a very good author but he never let anyone else have a go at Ernie, he became very protective of him, and that brought the relationship even closer.'

It also, to a large extent, mirrored the way they both were in real life, according to Michael Grade. 'If you wanted to upset them, to get them really riled, which was very difficult to do, you'd talk about the other one. You'd say, 'Well, Ernie wasn't very good tonight,' and Eric would just round on you—or vice versa. They were incredibly protective of their relationship, and of Morecambe and Wise Ltd. It went beyond the conventional comedy duo—way beyond that.'

It also gave Eric so much to bounce off, this vain character, snobbish, puritanical, mean, sexually naive, magnificently smug and given to delusions of artistic grandeur, claiming his plays were 'better than anything by Oscar and Wilde'. Almost all the humour came from Eric debunking Ernie's pretensions.

Braben recalls that Ernie reacted positively to the idea from the moment he read the very first sketch about the 'plays wot he wrote', telling Eric he'd written four plays that very day. 'What about the one coming up in the lift?' replies Eric. 'Oh I forgot about that one.' When Ernie read it he told Braben, 'This is marvellous. This is something I can really work at, something I can do. I'm no longer a straight man, I'm really performing now.' He was so enthusiastic.

It was a brilliant concept, a great comedic creation. What Braben had done was make Ernie's previous role as the straight man almost totally redundant. 'What we ended up with, in effect, was a double act without a straight man,' says the writer. 'We had two funny men instead. Ernie had become a comedy actor, because he played that character to perfection. He had gone beyond being a straight man; he was a comedy actor and a very, very good one.'

The character of the playwright caught on with the public almost immediately, it worked perfectly. 'Far, far better than we ever thought,' says Braben. 'Indeed, who would have thought that even today people talk about the plays what he wrote.'

In many ways that character and the way Ernie performed it was instrumental in the success of Morecambe and Wise during their golden age, the seventies. 'Almost the whole Morecambe and Wise act, at the height of their popularity, was based around Ernie's character as the arrogant would-be playwright with next to no talent,' identifies actor Ron Moody. 'That's where almost all the laughs came from. It wasn't just Ernie feeding Eric lines, as straight men generally do. Good heavens no. This was Ernie's show, in many respects. It was his character that the majority of the show was built around—and Eric was his comic. Not a bad one! But Eric was as much Ernie's comic as Ernie was his straight man. Don't get me wrong, Eric got all the big laughs as planned, but if you watch Ernie, in particular playing the playwright character, he became so much more than a straight man. Ernie played the character perfectly and always got the best out of Eric as well as himself.'

Miranda Hart, comedy actress and writer, and Morecambe and Wise fan, believes Ernie's brilliant portrayal puts the lie to the claim that he was merely Eric's stooge, a word Ernie actually despised. 'Ernie was very funny in his own right. His comic persona, particularly in the bedroom scenes and "play wot I wrote" scenes was inherently funny, with a comic perspective that would fit happily in any sitcom. His character in a sitcom wouldn't be the straight man. He was a fool with an inflated ego who thought he was right and extremely talented and that importance he placed on himself and his "talents" was very funny.'

It also worked in the new framework, introduced by Braben, of Eric and Ernie living together in an almost pseudo-sitcom world, sharing a flat—and even a bed! The boys initially baulked at the idea of two grown men in the same double bed, people would talk, wouldn't they? Braben just smiled and delivered the ace up his sleeve. 'If it's good enough for Laurel and Hardy, it's good enough for you,' he said. The argument was won. 'Actually, in the old days, it was accep-table that men slept in double beds together without people raising an eyebrow,'

182

said Ernie. Indeed, hadn't he and Eric done exactly that in digs to save money? 'The trouble was when I used to sleep with Eric in the double bed, he was a terrible snorer. He used to snore and I never got any sleep. But I cured it. One night I gave him a big kiss just before I went to sleep and he never took his eyes off me all night.'

Braben was also responsible for other personality traits and bits of business for Ernie that caught on massively with the public. 'Tea Ern?', for instance, was Braben's joke. 'I was very fond of that. When we had guest stars they almost begged to be given that line. We did it almost every week and every week it got a big laugh.'

Braben was also responsible for turning Ernie into a miser, someone careful with money, reluctant to take out his wallet and endlessly teased by Eric. Again, Ernie responded positively to the idea and based much of the characterization on a comic idol of his, the American stand-up Jack Benny. Whenever he was in America Ernie never failed to catch up with Benny's TV show. In one episode Benny opened his safe and there was an actual tiger cub inside, the joke being if anyone else put their hand in they'd be savaged. There was another sketch when he got up in the morning and picked up his trousers, which were hanging on the edge of a chair, and you could hear that the pockets were full of change, and he shook them and growled, 'There's a quarter missing!' Benny had a manservant called Rochester and he'd come in and start searching for the quarter. 'Ernie used to think all that was great,' says Doreen.

Again the joke caught on so much with the watching millions that everyone thought that Ernie was a total egocentric and mean. It was a touch unfair; yes Ernie was business-like with his finances in real life (once asked if he kept diaries the reply was no, he kept accounts), but far from mean. 'Ernie was extremely generous,' pleads Doreen. 'He lent a lot of money to friends, and gave them as much time as they needed to pay it back. He wasn't a sucker though. If they didn't repay it, he didn't lend them any more.'

Later on, as Ernie's fortune increased, people did try and tap him for money says Doreen. 'I think if you're a quiet person, which Ernie was, people assume you have a weakness, so people would sometimes target him. He certainly wasn't a pushover in that respect, but whenever people asked him in my earshot I used to say, "He hasn't got any money, I've spent it all!" And that used to do the trick.'

Maybe Ernie was his own worst enemy in this regard since he did love to play up to his supposed trait of meanness. 'We had a poodle once called Charlie,' says Doreen. 'He would sit next to Ernie while he was working in his study. Whenever Ernie wrote a cheque and tore it from the stub, Charlie would let out this terrible howl of pain. "Whoooooaw," he would go, like a banshee in agony. Ernie loved it. He'd tell Charlie, "Don't worry, I've still got enough to buy your biscuits."'

Then on holidays Ernie insisted on having photographs taken in front of banks. He was particularly happy with one taken in Sicily, 'because it made it look like we had influence with the Mafia,' says Doreen. 'Everywhere we stopped he'd say, "Oooh, look, another bank, get your camera out." He revelled in the fact that people thought he was obsessed with money.' For one Morecambe and Wise sketch Ernie even had a special wallet made with a dial from a safe on the front. He used to bring it out with him occasionally.

Certainly money was important to Ernie, he cheerfully admitted to being materialistic, often appreciating Noel Coward's famous quote: 'If you must have motivation, think of your pay cheque on Friday.' 'Oh yes, I like goodies,' Ernie once said, even treating himself to a yellow Rolls-Royce Silver Shadow which he called 'my aren't-I-doing-well car'. He felt that the public didn't begrudge him or Eric their wealth. 'When I'm driving through towns in the North people hate the Rolls until they see who's in it. Somehow they forgive us.'

Family friend Ray Crawford remembers when Ernie bought his very first Rolls-Royce and called him round to show it off and they drove into Beaconsfield for a glass of champagne to celebrate. 'It was an absolutely stunning car. So we sat there having a glass, and his hands were shaking.'

'Are you OK, Ernie?' Ray asked.

'Oh yes,' Ernie said. 'The shaking started when I signed the cheque and it hasn't stopped since. Not sure it ever will!'

Ernie also enjoyed dabbling in shares and was always worried about investments for the future. He rarely threw away old clothes. Again, this all harked back to his poverty-stricken childhood when the importance of money was drummed into him by his mother whose favourite saying went: 'When there's no money in the house, love flies out the window.'

There were two other trademarks, or long-running gags, developed around this time, not

185

by Braben but by Eric. The whole 'You can't see the join' bit and the fabricated line that Ernie wore a toupee was invented by Eric to deflect all the attention on to his partner and away from the fact that he was losing his own hair, something he was very conscious of and absolutely hated. And if you think about it, it worked. Everybody thinks of Ernie as somebody who wore a wig; nobody ever talks about Eric Morecambe as somebody who was going bald. It was psychologically extremely clever and it would have been very cruel if Ernie had cared or been thin-skinned. As it was he was always happy to play along, just so long as it was good for the act. Again the public were completely hoodwinked: when Ernie was out and about people would come up to him and want to see the join in his wig. 'They really don't believe I don't wear one,' Ernie said at the time. 'And I can see them searching for it with their eyes.'

Most iconic of all was the slap, a display of affection towards Ernie, however warped. The problem was, wherever Ernie went in public people wanted to slap his cheeks. 'That's all they ever wanted to do, you know, come up and slap him,' says Doreen. 'They'd say: "I always wanted to do this"—and they would, and he'd let them.' This in spite of the fact that he didn't enjoy it when people did it but felt obliged to let them have their fun. It was only after his stroke in 1994 that Ernie couldn't bear it any longer. 'In fact, he didn't want to go out at all,' admits Doreen. 'You see, it happened virtually every day. I honestly believe it could have contributed to the deafness he suffered later on.'

TWENTY-FIVE

DIDN'T THEY DO WELL?

That second series for the BBC, which began in July 1969, was a milestone. With Braben installed as writer and the running time extended to forty-five minutes, Eric and Ernie were beginning to hit a peak of artistic excellence that would last a decade, turning them into the nation's most beloved television entertainers. 'They were designed for television,' is how Sir Michael Parkinson sees it. 'I don't know what it was about the medium of television but it treated them perfectly. And whatever they did it never worked outside of television quite as well. They had this wonderful gift that the best TV performers have of being able to bring you into the magic box. The way they both engaged with the camera worked perfectly, a bit like Laurel and Hardy. That's the reason why Morecambe and Wise were great and that's the reason why they'll be remembered.'

The way the show was actually made was important, too. Due to the obvious concern for Eric's health, each one was rehearsed and put together over a three-week period with two days reserved for recording, a real luxury, time enough to perfect each and every aspect of the show and produce something of the highest quality. The boys also insisted on performing in front of a live audience; no canned laughter for them. The reactions and feedback they got from a real crowd were vital in giving their performance an edge and energy akin to a live gig.

It was one of the reasons why they'd failed on film; there was no audience to feed off. As Ernie claimed, 'It is the live audience that draws the best out of us. They are part of our act.'

That audience was important in another way, they were a link to where they'd come from, variety and live theatre. It was a connection also apparent in the fact that Eric and Ernie tried to lend their TV show an almost theatrical feel. Much of their banter, for example, was performed in front of a curtain, thus giving a mock impression that the show was coming from a theatre rather than a studio. And they'd have a specially built platform put in, slightly raised off the floor, to give them the feeling of being on a stage. It was complete artifice, but it worked.

So important was this shared past that the boys believed it was a vital component in their television success, as Ernie claimed in 1978. 'It's a fantastic thing because all we have done is adapt music hall on to the television and make it acceptable.'

A much-loved feature of the BBC series was the multitude of guest stars that competed with each other to get on the show. And the reason so many famous people were prepared to put their reputations at risk was the simple knowledge that there was no malice in the humour. They were never mocked, teased yes, but never mocked. 'We puncture them, but they are big enough stars to take it,' said Ernie. 'Everyone knows it's a joke and at our expense, not theirs.'

Many of the guest stars were distinguished actors, who fitted conveniently into the concept of the plays Ernie wrote. The boys rarely invited a fellow comic onto the show because of the natural rivalry that would emerge. They'd made that mistake during their inaugural BBC series when they allowed Bruce Forsyth to come on. 'And neither Eric nor Ernie particularly enjoyed the experience,' says Doreen. He'd filled in for Sammy Davis Jnr, whom the boys had rehearsed with but he'd fallen ill and couldn't continue.

The guests on *The Morecambe and Wise Show* were there as supporting players or stooges but Bruce didn't seem to have been told the ground rules. As a result, he and Eric were 'metaphorically slugging it out onstage', Ernie remembered, 'each trying to top the other with an ad-lib or one liner. I don't know what it did to the audience but it frightened the living daylights out of me. Neither was willing to back down, the two of them held centre stage, each trying to bludgeon the other with comic repartee.' By now the script had gone for a burton, although Ernie tried his best to get the thing back on track.

When Ernie made reference to this incident in an interview after Eric's death, how he believed Brucie had acted in a selfish way, the ructions from Forsyth Manor could be heard all the way across Wentworth Golf Club. Bruce felt wrongly accused and in the end wrote Ernie a letter defending himself against the accusation. Ernie duly replied and somewhere along the line they made it up. 'They always remained friends,' says Doreen. 'So it was all water under the bridge.'

According to Alan Bell, who acted as Ammonds' production assistant, it was Ernie who came up with the idea of getting as many classical actors as possible to come along and perform, say, a song-and-dance routine with the boys or something else out of their comfort zone. 'And one of the first was Eric Porter. We all thought it was possibly a good idea but John Ammonds wasn't sure if these kind of actors and actresses could actually dance. Anyway, Ernie then suggested that to make it easier we record it in small bits, which we thought was a very good idea. We tried this with Eric Porter and it worked brilliantly so Ernie was to thank for that. I always got the impression that Eric was going along in the jet stream, but Ernie was driving the plane. Ernie was very quiet and he considered things.'

According to Bell, Ernie, as well as Eric, would often think up good, usable ideas. 'He really was Mr Ideas and would come up with loads, but John Ammonds would often claim that Ernie's ideas were actually his. Ernie would come up with an idea and John would think about it and not say anything and in the morning John would come in and say, "I've had a marvellous idea," and everyone would look at Ernie and say, "I don't believe it."' Never once, though, did Bell ever see Ernie try to reclaim the glory for any of his ideas. 'Ernie always felt that as long as the show was right that was all that mattered.'

One idea Bell specifically remembers Ernie coming up with was the economy petrol sketch, in which Eric drives a car to prove how many miles it can go on one gallon of this new super fuel. First the 40-mile banner is passed, then 50, 54, 60, 180 miles and then as a running gag throughout the episode the car carries on to 962 miles, 25,301 and finally 112,000 miles. At the end Ernie the reporter asks Eric, 'What do you think of our economy petrol?' Looking at the camera Eric replies, 'The petrol's excellent, but my car's clapped out now, isn't it? It's ruined.' It's a great sketch worthy of Monty Python.

Guest stars, however distinguished, were always

required to rehearse with the boys for at least two days to nail down the routine. This meant a trip to the less-than-glamorous BBC rehearsal rooms in North Acton, in truth a community centre just behind Wormwood Scrubs. No one was exempt, not even Shirley Bassey, who'd suggested Eric and Ernie might prefer popping over to her Mayfair hotel suite instead.

Other guests reacted differently. Robert Morley was horrified, not so much by the surroundings but that lunch consisted of soup and sarnies. 'Can't we retire to a hostelry, dear boys?' It was habit that there was no lunch break, everyone worked straight through so they could start late and finish early. The next day Morley had his uniformed chauffeur bring the Rolls round with champagne and a Fortnum and Mason hamper.

Vanessa Redgrave once turned up in scruffy jeans handing out left-wing political leaflets to the BBC staff. At the canteen she tried to sell the boys the *Morning Star* paper. 'No thanks, luv,' they said. 'We're capitalists.'

'But do you *own* the BBC?'

Ernie looked about him, 'No—but we're willing to make them an offer.'

Come the day of recording Vanessa transformed spectacularly into a dancing peacock. 'The epitome of grace and elegance,' said Ernie, whereas on that rehearsal day, 'she looked more at home on a picket line than show business.'

Then there was Frank Finlay, who Ernie recalled played Casanova in a sketch as if he were on the stage of the National Theatre. But when it came time for him to appear as himself it so unnerved the actor that while the audience were laughing at a previous joke he whispered to Ernie, 'I've had enough. Get me off now, will you?'

And who can forget Glenda Jackson as Cleopatra emoting Ernie's legendary line: 'All men are fools and what makes them so is having beauty like what I have got.' Hollywood producer Melvin Frank caught that show and said, 'Gee, I didn't know that girl could do comedy,' and swiftly cast her in the lead in *A Touch of Class* and her performance won her an Oscar. 'Really, we felt a little insulted,' Ernie remarked. 'He didn't offer us anything.'

A few stars did turn them down, notably Michael Caine, John Gielgud and Albert Finney, who told Ernie he couldn't appear because, 'I find it difficult to play myself.' It's strange how actors, without the safety of make-up to hide behind or the shield of a character, find it hard to just be themselves. Ernie could relate to that. 'Once I get on the suit I'm wearing on the show and a bit of make-up, too, I'm somebody else, whatever that means.' Michael Caine's reason for turning down the show was that he wanted to be taken seriously as an actor. 'We would have taken him very seriously,' said Ernie. 'We might not have given him any laughs.' As for Sir John Gielgud, Ernie spotted him one afternoon in the BBC canteen. 'Excuse me, Mr Gielgud,' a faux pas that Ernie believed is what put the kibosh on it. 'Would you consider appearing in one of our shows?' The reply was non-committal at best. 'He continued eating his custard while glancing over to the far side of the room as if to say "rescue me" to anyone who would listen.'

Actually it was Ernie who did a lot of the asking, certainly not Eric, who admitted he didn't possess the bare-faced nerve to approach someone like Sir John. 'I can't face being turned down,' he confessed. Ernie was always cocksure enough to go up to any star, although all he would say was, 'Would you consider it?' nothing more. Many said yes, some replied, 'I'll consider it. No.' Actually, to be fair on Gielgud he did finally respond. 'I love you, boys, I think you're wonderful, but no.'

They did get Dame Flora Robson, who was delighted to be invited. 'People think I'm dead,' she told them. 'And that can sometimes lose me quite a lot of work.' The sketch had the celebrated actress play Queen Elizabeth I and during rehearsals Ernie dried, he couldn't for the life of him remember his lines. Flora stopped and just looked at Ernie. 'How could you forget them?' she said. 'After all, you wrote it!'

Perhaps the boys' biggest catch was Lord Olivier, but alas he didn't appear in the studio with them, only on a filmed insert, although it was a great gag. Eric and Ernie are phoning round trying to get stars to come on the show and everyone makes excuses why they can't. Olivier pretends to be a Chinese laundry: 'So solly, long number.' Priceless.

Curiously the only star guest ever to pull out was Sarah Miles. Due to appear in one of Ernie's 'plays wot I wrote' set on a tropical island, she turned up for the rehearsal wearing, as Ernie breathlessly recalled, 'the shortest miniskirt I have ever seen.' He remembered her as being extremely outgoing during rehearsals, very enthusiastic, and then they heard she wasn't coming back. Ernie could only assume that her famous playwright husband, Robert Bolt, the man who wrote *Lawrence of Arabia* and *A Man for All Seasons*, had read his play and told her on no account to appear in such a suicidal production.

There were other stars who were seemingly game to appear but for whom Eric and Ernie could not find the right routine or their schedules never worked out, notable among those were Sean Connery, Paul McCartney and Roger Moore. The one-time Saint and at the time the incumbent 007, Moore was asked many times to appear with the boys. 'But unfortunately whenever the Christmas show came up I was either filming *The Persuaders* or then Bond, or some other movie in a far-flung corner of the world and I was, alas, never around to accept their invitation. It was a great regret of mine. That was the reason I was delighted to do *The Play What I Wrote* in London and on Broadway. It was a joy. When my friends asked if I was working (in the hope of me paying for lunch perhaps?) I'd say, "Yes, I'm in the West End in *The Play What I Wrote*." It provoked the obvious, "I never knew you wrote as well."'

Moore first met Eric and Ernie in 1960 when the lads were appearing in variety at the Finsbury Park Empire and he'd gone to see them with his then wife, the singer Dorothy Squires. Much later, Moore got to know Ernie well when he was filming *Shout at the Devil* in Malta in 1975. 'I discovered that the Wises had a holiday home there. We were able to see one another a few times during my stay, and had great evenings together. I always enjoyed the company of both Ernie and Eric, two lovely men, and as entertainers they appealed to everyone.'

This was the reason why Morecambe and Wise were taken to the nation's hearts, this everyman quality they had, they were more loveable, more relatable, more 'boy next door' than other entertainers of their period. 'There was a simplicity to them,' says comedienne Miranda Hart. 'They weren't complicated, not wounded souls like Tommy Cooper sometimes came across as, or Hancock. Any pain they might have in real life would be checked at the studio door and there was a naïvety and playfulness that brought a true escapism to their comedy that no one else could match. Their double-act relationship was like a friendship we all recognized and laughed at. We recognized enough of the fool in ourselves to identify with them, but they took it to another level so we could escape out of ourselves as they made us laugh at their extreme clowning and foolishness.'

There was also a warmth and complete lack of cynicism about both Eric and Ernie that endeared you to them. 'They were quite childlike,' says Kevin Eldon. 'But they never got into any of the kind of mawkishness you could sometimes get with other double acts, say for example Dean Martin and Jerry Lewis. There was exuberance about both of them and it was very infectious.'

What the public loved about the duo was the complete absence of rancour. Beneath the relentless one-downmanship ('this man's a fool!'), there was a genuine affection and the public sensed it. 'Eric and Ernie weren't just liked by the public, they were loved,' says Angela Rippon. 'I find this now when people talk to me, they genuinely loved them.'

Another memorable feature of the BBC shows was the running gag disparaging the singing abilities of Des O'Connor, stuff like, 'That's the best record Des has ever made,' says Ernie. To which Eric replies, 'You mean there's nothing on it at all.' What the public didn't know was that Des was an old friend from variety days so the boys knew he wouldn't be too offended by their gentle jibes. Des first came across Eric and Ernie at one of his very first gigs in 1954 at the Regal Hull, a cinema that used to put on shows. 'Back then,' he remembers, 'I wasn't earning very much and one night I had to get back to Northampton where my mum and dad lived but I'd no money at all. Ernie and Doreen lived in Peterborough and they said, "We'll give you a lift as far as there." So we all piled into this tiny little car they had, a Triumph Mayflower. I'm sure they could have well done without another passenger and my big suitcase, but they didn't mind and they were wonderful; Ernie was just a lovely guy.'

Something else the public didn't know was that Des dreamt up some of those insults himself. 'And people would say to me after the show went out, "Did you hear what he said about you Saturday?" I'd say, "Yeah, I know." I couldn't tell them that I had written it. There was one exchange, I said, "I'm doing a one-man show," and Eric replied, "Well, let's hope two turn up next time." That was my joke! So, all that stuff, it was just a lovely part of my life, I really felt that I was connected with the boys.'

As it gathered momentum, each series seemed to get better and better and the whole production was a joy to work on, according to director Alan Bell, and highly disciplined, the two stars working off each other instinctively and brilliantly. 'Eric knew that Ernie would be there to handle whatever he did. Ernie wasn't an ad-libber; Ernie stuck to the lines. Eric knew that if anything went wrong Ernie would just keep going. One of their main rules was that they never wanted to stop once a sketch had begun. They didn't want all this business of stopping to adjust the camera etc., and that suited Ernie very well.'

There was even the odd perk, Bell recalls. 'The two guys used to have a tailor on Savile Row who used to come and visit the studio. One day this tailor suddenly started to measure me and I said, "What are you doing?" He told me, "Mr Morecambe and Mr Wise insist you have a new suit so sent me to measure you up." I was slightly aggrieved to be honest because I didn't think my current suit was all that bad. In fact I think I actually looked rather smart. Anyway, apparently it was something that they used to do for people that they liked.'

The boys were very particular about the clothes they wore onstage and on television. And whenever they had a suit made they only ever had one inside pocket; all the other pockets were false, including the trousers. It meant they hung better. One day back in the late fifties Ernie's dad was admiring his son's new suit, 'It doesn't half look good on you Ernie,' he said.

'If you like it, Dad, you can have it.'

Harry took it home proudly, only to discover the false pockets. 'Who on earth makes a suit without any pockets,' he grumbled. The next time he saw Ernie he brought the matter up. 'That was a funny suit; it didn't have any pockets in it. Anyway, I took it into Burtons the tailor and had some put in.'

Ernie was incredulous, 'WHAT?! What did you do that for?!'

Bell wasn't the only one Eric and Ernie had measured up for a suit. They had one made for Peter Lovell, who also worked on the show as the floor manager, and one for John Ammonds. 'Funnily enough,' says Bell, 'there were only three people in our production office back then where today you can have anything up to fifteen in one office. Maybe it was a case of less is more in those days.'

Eddie Braben certainly didn't clutter up the office, he hardly ever turned up, preferring to work at home and post in his scripts, which were then worked on by Eric and Ernie and Ammonds, bits and pieces added, and then sent back up to Liverpool for little rewrites. As Braben noted, 'I knew that if I wrote a bad script they would make it acceptable. If I wrote a good one, they could make it brilliant.'

TWENTY-SIX

MR FIFTEEN PER CENT

With the BBC series up and running and a huge success Ernie began to diversify, using his natural business talents to become an agent in 1971. His theatrical agency was called Wise Bookings and continued for around four years. The primary reason for starting it was to sort out all the contracts for shop openings and other personal appearances he and Eric engaged in, all the little things Billy Marsh didn't handle. Ernie also negotiated some deals for Eddie Braben, including his contract to write the 1972 Frankie Howerd film *Up the Front*.

It was quite a remarkable achievement all this, especially for someone whose schooling was so fractured. 'Ernie wasn't the most academic man in the world because he started in the business so early and was denied an education,' says friend Alan Curtis.

198

'But he had a very well rounded common-sense attitude to everything and was extraordinarily sharp. He was obviously the senior partner in Morecambe and Wise when it came to money and business and he very much impressed me.'

Sometimes Ernie amazed himself that he could hold his own and converse with the people at the top, 'because the higher you get the cleverer they are,' he said. Ernie was always trying to make up for his lack of a proper education. He particularly enjoyed visiting universities and talking to young people. When a group of school children once visited the TV studio during a recording of a show Eric just wanted to know what their favourite TV show was and if they liked *Morecambe and Wise* but Ernie wanted to know what they were doing at school and what were their favourite lessons. It was a thirst for knowledge. 'Ernie also experienced a great deal from an early age, and you often pick things up that you have a natural talent for,' offers Doreen. 'Ernie obviously had a natural talent for figures so I suppose he was like a sponge in that respect. And through his experiences and reading, he became a very bright man. He always did a crossword every night after a show.'

In fact, according to Doreen, Ernie made more money from property than he ever did from show business. Over the years his real estate portfolio was considerable, including three maisonettes that he used to let out. These were bought in the mid-sixties for something like £5,000, and later all sold at a huge profit. The couple also had a very nice detached house in Harrow that was later let out. And there was a villa in Malta. 'We bought it from a Scotsman who used to wear a tweed suit every day of the week, despite the heat,' Doreen recalls. It was another bargain, bought for just £8,000.

Their neighbours in Malta included Frankie Howerd, Brenda De Banzie, Reg Varney, Jean Kent and Dawn Addams. 'It was a nice little community,' says Doreen. 'We used to call it our kibbutz!' Ernie got on particularly well with Frankie Howerd. Of course he was aware of Howerd's homosexuality, but having virtually grown up in show business Ernie had lived and worked among gay people so was perfectly fine about it. He and Doreen often went to parties at Howerd's house where his partner Dennis Heymer, 'a lovely fellow,' says Doreen, would play host and cook superb meals. So there was nothing predatory in Howerd's behaviour towards Ernie, but that didn't stop him making enquiries about other people says Doreen. 'The thing with Frankie was that he was always trying to psychoanalyse people, and usually about sex. And if he used to meet anybody, especially from the armed forces, he used to give them hell. He was probably trying to find a dormant homosexual or something. But if Ernie met people and they told him they were in the forces, he'd say, "For God's sake don't tell Frankie!" But he was a dear man and Ernie and I loved seeing him and Dennis.'

A lot of Ernie and Frankie's time in Malta was spent playing tennis. 'Ernie was a very good tennis player actually and had a very good eye,' says Doreen. 'He also played cricket and wasn't bad with a bat. Probably for the same reason. He couldn't bowl though. He was awful!' Ernie played in quite a few Lord's Taverners cricket matches and was a huge fan of the sport, but Sir Michael Parkinson isn't quite so complimentary about his skills. 'Ernie was to cricket what Graham Norton is to rugby league. Ernie did, however, possess a bat a yard wide, which he produced at charity matches and placed in front of his wicket with the result he was never dismissed. That must be some kind of record.'

Back in England, Ernie and Doreen had left Peterborough and for a few years lived in Harrow-on-the-Hill until deciding they wanted a place on the river where they could keep a boat. Sailing was a real passion of theirs since buying a motor cruiser called *Gaye 4*, which was kept in South Walsham in Norfolk. This was when Eric and Ernie were doing Summer Season in Great Yarmouth. 'After every show we'd travel to the boat, stay the night and in the morning set sail!' remembers Doreen. 'While we were there we must have travelled along every single broad in Norfolk.' After that summer the boat was brought back home to Peterborough, until Ernie saw a thirty-foot cabin cruiser at the Boat Show and bought it. They ended up selling *Gaye 4* to Billy Cotton Jnr.

Dorney Reach in Maidenhead, its garden stretching down to the Thames, was a perfect place to moor Ernie's brand-new big boat. It was a real haven, except when the odd pleasure boat came past and there was a loud 'Ernie Wise lives here!' blasting out of the loudspeaker. They bought the house from Billy Walker, the boxer, in the mid-seventies and quickly moved the boat there. In time Ernie bought an even bigger vessel. 'We'd have had the Royal Yacht *Britannia* if we could have afforded it,' jokes Doreen. 'Or found a place for it!' It was Ernie's pride and joy and he christened it *The Lady Doreen*. At first Ernie wanted to call it something else. A running joke in their marriage was Ernie's insistence that it was Doreen who ran the show and gave all the orders. 'So Ernie wanted to call the boat *Sergeant-Major Doreen* but I wasn't having it.' One of his great pleasures was gently sailing it up and down that lovely stretch of the Thames.

The house itself was a large mock-Tudor affair. 'Hollywood-on-the-Thames,' Ernie called it, complete with a swimming pool. A near neighbour was the television presenter Frank Bough. Soon after Bough's high-profile sexual indiscretions came to light Ernie joked to visitors, 'I know that if lots of reporters turn up here Frank has been a daft bugger again.'

The road they lived on was private with just three houses on it and Eric and Doreen became friendly with all their neighbours. In the early eighties Jack and Maureen Culley moved in and remember Ernie with fondness. 'He used to take his dog Molly for a walk along the riverbank, and on his way back he'd pop round to our back door and say, "Any coffee on the go?" Then he'd pop in for a chat. He never talked about show business though. Never about Morecambe and Wise. He'd talk about his boat or food or something, things that interested him. Or interested me, for that matter.'

Ernie loved walking his dog. If he ever got bored sitting around the house he'd take the dog out. 'Then the dog would come back without Ernie,' recalls Doreen. 'And I'd say, "Where is he?" and he'd be down the road talking to somebody.'

Because where they lived was a private road

202

the residents were all responsible for its upkeep. However, whenever potholes appeared Maureen Culley remembers that Ernie would collect all the ash and cinders from his boiler, mix it with some water, put it in his wheelbarrow and go round with his trowel filling them all in. 'It didn't last very long but bought us all a few weeks. It was obviously a make-do-and-mend attitude. Very Yorkshire!'

Television presenter Michael Barratt, stalwart of *Nationwide*, the news and current affairs programme that was so much a part of early evening viewing in the seventies, had an office in Maidenhead not far from the Wises' home and has never forgotten his very first encounter with Ernie. 'He came up to me and said, "I love your programme. I love *Nationwide*, I really do. When I come home from the studios I'll have a meal, sit down in front of the TV and as soon as that wheel goes round and the title music comes on, I fall asleep. Sends me off a treat."'

After that first meeting Ernie would often pop into Barratt's office for a chat after happily wandering round town with his dog, Molly. Sometimes he'd come in and say, 'Michael, I wonder if you could help me. I have to send a fax but I have no idea what to do. What is a fax?' So Barratt would show him the fax machine and explain how it worked. 'I don't think Ernie was good at technology. But what I found very admirable about him, like many of the greatest entertainers, was his extraordinary modesty, which you only find among the real greats. With Ernie there was never the faintest hint of "I'm a celebrity" or any of that kind of stuff. He was just a very ordinary, lovely friend. He never pushed

203

himself, which is maybe one of the reasons why he's never had the recognition he deserves. That said, it obviously didn't mean a great deal to him. He was an extremely contented man.'

Ernie and Doreen would reside at Dorney Reach for over twenty years. It was a very special place for them. When Ernie died the house became too big for Doreen, with each room containing so many memories of Ernie, so she moved to a more modest but stylish apartment in Windsor. Today Dorney Reach has been drastically rebuilt, virtually knocked down. 'It doesn't mean anything to me now though,' says Doreen. 'Once you leave a house, and once the person you lived with has gone, it doesn't mean anything any more.'

TWENTY-SEVEN

ARM'S LENGTH

By the mid-seventies, Eric and Ernie were no longer just the country's favourite comedians, they'd become national institutions. Indeed, such was their fame and popularity that, according to secret papers released in 2005, Harold Wilson's government of 1975 wanted Morecambe and Wise to help raise the spirits of the people of Northern Ireland at the height of the troubles by performing their signature tune 'Bring Me Sunshine' on the lawns of Stormont. It was a ludicrous notion that never got off the ground.

Of course, this level of success brought with it a unique set of problems, principle among them the huge pressure of having to deliver quality shows every single time, knowing that there was an audience of millions out there waiting for them. Yet, in spite of this incredible popularity there remained a reassuring and pleasant humility about them both. Neither big-headed nor conceited, Eric and Ernie remained relatively humble about their success, a remarkable achievement in itself. 'The thing that always struck me about both of them,' says Angela Rippon, 'was that even though they were the biggest names on television there was nothing starry about them, they didn't behave like divas or superstars, they were just lovely people.' Glenda Jackson agrees, 'One of the things that I found surprising about them given the kind of success they had and given the love that audiences had for them, they were obedient to the director. They would sometimes say, "Oh but if he said this," or, "We want to do it some other way," but they never ever thought that they knew everything.'

Doreen and Joan perhaps deserve some credit here for providing the right kind of home life for their husbands, a 'normal' environment in which their feet were firmly kept on the ground. As Ernie admitted, 'Thank God I've got in Doreen a sensible wife who acts as a stabilizer in every facet of my life.' Angela Rippon noticed this down-to-earth quality about Ernie and found it both endearing and admirable. 'There was always a certain amount of, not self-deprecation because he never did that. He never made a song and dance about who he was or what he had achieved, he just didn't and I think that was a lovely thing about him. Ernie took all the praise and the adulation and all the prizes and everything else with great good humour and good grace, but there was never anything big-headed or bombastic or loud about Ernie Wise, he was always a very modest man.'

This shared level-headedness may have had something to do with both of their backgrounds. Far from taking this success for granted, they respected it because it had been hard won. 'They were still working-class lads in many ways,' said John Ammonds. Although they did turn up for rehearsals in their separate Rollers. People were always surprised by this, not that they drove Rolls-Royces, but that they showed up for rehearsals separately. Bill Cotton remembered them returning to the BBC to start on a new series and it was obvious the boys hadn't seen each other since the last time they'd worked. But something remained between them, something special.

It was also rare to see Eric and Ernie together at a social or showbiz function. Outside of their professional relationship the two men hardly saw each other. Understandable, since away from the cameras both were very different people, with different interests and outlooks on life. Ernie was placid, cheerful and easy-going, while Eric had a darker, more complex and tortured personality. 'I travelled with them when they were on the road, so I saw it first-hand,' says Doreen. 'Eric would either be laughing and joking or he'd burrow deep inside himself. He used to get terrible moments of depression and there was no getting to him then. He could be quite morose and lock himself away.' Doreen recalls one visit during summer season to Chesil Beach in Dorset where Eric barely came out of his room. 'Joan and the kids were on the beach with us, but he hardly saw anything of them.'

Apart from mood swings, Eric had a very bad temper. 'I remember once seeing him lose his rag in front of an audience,' claims Doreen. 'That was just Eric, though.' Something else, too. Eric had a saying which was: 'He's a personal friend of mine.' This meant that he didn't want you to get too close to him—'He's my mate, not yours.' Some people probably wondered why Ernie and Doreen were a bit distant with them, and that was the reason. 'Eric was extremely protective of his friends,' says Doreen.

Ernie often said he and Eric were opposites in many ways. 'I am what I would call a cautious optimist, while Eric is an incautious pessimist. I will say a theatre is half full; to him it's half empty.'

But there was something else, too, that led them to live quite separate lives. When they formed their double act Eric and Ernie virtually lived in each other's pockets, travelled everywhere together, ate together, went out together and stayed in the same grotty digs. Once they married new priorities took over and they deliberately separated their social and working lives and began to see less and less of each other. They also stopped sharing the same dressing room and while out on tour stayed at different hotels, often miles apart.

It also appears that they only went on holiday together once. That was in 1971 when Ernie and Doreen joined Eric and Joan for an Easter cruise aboard the recently launched QE2. The boys had done some promotion at Cunard's head office on Regent Street and the company rather obligingly offered them a free cruise. On board, Eric and Ernie didn't actively avoid each other; rather they were conscious of being seen in each other's company. 'Eric said that if we were always seen together they'd expect us to work,' Doreen remembers. 'So we just met up occasionally really.'

Walking the deck Eric was often accosted by fellow holidaymakers asking, 'Are you looking for Ernie?' Eric just smiled back and replied, 'No, I've got him in my pocket.' Shades here of the Oliver Hardy put-down about Stan to the Regent Street news vendor. Maybe Billy Marsh had told Eric that story and he'd been waiting years for an opportunity to use it.

Of course, the press used to seize on all of this as proof that they didn't get on, when in reality the opposite was true: it was the very reason their partnership worked so well. Millicent Martin believes the fact Eric and Ernie never socialized certainly helped the partnership thrive far longer than it would have otherwise. 'Both just knew that if they spent every waking hour together they would get bored of each other and the partnership would start to rot. So when they met up they would always spark off each other. And they respected each other professionally more than anyone I've ever met. They may not have been best friends but they were mates who just happened to be extraordinarily talented.'

Incredibly this arrangement never affected the act; they'd been together so long and so intensely that the bond between them could never be broken. Indeed, the mere fact they didn't have much of a private life together explains their durability, so when they did get together it was always a very happy occasion. They'd just sit down, say hello and get stuck into an enormous catch-up; all the gossip and whatever had been going on in each other's lives. 'I think they both looked forward to it,' says Barry Cryer. 'Familiarity may breed contempt but absence certainly makes the heart grow fonder, especially if you were as close as those two. Ernie once said to me, "Because we don't live in each other's pockets we're always pleased to see each other." I think that sums it up perfectly.'

And one must admit that their eventual success had as much to do with their staying power as anything else. Eric always said to Ernie that the reason they succeeded was because they stayed together. Simple, yet profound. And they lasted the course largely because of what they'd experienced on the way up the ladder in variety. 'They'd seen so many double acts end up not speaking to each other over the years,' says Michael Grade. 'Their early heroes, Ben Warriss and Jimmy Jewel being a case in point, and they were determined that they were never going to end up like that. They had a good business going.'

Whatever differences of opinion Eric and Ernie had it never descended into any personal animosity. 'There was never any friction between them in real life,' confirms Eddie Braben. 'They liked each other,' says Doreen simply. 'I was around them for years, so if there had been any tension at all, I would have known about it.' Of course sometimes they didn't agree on things, 'we have professional arguments, but that's all,' said Ernie. They were always mindful to keep such differences on a business footing because hidden underneath was the fear that if their personal relationship collapsed that was it, that was the end. 'I just have an immense amount of admiration for the length of their career,' says comedian and actor Ben Miller.

209

'And the fact they stuck at it. If only all of our careers were like Morecambe and Wise's. I think that part of the reason they were so bulletproof in the end is the fact that they'd had so many failures and missed chances in the early years. Actually Morecambe and Wise's early years run to about two decades. Can you imagine having to do an apprenticeship of twenty years before becoming famous? That's just incredible and would never happen today. Nobody would have the staying power. That's one of many things that make them so totally unique.'

And to a large extent we have Ernie to thank for that longevity. The boys never fell out largely because Ernie was so easy-going. Had he been burdened with Eric's temperament they'd have endlessly clashed and broken up and got back together a dozen times. Even in their very early days Ernie was prepared to allow Eric to let off steam by balling him out: 'You're not a bit good,' he'd yell or, 'You're supposed to have learnt this!' On one occasion Sadie was witness to this and couldn't stomach it any more so ordered Eric out of the room. 'You know, you shouldn't have interfered,' Ernie said once he'd left.

Sadie was quite taken aback by Ernie's reaction. 'But I'm sticking up for you,' she said.

'Don't you see? Eric is only trying to make me the best feed in the country, like Jerry Desmonde is to Sid Field. And shall I tell you something—Eric's going to be the best comic in the British Isles.'

Ernie never had a problem with this side of Eric; certainly he never allowed it to sour their relationship. 'Ernie was the most placid person you could meet,' says Doreen. 'We used to say he should have been a priest. He had known Eric all his life, and knew exactly how to handle him. I don't think they ever had a row because Ernie wouldn't do that.'

Ernie's placid nature also meant that he indulged Eric's ego by never trying to win the laughs from him onstage or moan in public that the spotlight was never really on him and that his partner got all the plaudits. 'Ernie didn't seem to mind that Eric was getting seventy-five per cent of the limelight and ninety per cent of the laughs,' says Des O'Connor. 'Though privately perhaps he did. You've got to give Ernie great credit for that. He would set up Eric's lines like a golf ball on a tee.' Ben Warriss, who along with Jimmy Jewel was a big influence on the boys, once told Ernie not to worry about being a straight man. 'It doesn't matter who gets the laughs as long as you get half the money.'

For the most part it was Doreen who got angry on her husband's behalf. When critics talked about Eric being the comic genius and Ernie being 'the other one', Doreen would be seething inside. 'I always got furious, but Ernie didn't. He'd just say, "Well, I know better." Ernie was content to let Eric have the spotlight. He'd invent marvellous comic lines and Eric would say, "It's your line, Ern, you say it," but Ernie would reply, "No, it'll be better coming from you." So, no, Ernie didn't resent Eric getting most of the attention.'

He was also happy to take the insults, just so long as they got the laughs. With good grace he took the swipes about his short, fat hairy legs, the wig, the slaps in the face, and Eric pointing out his solitary fan in the audience, Vernon from the wig boutique.

'He was very savvy,' says Ben Miller. 'It was a bit like John Lennon realizing that he could either

211

be the top dog in the band or step aside and let Paul McCartney sing most of the songs. Which is of course what he did. He could see Paul's talent as a singer so decided to forgo his ego in favour of a better voice. Because Ernie obviously saw enormous potential in Eric and nurtured that talent he was also prepared to forego what would have undoubtedly been a very successful solo career in pursuit of the perfect double act, which is of course what they became. Ernie should get credit for that because without his savvy and selflessness Morecambe and Wise would never have come into being.'

What did get Ernie's back up was people denigrating what he did. The straight man is invariably overlooked, it's the comic in a double act that is always favoured and remembered, especially in Eric's case when you had someone genuinely touched by genius. 'The only sadness with the relationship is that you kind of thought that Ernie felt he never got the kind of recognition he deserved,' says Sir Michael Parkinson. 'And there's something in that but inevitably people are attracted to the comic. But the difference here was that Eric was exactly the same offstage as he was onstage, so people always got the Eric Morecambe that they wanted. Subsequently everyone gravitated to him and Ernie was left being the more normal of the two but the less regarded.'

Perhaps Ernie took solace in the fact that such people misunderstood what constituted a good double act. That one without the other wouldn't work. 'What the act would have been without one of us—whichever one—was simple,' said Ernie. 'Not half as good.' It wasn't just behind the scenes that Ernie controlled matters, but onstage as well, allowing Eric the freedom and confidence to ad-lib or go off on flights of wild comic fancy, safe in the knowledge that Ernie was there to keep the act on course if things went too far. Ernie was the director, if you like, the one in control. 'Whatever Eric did, and he was brilliant running off into different directions, he knew Ernie was always there to right the ship,' recalls Des O'Connor. 'Wherever he'd gone Ernie was a rock and he was always going to pull him back to where he was.'

Eddie Braben once asked Ernie when he knew Eric was going to ad-lib and he replied, 'I can tell by his eyes.' Braben was astonished. 'But when you think they were together all that time it makes sense,' said the writer. 'It tells you a lot.'

On their TV shows Ernie also learnt all the guests' lines, so that if they wandered away from the script he could manoeuvre them on track again. Eric used to call him, 'The thin line of sanity.' But much of this work went unheralded: in the public's eye he was relegated to being the unfunny one, and the suggestion floating around that Eric was so funny he didn't need Ernie not unnaturally hurt him deeply. 'Even today I don't think we realize just how important Ernie was,' says Eddie Braben. 'He was so good nobody noticed him, that's how good he was. Without "and Wise" there wouldn't have been an act. They were inseparable. I wrote a line for Eric when they were doing their stand-up patter and Ernie had to go off to get a prop and Eric said, "Don't be too long because when you're away I get a cold draught down one side." And when he read it, I suppose this speaks volumes today, Eric told me, "That is right, that is so right, when he's not there I

213

feel lost." I think that tells you how important Ernie was.'

The truth is Eric felt uncomfortable being onstage on his own. He didn't just need Ernie there to feed him the lines; he needed Ernie on that stage with him for security.

Ronnie Corbett observed this while attending a showbiz charity do with Eric. 'He wouldn't even get to his feet to hand out a prize if Ernie wasn't there, at his side.' It's a strange phenomenon that affects a lot of double acts. Des O'Connor remembers years ago talking to Mike and Bernie Winters when they split up and Bernie confessing how terrible it was walking onstage by himself. Eric was the same, he didn't like standing out in the lights alone. He didn't like performing as a solo artist, whereas Ernie began on his own so felt much more comfortable with it. He was OK for a couple of minutes, Eric, and then he'd start to feel uncomfortable without Ernie. 'When Ernie wasn't there it didn't work,' says Braben. 'That's how important he was. He was the pillar; he was the pillar that held the act together.'

TWENTY-EIGHT

A SONG AND DANCE

By 1974 producer John Ammonds had left the team, replaced by Ernest Maxin, who like Ernie was a big fan of Hollywood musicals and brought to *The Morecambe and Wise Show* something new, those big MGM-style numbers, such as the brilliant

Singing in the Rain pastiche, which allowed Ernie to shine. Incredibly that number was shot in about twenty minutes, according to Maxin. 'They worked so hard in rehearsals they never made a mistake in the studio.'

Maxin and Ernie worked closely together on those numbers. After all, that's what Ernie always saw himself as, a song-and-dance man. Eric was a comic first and foremost, who could dance and sing passably, but it was the fusing of these talents that gave their act such broad scope and appeal. 'I'm not an out-and-out comic,' Ernie once confessed. 'Singing and dancing is what I like to do, and it's the one thing I don't do a lot of.'

Besides Hollywood musicals Ernie was also a big jazz fan and often went to Ronnie Scott's Jazz Club in London's Soho. One night he and Doreen took Alf Garnett's creator Johnny Speight with them to see the famous American trumpeter Harry James. 'Johnny was three sheets to the wind,' Doreen remembers. 'But we were all having a great night. Then in the interval Ernie went up to speak to Harry to tell him how much he was enjoying the show and Harry James said, "Hey, I know you— you're on the *Ed Sullivan Show*." So, in the second half he played the entire set right next to our table and straight at Ernie. It was such a lovely gesture, except that he almost blew Ernie's head off. The entire table was very nearly deafened and Ernie was going bright red. None of us could move, of course, because that would have been rude. We just had to sit and bear it. I think it actually sobered Johnny up, which was an achievement. What a wonderful night though.'

Perhaps the jewel in the crown of Morecambe

and Wise's musical numbers is the breakfast sketch where the boys do a hilarious pastiche of 'The Stripper'. It's a routine that has not only gone down in Morecambe and Wise legend but is generally perceived to be among the funniest sketches ever seen on British television.

The origin of that sketch is interesting. When the boys toured round in variety they always took with them a notebook in which they'd jot down jokes and ideas. One day the idea flashed into Ernie's mind of two guys making breakfast to the tune of 'The Stripper'. Eric agreed it was funny and so Ernie quickly scribbled the basic concept into one of the notebooks. It was another twelve years before the sketch actually saw fruition. And like the *Singing in the Rain* pastiche, Ernie was in his element here. 'If you watch the breakfast sketch Ernie's far more animated and seems to be enjoying himself a lot more,' says Maxin. 'It's his sketch really.'

Strangely, according to Doreen, Ernie could barely watch that routine without criticizing himself. 'There was one bit, where he was whisking the eggs that he hated. Every single time he'd say, "The timing was all wrong there. That could have been better. I came in too soon."'

This happened frequently. Continuing the habit that they had developed early in their career, Eric and Ernie always carried out a post-mortem on each one of their shows, analysing where things went wrong, considering where they went too slow or too fast, where things were mistimed, how they could have made it funnier. Nothing was ever perfect; things could always be improved.

In an extremely brave move the comedy duo Armstrong and Miller agreed to recreate the breakfast sketch for a gala show celebrating the sixtieth anniversary of BAFTA back in 2007. 'It was fiendishly difficult,' recalls Ben Miller. 'And it took weeks of rehearsal to be able to pull it off, as you can imagine. Ours was done in real time in front of a live audience but theirs was done in slots and when you see the transcript of the shooting day they did it in a remarkably short time, it was just one of a number of things they were recording that day. I think it was all shot in the morning.'

The idea was to recreate the sketch in every minute detail, so it was exactly how Eric and Ernie did it all those years before, which meant the pair had to watch the sketch countless times in order to get everything right. 'I don't know how many times I did that catching the egg bit,' says Miller, who assumed the Ernie role. 'But we basically just spent the whole day throwing eggs in the rehearsal room to get it right. We just spent hours and hours rehearsing it until it was absolute second nature because we didn't want to be nervous on the night. And also standing in Ernie Wise's shoes was really difficult. He was a fantastic dancer Ernie Wise and that bit at the end when the fridge door opens and they're larking around with the sausages, it looks really easy but isn't. It was consummate hoofer stuff, and remarkably complicated to reproduce—it certainly was for me anyway.'

Interestingly, Ant and Dec were originally asked to perform 'The Stripper' sketch at that BAFTA event and declined the offer straight away. 'We're such big fans for a start, and on top of that, the last thing we wanted people to think was that we were trying to become the next Eric and Ernie. It all felt very wrong. We'd love to do it on our own in one of our own kitchens, just for a laugh. That'd be excellent. I think half the country would want to do that. But on TV? No.'

With Maxin installed as the new producer, the show went from strength to strength, but already the boys were aching to move on and try something different, they'd been doing the same kind of comedy for so long it bored them. One very enticing idea was to try their hand at situation comedy and they actively looked for the right project. Ever the pragmatist, it was Ernie who knew it was impossible to break free of the formula they had established for themselves on television. The British public simply wouldn't accept them doing anything else; ultimately they were victims of their own success.

And there's no better example of how ingrained the boys had become in the British psyche than their Christmas show. It was for many the television highlight of the year, as much a part of the festive season as turkey and the Queen's speech. As Braben observed, 'People judged the quality of their Christmas by *The Morecambe and Wise Show*.'

Once invited to perform before the Queen at a special private show for the Royal Family at Windsor Castle, Prince Philip took Ernie to one side to tell him that the Royals always delayed their Christmas dinner until *The Morecambe and Wise Show* was over.

With that expectation came huge responsibility, of course, and added pressure. 'Other programmes can flop,' said Ernie. 'The Christmas ones must never be allowed to.' With that in mind five weeks were allotted to knock them into shape and it was always recorded as close to Christmas as possible so everyone could feel at least mildly festive, akin to

Roy Wood's band Wizzard recording the classic 'I Wish It Could Be Christmas Everyday' in mid-June and hanging decorations up all over the studio.

It is possibly for these festive specials that Eric and Ernie will be most fondly remembered. It was when they seemed to up their game, operate at a level of perfection that no other British entertainers have ever managed on television, when they strove to get the biggest guests and put on the biggest production numbers. They reached an unheard of peak when their 1977 Christmas show was watched by an estimated 28 million viewers, more than half the UK population. 'The popularity of their show was just ridiculous,' says Jeffrey Taylor, who was later Ernie's producer in the West End. 'And what was unique about Morecambe and Wise, compared to today, was that you would sit down and watch it with your grandmother and your son and all three generations enjoyed it, which was and still is totally unique. We now live in an era where we have different channels for everybody. Today a sixteen-year-old wouldn't be seen dead watching what a fortyor a sixty-year-old likes. Everything is so fragmented and segregated whereas in Morecambe and Wise's day it was different.'

Comedy actor Kevin Eldon makes a similar point. 'I remember sitting in the front room with my extended family at Christmas and everyone from us kids to the grandparents would be roaring with laughter. That's a mark of their brilliance, the fact that they appealed to such a broad range of people age-wise. And class-wise. People would be laughing in council houses and palaces alike.'

The highlights of those Christmas shows are many, Elton John wandering around the BBC like

219

a little lost boy searching for Eric and Ernie, Shirley Bassey getting her high heels unceremoniously replaced with hobnail boots and Grieg's piano concerto with André Previn, which elicited this classic exchange when the conductor exclaimed to Eric, 'You're playing all the wrong notes.' Incensed, Eric grabs Previn by the lapels. 'No, I'm playing all the right notes. But not necessarily in the right order.' It's a sketch that is an all-time favourite with comedienne Miranda Hart. 'All three of them were so funny in their different ways in that sketch. And it one hundred per cent holds up today when, even though I am a huge fan of theirs and hate to admit it, not all of them do. Some of them seem a little long and lacking in pace, which may not fare with today's TV remote-control flicking audiences but the André Previn sketch is total genius.'

And, of course, no Christmas show would be complete without at least one pop at poor old Des O'Connor, until finally he was able to turn the tables on them. 'There is one particular appearance I made on their Christmas show that is lovely, it shows us having a giggle and having a laugh. I wrote a bit that I'd used years ago in a panto where I smack Eric on the face to spell out a word. Little Ernie says "hard" and so I'm going H-A-R-D and then "rough" R-O-U-G-H, all the time hitting Eric in the face. Then I say to Ernie, can you think of any more words and he says "Unscrupulous" and it got a belting laugh. And the nice thing about that, it was one of the few times the audience could actually see Eric and Ernie ad-libbing. We did some real fun things together; nothing but happy memories.'

In 1976 they were joined by John Thaw and

Dennis Waterman, escaping their current *Sweeney* roles to play Germans in an amusing war skit. Thaw remembered feeling nervous on the first day of rehearsal. On *The Sweeney* it was usually a case of showing up on location, reading the scene a couple of times and then shooting it, the intense rehearsal period Eric and Ernie insisted upon was totally alien to them and both actors felt deeply anxious. Made to feel at home, Thaw and Waterman quickly grew in confidence and after the recording everyone met in the bar for a friendly drink. Half-jokingly Thaw suggested that now he and Dennis had done their show, Eric and Ernie ought really to guest star on theirs. This could have been laughed off, but Ernie immediately picked up on it. 'You mean come on *The Sweeney*?' Pleasantly surprised that the suggestion was being taken seriously Thaw replied, 'Why not?' 'God, I'd love that,' said Ernie. Everyone thought it was a great idea and the boys did appear as themselves in one of the last ever *Sweeney* episodes, broadcast in 1978.

The 1976 Christmas show was also famous for an appearance of a pair of legs that made newspaper headlines. They belonged to Angela Rippon. The concept of taking a guest out of their normal sphere and plonking them in the most unexpected situation was perhaps epitomized best here. Along with Anna Ford, Angela was the only woman back then on television reading the news, or even connected in some way with a serious current affairs programme. She therefore had the sort of high profile the boys always looked for in a guest and they especially knew the public anticipated a surprise or two in their Christmas show, like an unexpected extra present at the bottom of your stocking.

The idea was for Angela to front a news broadcast that suddenly became a glitzy dance number, which like everything else the boys did was meticulously planned and rehearsed. 'Ernie was a good dancer,' reveals Angela. 'He was a much better dancer than Eric of course because he'd been dancing since he was very young; he did know what he was doing. Eric was a great hoofer. So Ernie danced like a straight man and Eric danced like a comic. Eric made fun of what he was doing, but Ernie did know how to dance.'

Angela's appearance was almost ground-breaking and she was delighted to be approached. 'But remember: I would not have been allowed to do it had I not been given permission by the editor of television news at the time.' Of course, everyone at the BBC news office watched the show and when Angela returned to work the response was something quite extraordinary. 'Actually, Ernest Maxin told me subsequently that within weeks of the New Year some of the male newsreaders and some of the other men in current affairs went to his office and asked, "Do you think we might be able to do something like that?" And if you remember on the following year's Christmas special Eric and Ernie did a parody of *South Pacific's* "There is Nothing like a Dame" with a few male newsreaders, Michael Parkinson, sports and current affairs presenters, all of the blokes were given their moment in the spotlight.'

It was Maxin himself who came up with that idea and ran it past the boys during a production meeting. 'Ernie was immediately hooked. He loved it and could visualize exactly what I had in mind, which was to cut in shots of body doubles doing elaborate gymnastic moves, with the upper bodies of the guests. Eric though, didn't like it at all. He just couldn't get his head round it. Partly because he was a born worrier. His tendency to worry could sometimes impede his ability to run with an idea. By that I mean that if he couldn't visualize what somebody had in mind, he would block it out and lose all enthusiasm. Ernie, on the other hand, had been dancing since he was a boy and had a genuine love for song-and-dance routines. He could be quite a visionary at times, especially with this kind of thing. Ernie was always a lot more involved with the song-and-dance routines.'

Eric only came round to the routine when he sat and watched it being edited, at Ernie's insistence, according to Maxin. 'Ernie had to go and persuade Eric to come and watch the sketch being edited. That was the only way I'd be able to show him how it would work. We recorded it on the Friday and edited that evening—to be shown at the recording of the show on the Saturday. Anyway, Ernie eventually persuaded Eric to come and watch me edit the routine, and it worked, thank God! After it was done, Eric kissed me on the cheek, said "thank you" and went home.'

The *South Pacific* spoof was but one of many gems from the 1977 Christmas show. It was another stellar cast list: Elton John, Penelope Keith, Francis Matthews and cameos from Formula One champion James Hunt and the *Dad's Army* cast. Angharad Rees, then starring in one of the BBC's top dramas *Poldark*, also appeared. By now being invited on *The Morecambe and Wise Christmas Show* was seen as the ultimate accolade, and

Angharad has never forgotten the experience. 'They couldn't have been lovelier to work with, such fun. They taught me so much about comedy, about timing and delivering a funny line. Working with them I noticed they each had different strengths, Eric seemed the more forceful but Ernie knew just how to handle him. He was very good-natured with Eric.'

What Angharad didn't expect was the level of intense rehearsal that she was put through. 'Eric and Ernie were terrifically disciplined and great sticklers for everything being absolutely right, going over and over and over something and improving it. And sometimes it changed in rehearsal, they'd realize a joke or something wasn't quite right so they'd change it until it was perfect in their eyes. They were total perfectionists.'

And being perfectionists, it was really no surprise that the boys approached each rehearsal with total thoroughness. They'd start about 10.30 in the morning and work through till three but always cultivated, 'a wonderful happy, family atmosphere', according to their frequent co-star Ann Hamilton, while at the same time expecting everyone to put a shift in. As the maverick theatre director Joan Littlewood said, 'Rehearsal is the work, performance is the relaxation.' This was the boys' credo, too, they worked and worked until they knew the last bolt of everything so when the cameras rolled they were supremely confident in what they were doing and could relax and enjoy themselves. And it showed. 'And because they worked and rehearsed very hard,' says Glenda Jackson, 'because they didn't leave stuff to chance, that's why it looked as though they were making it up as they went along, that those shows had an air of spontaneity. But it was the result of painstaking rehearsal. As Fred Astaire said, "If it doesn't look easy we haven't worked hard enough," and that was their baseline.'

Even the ad-libs were more often than not scripted and rehearsed over and over again. 'It's interesting to find out that they rehearsed stuff really assiduously,' says Kevin Eldon. 'They'd go over and over routines, sketches etc. so they knew exactly what they were doing. In comedy an element of spontaneity and natural funniness is really valuable but in most cases it also needs technical application. So that excellence of theirs had two aspects. It was natural *and* it was worked at.'

TWENTY-NINE

BYE BYE AUNTIE

With their long experience in variety both Eric and Ernie knew full well that once you'd made the top of the bill there really wasn't anywhere else to go. A similar thought must have registered with them when the viewing figures of their 1977 Christmas show were released. Just how do you trump 28 million viewers? The answer was you can't, it was a feat that simply couldn't be beaten.

For much of the early part of 1978 Philip Jones, Head of Light Entertainment at Thames Television and a long-time friend of Ernie's, had being wooing the boys to defect over to ITV. The inducement was a mouth-watering hike in their salary; Ernie was to recall that it was three times more than what they were presently being paid. When news filtered back to the BBC governors about ITV's attempt to snatch their star team they approved a matching bid. But things weren't quite as simple as who was prepared to pay the most, there were other factors at play. For one, a move away from the BBC, their home now for almost a decade, would offer Eric and Ernie a new challenge. But it was the prospect of making another feature film that ultimately proved the clincher, and something the BBC just couldn't match. Unlike dear old Auntie, Thames had a movie-making division by the name of Euston Films, who'd made the *Sweeney* movies. The boys had always wanted another shot at making a comedy picture and this was their chance. It was too good an opportunity to refuse and in early 1978 they made the switch.

The repercussions were huge. Of course it made front-page headlines, but so devastating a blow was it to the BBC that its governors actually planned to lobby the government to have ITV penalized. The poaching of Morecambe and Wise raised fears about the massive spending power of the independent television companies and the BBC wanted them reined in, otherwise the organization would continue to lose out in high-profile bidding wars; as it eventually did when Bruce Forsyth and Mike Yarwood, both huge draws for the BBC, jumped ship to ITV in the wake of Morecambe and Wise's departure. There was even a suggestion of asking for a 'levy' to be placed on ITV profits so that the BBC could operate on a level-playing field.

For Ernie, the decision to leave the BBC was

purely business-based. Not for one minute did he think he and Eric acted disloyally, as some said they had. After all, would the BBC have stayed loyal to them had they begun producing lousy shows that no one watched? 'The simple fact is that we were unique and uniqueness sets its own price,' said Ernie. His one personal regret was the hurt inflicted upon Bill Cotton, the man who had done so much for them, especially when Eric had his heart attack. Their old boss was in America when the news broke and he was left devastated. 'I just felt completely and utterly empty.'

Thames had no intention of changing the format of the show, as they pointed out, when you buy a Rolls-Royce what's the point in converting it into an Austin 7? The only obvious difference was the commercial breaks, which in hindsight Ernie believed harmed them. It was, however, a whole new production team; Ernest Maxin had refused to leave the BBC, as did Eddie Braben, who felt comfortable with the network, 'like a favourite cardigan.' So a new writer was required and as the shoes they were filling were rather on the large side Thames brought in two vastly experienced new guys, Barry Cryer and John Junkin. Cryer knew the boys from way back in variety days and was good friends with both of them. In fact, he became their warm-up man at the BBC. He remembers Eric and Ernie sitting Junkin and himself down and giving them the whole idea for their Thames Christmas show—there and then. 'So we went away and wrote it to order. John and I did our very best, but we had to admit that it wasn't one of their classics. After the show was broadcast John and I asked the boys out to lunch. They must have thought it was a bit strange, a couple of writers taking them out.' During the meal, which was convivial and full of laughter, Cryer could see Junkin looking at him, as if to say, 'Look, we've got to mention it.' So he took the cue.

'Look boys, we're off. We're leaving.'

Eric and Ernie looked puzzled. 'Why?'

'Well, the Christmas Show wasn't that good,' said Cryer.

'Yes it was!'

'Well it wasn't one of your best, boys, let's be honest. John and I wrote it so it's only right that we should take the flak.'

And quick as a flash Ernie said, 'Do you mean we can be as bad as we like?'

In the end Junkin and Cryer just wrote two specials for Eric and Ernie but it was certainly an experience and Cryer has never forgotten the occasion he actually had a heart murmur during a script conference with the boys at Thames' offices on the Euston Road. 'There were a whole gang of people in the room and I suddenly started to feel very ill and Eric, who was obviously an expert in this field, noticed the signs straight away and got to work. He had an ambulance called and laid me down (which was apparently the wrong thing to do!) and made sure I was comfortable etc. So while we're waiting for the ambulance to come, Eric looks around for Ernie, and Ernie's sitting there behind his script, and Eric shouts, "Hey, Ern, do you know what's happening here? Come on, give us a hand." And Ernie looked up from his script and said, "Yes, I know what the problem is. We come in too early in this sketch!" It was hilarious. He was so engrossed in the script he had no idea what was going on. That nearly finished me off!'

There was another occasion when Cryer was asked to write a two or three-minute bit for Eric. 'I forget what for but it was to be delivered straight to camera. So I brought it into the production office, and the room's full of people and Eric looked at it and said, "No, this is wrong. This isn't what I asked for. You weren't listening to me Barry, go and do it again." So I went off to the bar and sulked. Well, I found it really humiliating. So after a bit Eric came in and said, "Why the long face?" So I said, "You just bollocked me in front of everybody," and he said, "That was there, this is here, sunshine—what are you drinking?" It was like, that was business and this is friendship. And I never forgot that. Both Eric and Ernie were the ultimate professionals, but would never let it affect a friendship.'

The boys' new career at Thames had only really just got started when in March 1979 Eric suffered another heart attack, this time when he was relaxing at home in his kitchen. It led to a life-saving triple bypass operation at Harefield hospital that took seven hours. It was judged a success and he left hospital after nine days in a media blitz; the principal reason why Ernie never visited his partner was because the press were camped outside the hospital day and night.

Again all Ernie could do was wait anxiously for his partner to recuperate, his life on hold. The same thing happened of course, every time he left the house people came up to him asking how Eric was. Ernie understood they were well intentioned but did get rather sick and tired of it, so much so that he took to wearing a badge on his lapel. It read: 'Eric's getting much better. PS: I don't feel so good, though.' He met Princess Margaret at a reception during this time and she'd just begun to say, 'How's Eric . . .' when Ernie pointed at the badge. Princess Margaret didn't have her glasses on and Ernie overheard her asking her lady-in-waiting, 'What did it say?'

Again, Ernie was offered solo work. He was asked to star with Bill Maynard in a revival of *The Odd Couple* onstage and approached by producers to front an *Opportunity Knocks/New Faces* type of TV programme focusing on amateur entertainers. He turned everything down: 'they smacked too much of disloyalty on my part to even consider them.'

When Eric returned, jaded but seemingly game to carry on working, what was needed was a few familiar faces around him and so John Ammonds returned as producer. Ammonds' first task was to get Eddie Braben back on board, knowing full well that he was the only writer to have really captured the boys' unique personal style.

The ITV shows have had a bad press over the years but the quality is substantial although, according to Ammonds, 'I don't think, to be honest, that Eric and Ernie really knew why they were doing it any more.' Even if that were true, they remained as professional as ever. 'But the spark had gone,' said Ammonds. This may have been due to the fact they were deliberately slowing down due to Eric's health. He had been told by his doctor to take it easy and look after himself, but Eric being Eric sometimes he still went at things full throttle.

What those ITV shows did succeed in doing was attracting a consistent level of top-name star guests, starting with Dame Judi Dench on their first special. An avid fan, she was absolutely delighted to have been asked and jumped at the opportunity. 'Although it was daunting to say the least because I had seen all their shows and they were my heroes. They also made me laugh the whole time, which was not supposed to be part of the show.'

What was even more disconcerting was Eric's habit of constantly calling Dame Judi, 'young man'. He also taught her his famous paper bag trick. 'Watching them work together, they were very professional. It was a total partnership. I think they had great admiration for each other and a wonderful rapport, which was what made the shows so irresistible. Also Eric was a great ad-libber, but Ernie always had a response.'

Robert Hardy was another guest and very much in the public eye at the time with his role in popular BBC drama *All Creatures Great and Small.* 'I can remember that we rehearsed meticulously as they always did and they were kindness itself. When it came to the recording, on cue I had to knock on the door. Eric and Ernie were both in bed and one of them shouted, "Come in," which I heard, pushed open the door and the entire flat collapsed and fell down. That wasn't an intended part of the script, by the way, so there I was like the man in the film standing up in the doorway and they were in hysterics. Everything obviously stopped and we chatted while they reconstructed the actual flat and on we went.'

As a young actor Hardy recalls seeing Morecambe and Wise performing in panto. 'They were right down the bill. I don't remember what parts they played but I was certainly one of the first ones to see them as Morecambe and Wise.

And although they were a little bit rough around the edges they were certainly good together and even though it was very early on in their career they stayed with me and I remembered them.'

Hardy made two subsequent appearances on the show, both highly memorable. 'One was a song-and-dance number and I'm a very bad dancer and there was a row of us, all well-known folk. We actually did the act again at the Royal Variety performance and I remember Prince Philip coming along shaking hands afterwards and I'd met him before and he looked me in the eye and said, "Not much time to rehearse then, eh." It wouldn't have mattered if I'd rehearsed since Christmas, I'd still have been awful!'

Another venerable guest was Sir Ralph Richardson. Ernie visited him at his London home near Hyde Park, and during high tea persuaded the extremely weary thesp to come on their Christmas show. During rehearsal the boys quickly discovered that dear old Ralph was not a regular viewer, it was his wife who was the fan, so the theatrical knight didn't get the humour at all and even made the suggestion that they bring in someone like Harold Pinter to make Ernie's 'play wot I wrote' better. It took his wife quite a while to explain that it was supposed to be rubbish.

At one point during rehearsals, Eric took aside fellow guest Ian Ogilvy and asked him why Sir Ralph seemed to be questioning every one of his lines. 'Why am I saying this? he'd ask, to which the boys would reply, 'Because it's funny, Sir Ralph.' And Ralph would reply, 'Ohhhh . . . Funny! Oh, I see!' Ogilvy gave his opinion that Sir Ralph was probably amusing himself at their expense. 'The old bugger!' said Eric.

Robert Hardy was also a guest on that episode and tried to help dear old Ralph along. 'Ralph didn't know what he was doing and it was up to me to lead Ralph Richardson about by his elbow and take him through. Eric was obviously worried as to whether Richardson would actually do as he was told, but once we were on the adrenalin flowed and everything went wonderfully.'

Richardson was fairly ancient by this time and Eric and Ernie told him that he didn't need to do the little obligatory skipping dance at the end of the show. Ogilvy recalls that Richardson replied hotly that he was absolutely going to do the little dance at the end because that was the only reason he'd agreed to do the show in the first place.

Ogilvy had appeared briefly on a previous *Morecambe and Wise Show* during the height of his tenure as the Saint. 'I remember them both being wonderfully welcoming and enthusiastic and even grateful for their guests agreeing to be on their show at all, which was very endearing, given the enormous kudos attached to appearing with them.' Back for the Christmas show, he could observe them at his leisure and was struck by the way they operated as a team. 'Ernie had lots of ideas, some good, some not so good. Eric would enthuse about all of them and we'd try them out and then Ernie would say, "That doesn't really work, does it?" And Eric would say, "Not really, Ern." But he'd never squash any of Ernie's ideas before letting us try them out first. There seemed to be a genuine affection between the two of them and there was never an argument.'

One celebrity that came mighty close to

appearing on one of the Thames shows was Jeffrey Archer; this was around the time of the huge success of his novel *Kane and Abel,* when it was number one on most of the bestseller lists around the world. Like Hardy, Archer had seen Morecambe and Wise in their early days. 'I first saw Morecambe and Wise in Weston-Super-Mare in, I think, 1957. I would have been about sixteen. They were top of the bill and were superb. Brilliant.'

It was Ernie who approached Archer to see if he would guest star. 'And I was so desperate to do it, as it would have been a win-win situation for me.' Archer had just begun to garner a celebrity image for himself by appearing on successive television shows. 'But Morecambe and Wise would have been the pinnacle. Also around the same time I received a call from Barry Humphries who said, "Jeffrey you're going to do my *Dame Edna Christmas Show.* The idea is that you turn up at my flat, I see you on the intercom and I refuse to let you in. I'll say, God it's that dreadful Jeffrey Archer, I'm not letting him in. All he'll try and do is sell me some awful book he's written." I said, "I'm not going to do that, it'll make me look like a complete idiot, no, absolutely not." To which Barry replied, "Jeffrey, you will do it. There are three shows, Sean Connery is doing one, Jane Fonda is doing one and you're doing one." To which I replied, "OK, I'll be there."'

Ernie visited Archer at his London home and together they went through the sketch that had been planned for him. The idea was that Archer would be sitting in a small room offstage with a typewriter and Ernie would pop in from time to time and take what he'd written, return and hand it to Eric, who would say, 'Hey! This isn't bad!' It was actually quite a funny idea and you can see how it would have worked very well. 'So I would be sitting there made up to look very old and overworked,' reveals Archer. 'And I would be forced to type away furiously penning Ernie Wise's new "play wot I wrote". This would be a running sketch throughout the episode, which from time to time would flip back to Ernie running in frantically saying to me, "More more, I need more quickly," and I would hand in what I'd written and he would run out. Then at the end of the episode they would act out what I was supposed to have written and Ernie would take all the praise. I had no lines. The plan was that I wouldn't speak, I would simply type and type and type until Ernie had his masterpiece. As far as I know it was his idea.'

In the end the sketch never happened, due to scheduling conflicts, but Archer does recall a particularly memorable meeting with Eric at Wimbledon which wonderfully illustrates the affection the comic had for Ernie. 'Eric could never stop entertaining and we were on a fairly distinguished table for lunch, but Eric refused to stop playing the clown. When asked where Ernie was he said, "He's here under the table," and proceeded throughout lunch to pretend to everybody that Ernie was indeed underneath being fed and looked after by Eric and he did it with such genuine affection.'

As an interesting side note, Archer reveals another occasion he encountered the boys. 'Eric and Ernie came to see me privately and asked me to put a question to Margaret Thatcher who was of course then the Prime Minister. And the question was, why aren't comedians treated the same as Shakespearean actors? In their opinion it was grotesquely unfair that, say, Tony Hancock was never given a knighthood, yet three or four lesser Shakespearean actors would all get one. What I think they meant (although they didn't actually say it) was that why had certain grand actors been given a knighthood and they had not. I thought they had every right to make that complaint. Subsequently, of course, Norman Wisdom and one or two others have actually been given a knighthood, but their point was a good one in that it is every bit as difficult to be a world-class entertainer or comedian as it is to be a world-class actor. And I took that very much on-board and I reported this back to Mrs Thatcher, or I reported the concept to Mrs Thatcher. She nodded but didn't really say much as she was never really into the world of entertainment.'

To distinguish the Thames shows from the BBC ones, Ammonds didn't want Eric and Ernie to do their famous dance-off at the end, but what could possibly replace it? Eric came up with an idea to have a tenor singing an impossibly long note while some funny business happens around them each week. A couple of these were shot but Ammonds quickly realized it wasn't working and told Ernie, who replied, 'It isn't really, is it, but it's Eric's idea.' Ernie didn't want to be the one to tell Eric that they were dropping it. In the end Ammonds did the deed and Eric totally agreed, in fact he'd been waiting for someone to say it. Ultimately Ernie sang a duet each week with the guest star while Eric walked off home in flat cap and overcoat carrying a plastic shopping bag thinking the show had ended and that worked very well. What's illuminating about this anecdote is that Ernie's incredible loyalty to Eric could sometimes cloud his judgement and get in the way of his making a professional decision. He knew Eric's idea wasn't working but was unwilling to raise it for fear of hurting his feelings.

Or was it much deeper than that? Was Ernie by this time walking on eggshells around Eric, aware that the very future of Morecambe and Wise was in the balance? He'd had a feeling for some time that Eric was preparing to throw in the towel for good.

THIRTY

NIGHT TRAIN TO DISASTER

One day after rehearsals Eric walked into Ernie's dressing room and sat down. 'I'm not enjoying this any more,' he said finally, looking at Ernie. 'I've had enough. I think I ought to stop it. What do you think I should do?'

After a long and heartfelt conversation, Ernie said in conclusion, 'That, Eric, is something only you can decide.'

As the eighties began, Ernie could still tap into a vast reservoir of ambition, he still entertained those same old dreams of Hollywood fame he'd had as a kid. Eric, on the other hand, had grown visibly tired of the conveyor belt existence of churning out successive TV shows. Ernie saw his old friend arrive for rehearsals 'drained of real enthusiasm'. Even during the actual recording, when the adrenalin hits a performer, Ernie could see that the drive to perform just wasn't there any more. It was as if he'd fallen out of love with entertaining.

After the bypass operation and another bout of recuperation Eric had begun to think afresh. He wanted to be around Joan and the children more, and he'd begun to write novels and found great peace and satisfaction in being an author. As a result, never were the differences between Eric and Ernie more marked than they were at this point, with Eric also pursuing hobbies like fishing and birdwatching, solitary pursuits that, along with a desired quiet life at home, were all indicative of a withdrawal from the limelight. Ernie and Doreen were the complete opposite and much more showbiz-centric in their lifestyle. For years the couple hosted parties for their large coterie of friends like Harry Worth, Billy Dainty, Norman Vaughan and Pearl Carr and Teddy Johnson, or dropping in on pals, as Francis Matthews recalls. 'Funnily enough I was probably closer to Eric than Ernie, but Eric would never come and visit. Never. Ernie and Doreen always would though, which was a delight.'

And it was Ernie, not Eric, who was the one always popping over to America on business trips helping the BBC sell their old shows to the networks. In 1980 Ernie was instrumental in brokering a deal the BBC made with Time-Life to show *The Morecambe and Wise Show* on local channels up and down the nation. In the wake of successful British comedy exports like Monty Python and Benny Hill, Ernie badgered the BBC that they weren't doing enough to sell their shows to America. 'Ninety per cent of the work was done by Ernie,' said Eric. 'I was lying in hospital and he went out and did it.'

Another reason why Eric had grown disenchanted with the shows was a feeling of being trapped in the same format since the late 1960s. Ernie felt the same way, too, ever eager to surge forward and embrace new creative challenges, but like Eric was only too well aware that the public wanted things kept the same way, that they'd never accept them as anything other than a single life-form. It's the reason why neither had pursued solo projects like a sitcom starring just Eric or just Ernie, or one of them appearing on his own in a West End show. Ernie did later regret that they never found a sitcom both could have done together, maybe an extension of their sketches in their flat. Ernie was a great fan of *Only Fools and Horses*, but the scripts they were sent were not of equal quality. And now Eric had finally grown tired of it all. Not even the prospect of an upcoming movie for Thames could rekindle the old magic.

As we've seen, one of the carrots dangled in front of the boys' faces that lured them away from the BBC was the prospect of making a movie. As early as 1980 plans were drawn up for Morecambe and Wise's return to the silver screen. One plot had the boys encountering comedic misadventures in America opposite Vincent Price, only for the project to fall on fallow ground or get postponed, largely due to Eric's health.

When a film eventually got off the ground the fact it was to be shot on videotape and intended for television broadcast rather than cinema distribution was like a kick in the teeth for the boys. Making the best of a bad lot, Eric and Ernie worked on the script with director Joe McGrath and the result, entitled *Night Train to Murder*, was a rather jaded send-up of every Agatha Christie and Edgar Wallace thriller you've ever seen, featuring the boys as a pair of comics who get mixed up with murder and mystery in the obligatory spooky mansion. McGrath remembers Ernie as a good-natured hard worker who took criticism well and usually went straight home after the day's filming. 'Eric, on the other hand, stayed behind to have a glass and discuss what had been done and to have a look at any edited material. When Ernie left the set Eric (with his hand to his ear) would say, "It's very difficult to hear a Mercedes door close—beautifully made cars. In ten minutes Doreen will be on the phone asking if he's left." There was definitely a certain amount of animosity or jealousy in the air—on Eric's part, anyway.' One can understand Eric's annoyance that once work was finished Ernie was always keen to leave as quickly as possible, but then Ernie didn't feel the need to hang around the studio afterwards the way Eric did, sometimes taking an hour or more to unwind. Eric always begrudged Ernie the fact that he could shut the door completely on the business and relax. It was a luxury Eric never truly enjoyed.

Night Train to Murder did not really find favour with anyone. Eric in particular wanted Thames to shelve it or play it so late at night that the only people who might catch it were either insomniacs or burglars. 'Eric never wanted *Night Train* to be shown,' confirms Doreen. 'He hated the finished product because he looked old and quite dishevelled. He didn't come out of it looking quite like he'd hoped. He also made Ernie's character wear a neck brace most of the way through the production. He insisted on it, for some reason.'

Tragically, by the time Thames did broadcast

the movie, Eric Morecambe had died. 'After the film was released Ernie wrote to me saying that in his opinion *Night Train to Murder* was the best film they had made,' says McGrath. 'Eric didn't agree and was disappointed in it. Ernie thought this was because of Eric's physical condition when making it. He wasn't in particularly good shape then, after all, it was only a year or so before he passed away. Ernie also said that Eric usually reacted like this even after doing a show that was well received. He always felt that they could have done better, and it took some time for his depression to lift.'

THIRTY-ONE

TWO BECOMES ONE

By 1984 Eric's thoughts had turned once again to leaving Morecambe and Wise, and possibly retiring from show business altogether. It showed on Eric, this weariness. He wanted to ease back, see more of his grandchildren, and he was enjoying planning trips abroad with Joan, to spend quality time together, memories to share for the future.

Ernie had a sneaky feeling that Eric could never have faced retiring completely, that he needed an audience's applause just as much as he did. This was the dichotomy that ruled his life. 'Eric was a mass of contradictions,' said Ernie. 'At the start of his career he'd had Sadie to make all the decisions. Later on, I did it all. Towards the end of his life he was torn between his lack of enthusiasm to carry on and his compulsion to perform.' Ernie believes that

241

had Eric lived longer than he did it was inevitable they would have worked less and less together, almost gone into semi-retirement, performing only the odd charity event or maybe a Christmas special once a year.

But the plain fact was Eric's health couldn't take another heavy workload, or any more stress. Fearful that another full Morecambe and Wise series could bring on another heart attack, this time a fatal one, he loved life too much to want to jeopardize it. One night in April, Eric sat down with 12 and a half million other people to watch the ITV variety show *Live from Her Majesty's*, only to witness the terrible spectacle of his dear friend Tommy Cooper collapsing and dying right in front of him. That terrible tragedy merely served to reinforce his fears, and convinced him that he was making the right decision in stepping back. Poor Tommy dying onstage, that wasn't going to happen to him.

All through that early spring Eric had been unwell, he'd complained of difficulties breathing, looked haggard, and an ECG examination had revealed an enlarged heart. Told to visit Harefield hospital, Eric promised that he would right after he'd honoured a commitment to appear with his old variety friend Stan Stennett at a small charity event.

Stennett ran the Roses Theatre in Tewkesbury and asked Eric to come along for an informal evening of nostalgic chat about the old variety days. Eric had thought that it was a good idea, and that it wouldn't be too much of a strain talking about his life and career; if it went well it could be something he'd be able to do periodically. Ernie was worried. 'He knew Eric shouldn't have done it because he

Eric and Ernie cross swords during their first series for Lew Grade's ATV in 1961. This time, they were armed with exactly what they needed to make it work: confidence, experience, one of the best agents in the business and a great team of writers.

Roy Castle films the boys playing a parachute prank in the mid 1960s.

Ernie drags up for
*The Intelligence
Men*, 1965. Some
would probably
say that the photo
was funnier than
the film.

I don't get it?

Now I get it! The
boys do their best
to get a laugh
from Doreen's
dad, on the set of
*That Riviera
Touch*, 1966.

Producer Hugh Stewart presides over the cutting of Ernie's birthday cake. Ernie is flanked by Doreen on the left and leading lady Suzanne Lloyd on the right. Pinewood Studios, 1966.

Men from the Ministry! Eric and Ernie go for a stroll with pal Harry Secombe.

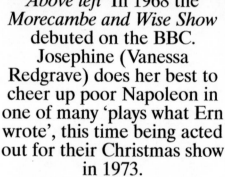

Above left In 1968 the *Morecambe and Wise Show* debuted on the BBC. Josephine (Vanessa Redgrave) does her best to cheer up poor Napoleon in one of many 'plays what Ern wrote', this time being acted out for their Christmas show in 1973.

Above Ernie with the sublime Glenda Jackson, playing Prince Albert and Queen Victoria in the 1972 Christmas show.

Left Howzat for a bat! Ernie brandishes his secret weapon.

Opposite page above Ernie with his 'Aren't I doing well' car.

Opposite page below Arr, Jim Lad! Eric and Ernie pose for the cameras at a promotional event in the early 1980s.

Above The boys with Rula Lenska, in the finale to the Yukon Gold Rush sketch, featured on the *Morecambe and Wise Show* in 1982. By this time they were back at Thames.

Left Billy Marsh, Prince Charles and the boys, backstage at the Theatre Royal Windsor in the early 1980s.

Ernie (and Molly) with his siblings in the mid 1990s.
From left to right, Annie, Gordon and Constance.

A publicity shot
for *The Mystery of
Edwin Drood*.
Although not a
commercial
success, Ernie did
well in the role
and gave it his all.

One of Doreen's favourite photographs of Ernie: going for a stroll with a feline friend.

knew he'd overdo it,' says Doreen.

So Eric went down, Stennett believes, because he just wanted to do something a little different than being in a double act. 'He might have wanted to prove something to himself, you know, that he could go on without Ernie if need be. I knew he'd been ill on and off and I did try to make sure that he was OK to attend. He'd promised to come but several times I rang and spoke to Joan and said, "Is he OK? Don't forget, if he can't make it at all, just let me know. I'll understand." But no, he didn't let me down and he arrived. And we spent quite a lot of the afternoon just laughing and reminiscing and that carried over into the evening when we did the show.'

The evening went very well. Eric spoke with clarity and humour about his childhood and those early days with Ernie, even his distress at the manner of Tommy Cooper's recent death. When it was all finished the packed house roared their approval. He couldn't help himself, it was the applause, the very thing that had fed and nurtured Eric his whole life, he had to respond to it, it was in his DNA. It began with him horsing around with the members of the band and then developed into a bit of knockabout physical comedy, running up and down the stage or playing around on the piano. When he left the stage he was roared back on. Joan was watching from the audience, almost squirming in her seat, desperate for him to stop, but Eric was in his element, doing what he was born to do.

Finally after six curtain calls Eric brought the nonsense to an end and said his farewells. It was almost as if he'd timed it to perfection, perhaps he sensed he was going to collapse but didn't want to do it in front of his public, because the second he was in the wings, out of sight, he keeled forward and dropped like a stone.

The audience were still applauding when the tannoy crackled into life and the almost clichéd announcement, 'Is there a doctor in the house?' was made. Joan raced backstage accompanied by her guest the mayor, who just happened to be a doctor. They found Eric crumpled on the ground, not moving. The mayor administered the kiss of life to get his heart beating again and to keep him alive until the ambulance arrived. Unconscious, Eric was taken to intensive care at Cheltenham General Hospital.

It was a nightmare Joan had lived through before but this time she sensed Eric didn't have the strength to pull himself back, though it was apparent he could sense what was going on, with gentle squeezes on her hand. Then something happened on the monitors and Joan was hurriedly led outside. Outside in the corridor she was in a daze, seconds and minutes passed without meaning; time had stood still. Then the door opened. 'We're terribly sorry, Mrs Morecambe.' It was one of the doctors; his face told the whole story. 'We couldn't save your husband. His heart just couldn't take any more.' He was fifty-eight.

After phoning the children Joan dialled Ernie's number. 'We heard the news when the phone rang at 2 a.m.,' recalls Doreen. 'And from that time on, if the phone ever went late at night, Ernie would get so upset. Eric had been a part of his life for so long. I suppose it was like losing a part of himself. Ernie was inconsolable.'

An hour after learning of Eric's death Ernie got

dressed and drove into London. He was expected at the *TV-AM* studios for a pre-arranged interview. 'I thought twice about going, but in the end it seemed the right thing to do,' he explained. It also allowed him to offer the first of what would be many public tributes: 'I am very, very proud to have been his partner. Through the years people will realize how great he was.'

For the next few days Ernie was in a complete daze as he endured interview after interview. Robert Hardy was visiting BBC centre during that period and has never forgotten encountering Ernie. 'I think it must have been the morning after Eric's passing and I got a call from the BBC asking if I would say something and of course I was honoured and thrilled to do so, so I turned up at Television Centre. And I walked down the corridor and there was a small figure coming towards me, a sort of figure of defeat and as we got closer to each other the figure raised his head and I realized who it was, with a look of absolute despair across it, it was the face of Ernie Wise. We looked at each other, stopped, hugged and I think I said something stupid like, "I'm so sorry." And there was nothing else to say really, I mean what else can you say, and we parted company. And then we were together briefly at the tribute programme for Eric but I never saw Ernie again after that.'

In the flurry of activity that followed the tragedy of Eric's death, among the glowing tributes and warm memories, there was one sour note. Just nine hours after the event George Bartram, press agent for Morecambe and Wise, received a call from a theatre not too far from the hospital where Eric lay dead. The enquiry was to find out if Ernie Wise would be available for pantomime. It was heartless beyond words.

One emotion coursing through Ernie was anger, anger that Eric had been robbed of the retirement he so richly deserved. Ernie felt sorrow, too, that he was never given the chance to say goodbye. The last time Eric and Ernie saw each other was a week or two before Eric's death at a restaurant called Maxim's. Ernie and Doreen were sitting with the television actor Tony Selby. 'The table was full,' recalls Doreen. 'And Eric turned up and I think he was expecting Tony Selby to get up and give him his seat, but he didn't. Eric went off and sat somewhere else with Joan. They did exchange pleasantries but nothing more.' It was the last time Eric and Ernie were ever together, as nondescript a goodbye as you can get.

Mixed in among feelings of shock and grief was another emotion, this one stronger and overpowering: guilt. Just days after the tragic news broke Ernie confided to his friend Alan Curtis that Eric should never have gone to that event alone, that he should have been there with him. 'Eric shouldn't have been working and he shouldn't have been at that theatre. I'd have looked after him. I'd have made sure he was OK. He shouldn't have been there!'

As Ernie spoke Curtis identified a very real desperation in his voice. 'It was so sad. Eric was his partner, his friend, his brother, really. If Eric was working it should have been with *him*, not anyone else. Ernie was always aware of Eric's vulnerabilities and was often quite protective of him. After all, he was basically put in charge of Eric when his mother Sadie was sent back to

Morecambe. Ernie wanted to save Eric but it was obviously too late. The whole thing was horribly sad.'

After those first few painful days, when Eric's death had finally sunk in, Ern was able to speak with honesty about it. 'He wore himself out. Simple as that. When he was onstage he was very dedicated. I don't have the same temperament as his, and I've always held something back. I don't go flat out when I'm performing, but Eric did. When he came onstage, he gave the audience everything he had. And he didn't relax or hold back enough and that's what killed him. It was stress.'

Over the years much has been written about Eric, his gifts as a comedian and the great loss his early death was to British comedy, denying us more years of laughter and shouts of 'get off' and 'this man's a fool' and catching invisible balls in paper bags. Often with Eric it was the simple things that made us laugh the most. And nothing was as simple and as pure as his partnership with Ernie, a partnership equalled perhaps only by Laurel and Hardy in its appeal and endearment. It was magic.

Within that partnership Ernie spared Eric a great deal of potential anguish regarding money and career decisions, Eric reciprocated by ensuring the partnership got plenty of laughs. And after all, what's a comedy duo when it's not getting laughs? 'Mike and Bernie Winters', might well have been Eric's answer.

The enduring fascination with Eric is easy to understand. First of all there was his nature—a nature so incredibly personable that he could win over entire continents just by asking the question, 'What do you think of it so far?' And secondly

247

there was his wit. Eric Morecambe's ability to make people laugh was truly biblical. Putting him up against today's crop would be like watching one Stanley Matthews run rings round a thousand Ronaldos. And thirdly, of course, there was his sense of timing—a genuine God-given talent that few possess and even fewer actually master. Luckily though, another 'one of the few' happened to be Ernie.

*   *   *

Eric's funeral took place at his beloved Harpenden. Ernie was touched by the fact that thousands of people had turned up to line the streets outside the simple church, 'to make a public farewell to the man who'd brought so much laughter into their lives.' Among the floral tributes the card on Ernie's wreath read: 'Goodbye, Sunshine. Miss you, your little fat friend.'

There were many speeches and eulogies that day, from Roy Castle, Dickie Henderson and others, it was a celebration really, his life remembered not by the sound of crying or mourning, but of laughter. Then it was Ernie's turn to stand up and speak. A hush fell over the church. Ann Hamilton, who was there, recalled that everyone wondered how he was going to follow all the wonderful speeches and sentiments already spoken. He didn't. He simply recited the words to 'Bring Me Sunshine'.

'We'd all been very brave until then,' Ann recalled. 'But those words moved us to tears.'

THIRTY-TWO

BACK TO THE BEGINNING

Amid the confusion of those appalling moments of grief after Eric died, the pain and the unavoidable sense of guilt, Ernie had what he later confessed to be a terrifying and unworthy thought. How could Eric go and die on him like that? After all they'd gone through together how could he desert him? This reaction of feeling abandoned is not uncommon in bereaved spouses and is totally understandable; after all, Ernie had not only lost his comedy partner but also his best friend. Almost fifty years of his life was tied up in that one person, so who can blame him for thinking, what is to become of me now? Ernie not only had to face the trauma of losing arguably the closest person in his life, but his professional livelihood, too.

Ernie was just fifty-nine when Eric died, healthy and still ambitious, but staring into a future that was far from certain. His first reaction was to pack everything in and throw in the towel. 'Ernie didn't want to work again,' reveals Doreen. 'When Eric died, he wanted to put down the shutters there and then.' Would the public who had so loved Morecambe and Wise accept him going on without Eric? 'Professionally, it was hard for him,' says Doreen. 'He did agonize about whether he should go on. I remember him saying, "I can't, because people won't accept me on my own."'

When Oliver Hardy died a French newspaper headlined the story *Laurel et Hardy est mort*, and Stan, realizing the truth of this statement, hardly ever made another public appearance. But Ernie was different. Financially made for life and in good health, he swam most days and had never missed a show during his long career, he could have put his feet up by the pool; did he really need the hassle of going out to look for work? And yet it was all he had ever known, performing ran in Ernie's blood, it was his life force, more perhaps than it was Eric's. Retirement was anathema to Ernie. He needed to be constantly on the move, facing new challenges. That's the way he was, that's the way it had always been. He also wanted to remain part of the business he loved. He still wanted to give something back to it. Although happily married, Ernie 'felt that my life was my work and my work my life'. Doreen puts it more bluntly: 'He was a performing seal. He didn't know any different.'

What he faced looked like an insurmountable obstacle. Ernie was famous only as part of Morecambe and Wise, exactly the same problem Eric would have faced had the roles been reversed, as Glenda Jackson observes. 'I think if it had been the other way round, if Ernie had gone first, I think Eric would have experienced, not to the same degree, but it would have been difficult for Eric to work on his own and it would have been very very difficult for the British public to accept one of them on their own.'

Approaching sixty, Ernie had to essentially reinvent himself and create a whole new career, to prove himself all over again—and in the shadow of Eric. It was a courageous feat even to attempt it.

Not just that, although the edges had become blurred within the partnership, the public and the industry still labelled Ernie as the straight man, the less funny one. And once the sympathy over losing his partner had worn off, Ernie found show business as tough as ever, coupled with the realization that on his own he had no clout whatsoever. 'I had the respect and reputation but not the power to call the tune.'

Could he hack it as a solo performer people were asking? In most double acts once one partner dies, the other almost disappears into the ether. One of the few exceptions has been Ronnie Corbett who was able to pursue his own career after Ronnie Barker died because he had always done solo projects in-between *The Two Ronnies*, such as the long-running sitcom *Sorry*. Indeed, he had made a name for himself as a television entertainer prior to teaming up with Ronnie Barker so the public were accustomed to seeing him work as a separate artist. That wasn't the case with Ernie.

Some suggested Ernie find another partner, as if he could or indeed wanted to replace Eric. Bernie Winters' name was bandied around and there was an idea he might team up with Eric Sykes; it would be Eric and Ernie once more. This was rejected: Ernie didn't want the comparisons if he joined another double act, but most importantly he wanted to leave the heritage of Morecambe and Wise unsullied.

For his future he looked to his past, deciding to go back to his roots as a song-and-dance man. He'd come full circle, back to where it all began. An Australian promoter called Lionel Abrahams had approached Ernie to tour a one-man show in Australia. Agreeing without hesitation, Ernie concocted an hour-long cabaret act, which he described as, 'A gentle celebration of a life in show business rather than a professional obituary, a mellow evening of song-and-dance and reminiscences.'

On the flight over he bumped into the newest British comedy star Rowan Atkinson. 'I recall wishing Ernie the best of luck with it more sincerely than I've ever wished anyone the best of luck with anything.' Atkinson got the impression that if his tour went well Ernie hoped to bring it to the UK.

The Morecambe and Wise shows had been hugely popular Down Under and Ernie was welcomed with genuine warmth and encouragement. Still, the first night was nerve-racking, waiting for that curtain to rise and to walk on a stage for the first time in forty years as a solo performer. Once on, however, the born entertainer took over. Strange, though, sometimes on that stage Ernie felt himself missing Eric, one wonders if he ever looked to his side and was mildly shocked to see that he wasn't there. He certainly sensed that the audience, too, felt a tangible sadness that both of them weren't there together. Des O'Connor feels that whenever Ernie performed he must have felt this twinge of loss. 'After Eric went I wondered what Ernie would do. Ernie was always capable; I just felt he didn't ever feel quite whole once Eric had passed on. You are almost walking on knowing that the audience is thinking, "it's not going to be the same". So it was difficult for him, but he was more than competent, he could dance and he could sing and he knew how to get that across.'

Playing theatres and nightclubs in Perth, Adelaide and Sydney Ernie always began the show with a medley of 'Bring me Sunshine' and 'Following You Around', accompanied by a small orchestra. This was followed by a few gags and a

252

little dance routine. More songs followed next from the golden age of music hall, songs made famous by the likes of Flanagan and Allen. There was a heavy ambience of nostalgia about the show, and sadness, not least when Ernie projected slides on a screen of Eric and himself and talked about the old days. Ernie always took questions from the audience at the end, his favourite part of the evening because it allowed him to engage with people, something he always enjoyed.

It was lovely to be back in Australia again and Ernie and Doreen made the most of it, although there was the odd mishap. 'I remember once in Sydney we went to a Japanese restaurant,' Doreen recalls. 'You know the green mustard stuff that they have, wasabi, it's very hot. Ernie saw this pot of wasabi on the table and thought it was avocado, so he put in his spoon and had a huge mouthful. He had to have all sorts of things stuffed down his throat to cool him down, in fact, at one point I thought he was going to die! It was hilarious.'

Almost halfway through the tour news reached them that Connie, Ernie's mum, had died. She was eighty-five. With his commitments and being so very far from home Ernie was unable to attend the funeral so Doreen came up with a considerate alternative. 'His mum was a big churchgoer so instead we went to a church in the centre of Adelaide and reminisced about her for a while. It was a very private occasion and was the right thing to do. I think it made Ernie feel a bit better.'

Despite the entire tour being a sell-out, which helped Ernie regain some confidence, the shows were never performed again, in spite of several offers to put them on in Britain. By this time he'd already made a small piece of history in his homeland, becoming the first person to make a mobile phone call in the British Isles. Using the Vodafone network the call was made from St Katherine's Dock on 1 January 1985 to Vodafone's head office in Newbury, which at the time was over a curry house, then on to the captain of the QE2 in Sydney harbour.

Later in 1985 Ernie finally made it to Hollywood when he was invited to guest star in an episode of the long-running American sitcom *Too Close for Comfort* starring Ted Knight. In a role especially written for him in an episode called 'The British are Coming', Ernie thoroughly enjoyed the experience and the knowledge that the show was seen by something like 40 million viewers.

THIRTY-THREE

ERN UP WEST!

In 1987, at the age of sixty-one, Ernie finally made it back to the West End, the first time he'd played a theatre there since his days as a child star with Jack Hylton. *The Mystery of Edwin Drood* was a musical based on Charles Dickens' last unfinished novel and had been a huge success on Broadway when it opened in 1985, running for 608 performances and winning five Tony awards, including Best Musical. It was an obvious candidate for a London transfer.

It was a fascinating concept, a play within a play featuring an Edwardian music-hall company putting on the show 'The Mystery of Edwin Drood'.

In essence you had a bunch of actors playing actors playing Dickensian characters. There was also something totally unique about the production, something that had never been done before. Because Dickens never came up with a finale for his novel, every night the audience could vote who they wanted to be the murderer.

Ernie was sent the script by theatre producer Jeffrey Taylor who thought he was ideal. 'Ron Moody was briefly considered but we went with Ernie simply for bums on seats because nobody had the cachet that Ernie had. He was just loved by everyone. And he was somebody who would also understand the piece.'

Reading the script Ernie was entranced immediately and because it was still running in New York he and Doreen went over to see it. Obviously he recognized this was a great departure for him and starring in a West End musical had always been an unfulfilled ambition, so Ernie was eager to do it and went to meet Taylor at his office to discuss matters. 'And one thing that stands out like mad about that meeting,' recalls the producer, 'is that I'd actually been introduced to Eric Morecambe in years gone by when I was doing a charity event and what struck me about Eric is that he was a really tough guy, very amusing but very tough. And then when I met Ernie, well, I've never met a sweeter man.'

However, at the back of Ernie's mind was a fear that was preventing him from accepting the offer, as Doreen explains. 'The actual thought of doing an audition terrified him. He hadn't had to do one for so many years. I told him to just jump around a bit! They gave him something to read and in the end he sailed through it.'

Ernie signed on to play the pivotal role of William Cartwright, a character that was onstage for the duration of the show. In many ways, he was the narrator of the piece; 'I was the lynch-pin with the responsibility of moving the show on from sequence to sequence.' The pace of the show largely depended on him, it was a huge responsibility and one that Taylor had no hesitation believing Ernie could rise to. 'He was such an obvious choice as he was a household name and I knew that he had experience with song and dance. So I thought everyone who came to see the show would be so surprised that a performer who we all knew and loved could actually do a musical.'

Fully aware that the focus of critics and audiences would be on him, this being his first high-profile outing since Eric's death, Ernie began work three months ahead of time. Often in the past he'd found it hard to learn lines, so Ernie wanted to make sure that he arrived word perfect on the first day of rehearsal. He had no intention of letting anyone down.

Ernie also wanted to take his responsibilities as the star of the show seriously and was keen to engage with the rest of the company, but according to actor and co-star Martin Wimbush it didn't quite work out that way. 'Ernie did enjoy being part of the company but I think he was a bit nervous and I think that nervousness made him slightly defensive and he drew back from total engagement during rehearsals at the beginning. He was very cautious because he was used to a way of working with Eric and now he was in a different kind of environment where we all worked together in a big company and he had to be part of that. It took him a while to understand that way of working and it was slow going. I think he was always slightly unsettled about being within a big company. I always felt frustrated when he addressed me by my character's name and not my real name. I don't think he actually called me Martin throughout the entire run.'

Those five weeks of rehearsals were something of an eye-opener for Ernie. The team behind the American production were brought over to drill the London cast and it was like Fort Bragg, everyone was worked flat out until every dance step and movement was knocked into them. Most of the musical theatre actors were used to this full-on method, of course, but it was particularly hard on Ernie who with Eric had rehearsed their television shows in a different way, just as tough, but in a more relaxed atmosphere. It was a real culture shock and some of the cast felt Ernie was intimidated by the American crew. Wimbush recalls: 'At first it did start to get a little bit nervy because the American team was so intense about the way they wanted it to go. They wanted to direct it in a very straight almost mechanical way, very regimented, and I think English performers can't really work like that and I think that started to annoy Ernie because he wanted to be a bit more fluid and a little less disciplined, which I can totally understand. When Eric and Ernie were working with John Ammonds and Ernest Maxin they were allowed a certain amount of freedom and used to work the audience and the cameras, partly by using this freedom, but within this particular show it was frowned upon.'

Those tensions got to Ernie at the dress

257

rehearsal when during his main speech he dried. Onstage alone, his mind just went blank. His first emotion was one of embarrassment and then guilt, he'd so wanted to impress everyone and now he felt he'd let everyone down. Somehow he managed to claw his way back and finish the speech. It had been a test of nerves. There would be no more slip-ups.

Opening night on the Saturday went well and the audience reaction was good. Coming offstage Ernie collapsed in his dressing room and back home went straight to bed and didn't wake up until Monday afternoon. So physically draining was the run that Doreen is of the opinion that the *Drood* musical contributed to Ernie's first stroke. 'You see, he was onstage for the whole show, from start to finish, and it really exhausted him.'

When Ernie woke up that Monday the first reviews did not make for pleasant reading. The critics had lambasted the show. The company were devastated. Ernie felt particularly low; as the star he'd wanted to lead from the front but had been distracted by the difficulties he was experiencing with the role. The part of Cartwright would have been a stretch for even the most experienced stage actor, let alone someone who had been solely part of a double act. 'I think it fazed him a little bit,' says Wimbush. 'Having to get used to playing not only someone else, but someone else playing someone else.'

Maybe Ernie was miscast; the role didn't suit his style, although Jeffrey Taylor stands by his casting choice. 'Ernie reminded me of a slightly younger version of George Burns. When George Burns was ninety or something and still performing I knew somebody who was his PA and they said,

"You know the man died twenty years ago, but if you wind him up and get him onstage, he suddenly comes to life." And I could imagine that being the case with Ernie. The light goes on and they perform. But it was a bloody hard show to do, lots of singing and dancing, but I thought Ernie did it really well. In fact, I remember being a bit worried, you couldn't believe that this man could go onstage and sing and dance because he was so incredibly gentle. Doreen came with him every night, put him in the dressing room and made sure everything was OK and really protected him and looked after him. And what kind of amused me was the public must have thought that Ernie was the tough one and made all the decisions, which could have been the case, but in my experience he was just a very kind and gentle man.'

On Broadway the role of Cartwright had been played by George Rose, an avuncular actor well known for playing larger-than-life characters, which is what Chairman Cartwright was. 'Ernie on the other hand was very contained; he liked to perform in a closed, well rehearsed, neat way,' remembers Wimbush. 'There was not much room for improvisation. The part, in a way, was too big for him in that sense. I remember on the first night when he didn't get the immediate affection and laughter that he was used to, I think that slightly concerned him and you could feel the tension in his performance and, of course, as soon as the performer gets tense the audience gets tense. He probably hadn't experienced that for a long time. Whenever he stepped onstage with Eric everybody loved him and he had that immediate recognition, but here he was suddenly being judged in a new show by an audience kind of saying, OK, show us what you can do.'

Ernie probably knew the acting requirements were perhaps out of his reach in what was too strong and dominant a character for him. But everyone could see that during the song-and-dance aspects of the show Ernie was in his element, and much more comfortable. It was something Wimbush certainly sensed. 'When Ernie was engaged in music and dancing with the other performers you could see that natural rhythm and that natural style within him in his performance, he could really sell a number. And suddenly that tension with the audience went and you had a different performer. All that, of course, harks right back to those early days as a young performer, you could really see the smile coming back onto his face and that's what the audience wanted to see, they wanted to see Ernie Wise enjoying himself.'

As the weeks went by the audiences who came to see the show seemed to enjoy it, but something was missing, something didn't quite click. The Broadway production had been something of a bastardized version of Dickens, with Dick Van Dyke-type annoying cockneyisms which Broadway audiences lapped up but in London looked totally false. The show was transplanted into the West End lock, stock and barrel, where perhaps had it been adapted to appeal better to a British audience it might have worked. As it was the show never got over those poor initial notices and as a result audiences began to tail off, which affected Ernie quite badly. As the 'big name' performer he took it personally that people weren't coming along in sufficient numbers and where before he'd strived to be part of the ensemble, now most of his time was spent alone according to Wimbush. 'Towards the end of the run I felt him withdraw from the company. He would stay in his dressing room longer and stay away from us. I don't think he knew how to deal with it, I think his way was to retreat.'

After ten weeks the producers finally pulled the show. Everyone who'd had such faith in it was bitterly disappointed. Jeffrey Taylor believes its failure may have had something to do with the choice of venue, the Savoy Theatre. 'One night I was sitting on the steps next to the stage with Michael White, who is a great producer, and he looked at me and said, "You know we're in the wrong theatre, don't you," and I said "Now you bloody tell me." And he was absolutely right, because the Savoy Theatre was in the wrong place. In the world of theatre for a musical the best place you can get is the Prince of Wales or the Prince Edward Theatre in Soho because they've got the best "carriage trade", in other words, half the world walks past there. The Savoy Theatre had a certain cachet to it, in the sense that it's part of the Savoy hotel, but what on earth were we doing in there with a musical? The Savoy Theatre was for a long time the home of the D'Oyly Carte Opera Company, which had a very dedicated audience. They didn't really rely on passing trade so Michael was right, it was the wrong venue.'

It also didn't help that after the first night and the bad reviews the whole American production team disappeared back to New York. 'And that really hurt everyone,' says Wimbush. 'They obviously lost faith, figured we weren't going to

261

make them any money and so decided to hop it. That was an awful thing to do.'

In spite of the failure, Wimbush enjoyed the experience and that of working with Ernie, of whom he still retains fond memories. 'The one thing I learnt from Ernie was charm. He had enormous charm and that really shone through, not only toward the company but to the audiences and everyone around him. I'm not sure if you can learn charm but Ernie taught me how to be charming. Charm is something that is inherent and instinctive. I also learnt about comic timing and how to time a line cleanly when it mattered. He was a master at that. He was also a decent man and a good man and a man who cared for his work very strongly and that was something I took with me. And even though he probably felt upset that the show didn't take off, the experience of working with a legend is always something very special.'

Ernie did take the failure of *Edwin Drood* personally. It was a great disappointment, especially since he'd begun getting into the swing of it. Although the part didn't really suit him, he'd begun to relax after several performances and make it his own. A failure, then, but Ernie also judged it to have been something of an achievement. He wanted more of the same.

THIRTY-FOUR

A TOUCH OF FARCE

A few months after *Drood*'s ignoble exit from the West End, Ernie was approached by legendary farceur Ray Cooney to appear in his hit comedy play *Run for Your Wife*. The play had been running at the Criterion Theatre for so long now Cooney had devised a policy to change a few of the cast members every four months or so to keep it fresh. Ernie was to take over the role of Detective Sergeant Porterhouse, then being played by Eric Sykes.

Ernie reacted positively to Cooney's offer and came one night with Doreen to see the play before accepting the offer. 'He thought it was great,' says Cooney. 'And he loved hearing that laughter every night. He thrived on that. Ernie was just such a nice guy to pop in and see and say hello to, and we often had a drink after the end of the show. Lovely.' Cooney would pop in probably once a week to see how everything was faring and give the odd note, which Ernie loved. 'Once I went in and he said, "Haven't you got any notes for me Ray?" And I said, "No." And he said, "God, I must have been awful!"'

Cooney recalls that Ernie fitted in extremely well with the existing cast. 'He was a great guy to have in the company. He was a terrific company member. Sometimes when you have people who've come from a variety background, because they're solo performers, they're not used to acting in a team. Yet the wonderful thing about Ernie was that he was so much part of the team. He was really great. And again if you have, in inverted commas "comics", they sometimes feel that if they're not getting laughs within the first five seconds they've got to either trip over or do something stupid to get a laugh, which is just what you don't need in my plays. That never occurred to Ernie. Ernie just wanted to know what to do to serve the play. He was terrific.'

As a consummate exponent of the art of comedy, Cooney is perhaps as well placed as anyone to comment on what Ernie brought to that famous partnership. 'In nearly all the double acts, the straight guy is, if anything, more important than the guy who "gets the laughs". And especially in my plays you need that man to bounce the laughs off. You need this authority figure and the dead-pan face that looks at you and says, "Are you being serious?!" And Ernie had it and, of course, even though it was a different kind of double act, Laurel and Hardy had it. Ernie Wise had been a comedian all his life but he could, if he'd decided to, have taken up straight acting, which probably would have bored him to death, but he would have been very good and that's what I'm looking for in my plays.'

Ernie enjoyed his time in *Run for Your Wife*, though niggling away at the back of his mind during performances was always the thought that audiences might be out there going, 'Oh, what a shame. What's he doing that for? He and Eric were so good together and look at him now.' And that was the dilemma he faced: balancing this need to perform while being careful about what he accepted.

He also appreciated the gesture of being given the theatre's number one dressing room, even though by rights co-star Patrick Mower, whose role was more substantial, should have had it. Ernie still vehemently believed he was a star, although he wasn't naïve enough to think he had the same clout he used to have when Eric was around.

Still, there was an element of professional pride that remained important to performers like Ernie. It wasn't ego or vanity, if anything it was professional etiquette that those at the top of the bill or people of a certain stature were always treated with special respect and got the number one dressing room. When on occasions he wasn't given that courtesy or offered work that he felt was beneath him he'd simply turn it down in the belief that producers weren't paying him the respect he deserved. 'At my time of life a four-week season as Mother Goose in a winter run on Tyneside held only marginal attractions.'

Following his duet of West End appearances Ernie seemed to take a back seat. The offers of work coming in were either of such poor quality or simply didn't interest him. But he was always on the look out for suitable projects. During a trip to New York he saw the latest Broadway smash musical, a revival of *Anything Goes*, and was particularly drawn to the character of Moonface Martin, a sort of comedic priest. When he heard the show was coming to London in 1989 he was desperate to play the part and personally contacted one of its producers, the lyricist Tim Rice. In the end the role went to Bernard Cribbins. Ernie was bitterly disappointed since the show went on to be a huge success featuring Elaine Page and a young

John Barrowman. A role in *Anything Goes* would certainly have made up for the disappointment of *Edwin Drood*. But it was not to be.

Instead, he agreed to participate in an unusual charity event that year, raising money and awareness for the Quarter Heart Charity. The idea was that Ernie would step into the shoes of the famous Jules Verne character Phileas Fogg and go 'Around the World in 80 Hours', with Marty Kristian of The New Seekers as his Passepartout. 'We started and finished the trip at the Horse of the Year Show,' recalls Kristian. 'And with the clock ticking we made our way to Heathrow where we boarded Concorde. I'd never been on Concorde. I'd been all over the world with The New Seekers but had never flown Concorde before, so it was very exciting for me. I have to say that every country we went to gave us a lot of publicity and exposure, and helped us raise a huge amount of money for the charity. Everyone was extremely welcoming too. It was a fabulous experience for both of us.'

Even though he was with Ernie for only a short period of time, Kristian got to know him well, cooped up in boats and planes for hours on end, you would. Maybe in those long hours he saw the real Ernie, as opposed to the one people met in a TV studio or a theatre dressing room. 'I felt a little sadness around Ernie at that time. He'd obviously lost his friend and partner some time ago and I think the press had been less than kind to him. Or to put it another way, they'd given so much coverage to Eric's death and what Eric meant to the country that I think Ernie had been marginalized a little. There were moments when he felt he needed to justify his contribution to the partnership. It was like him expressing his ego. You could tell it was born of something else though. Ernie wasn't an egotistical man. He just felt the need to put across his contribution because he felt marginalized. You couldn't blame him. In quieter moments when he was talking to friends there was a sort of self-obsession there, which I suppose was born of being undervalued.'

What Ernie wanted to do most of all was work and to get a bit more of the, as he said, 'VIP treatment' rather than the 'RIP treatment'. At the start of 1990 he made twelve appearances in Dictionary Corner on Channel 4's top-rated game show *Countdown*. Carol Vorderman, who made her name on the programme, remembers Ernie well. 'It was wonderful for Richard and I when Ernie appeared on *Countdown* as he was a real comedy hero and it was our privilege to host him. When he walked into the studio it was obvious that our audience adored him, as we all had for decades before. We had some wonderful days with him. I always found it slightly overwhelming when he was on the programme, as he had been such an icon as I was growing up. Like half of Britain we all stopped on Christmas Day for *The Morecambe and Wise* special in our house and laughed till we cried happy tears. Ernie Wise—a happy gentleman.'

There were other panel show appearances, too, such as *What's My Line*. One wonders why Ernie did shows like this; they were hardly the most creative or taxing things. The plain and simple truth was that it was work and also kept Ernie and Doreen in the showbiz mix, 'in the company of the people we know, understand and love,' said Ernie.

Later in the year he appeared on that

broadcasting institution *Desert Island Discs*. Considering his love and yearning for Hollywood, it was no surprise that many of his favourite songs derived from the great musicals, including Gene Kelly's *Singing in the Rain,* which of course harked back to that great sketch. Ernie also mischievously chose David Rose & His Orchestra performing 'The Stripper'. As for his all-time favourite track, could it have been anything other than he and Eric performing 'Bring Me Sunshine'?

As a change of pace, Ernie enjoyed his own gardening column for a few years in the *News of the World*: 'Dig the dirt with Ern!' it was called rather unimaginatively. Ernie loved nothing better than pottering around in his garden but refrained from doing too much since, as Doreen claims, 'If I'd let him loose on his own in our garden we'd have lost all the flowers. He'd have thought they were all weeds. He did the gardening column for about three years and then started to feel guilty so gave in. He went to Hampton Court once and a keen gardener asked him for some advice. When Ernie tried to give an answer she said, "You don't really know about gardening." After that he knew it was time to give up!'

In September 1990 Ernie heard the news that his long time agent and friend Billy Marsh had suffered a stroke. At the office his assistant Jan Kennedy was more or less left holding the fort while friends Michael Grade and Bill Cotton helped by ringing up all the clients to tell them what had happened, 'Billy's not very well, but don't worry, Jan's looking after things and we're behind her all the way.' It was beyond kindness to have helped out at such a difficult time. 'So when all the talent were told that Billy had had this stroke,' recalls Jan, 'Ernie actually gave me quite a tough time. One day he rang me and said, "I was out at a party last night and someone said they spoke to my agent Jan Kennedy, I told them that you're not my agent." I suppose that comment came from his distress for Billy, out of loyalty to Billy, but I was so hurt because I'd really worked hard for him. So I said, "No, Ernie, I'm not, I'm holding the reins for Billy, but I hope one day you have enough faith in me to realize that I can do this for you." And then eight months later when I did one of my first big contracts for Ernie he said, "I don't think Billy Marsh could have done it quite as well," and to me that was the greatest compliment he could have paid to me. He'd entrusted this great career in my hands, an unknown girl really, as did Bruce Forsyth and several others, and then he gave me that marvellous compliment and I won't forget that.'

Jan has a curious history with Morecambe and Wise, first encountering them in 1965 when she was eighteen and Blackpool's Girl of the Year and on the same judging panel as the boys at a talent competition. 'They were lovely and very warm. I was in total awe of them at the time, they were very funny, they made the whole panel laugh and put everyone at their ease. I never realized that years later I would actually be representing them.'

Sadly, Billy Marsh was never able to return to work again and passed away in 1995. Taking over, Jan would work closely with Ernie for the remaining years of his life and got to know him well. 'He was tough to deal with, but he knew the business and he never suffered fools gladly.'

Over the years Ernie has been unfairly portrayed

by commentators as being quite naïve and too trusting an individual. Perhaps his shy and reserved nature led them to such a conclusion. According to Doreen this couldn't have been further from the truth. 'Ernie was very streetwise and could sum people up in about ten minutes. He was quiet and probably a bit shy, but what people took for him not knowing what was going on was them actually being X-rayed by Ernie.'

Certainly he knew what he wanted out of show business. 'Being the business brains of the partnership Ernie was the one that made sure the fees were right and the contracts were right,' says Jan. 'He was methodical, he kept his paperwork.' When Ernie died all the old Morecambe and Wise contracts that Ernie had kept were given over to Billy Marsh Associates, where they continue to make valid use of them when referring to repeat shows; they're invaluable.

Contracts weren't the only thing Ernie hoarded. Tucked away in an old cardboard box and two dusty suitcases in his garage were stacks of old 78 acetate records and hundreds of feet of reel-to-reel tape, some from studio engineers, recorded at the request of Ernie, others produced by Ernie himself. Doreen only discovered these years after Ernie's death when she was moving out of Dorney Reach and into new accommodation.

Sadly, by the time Doreen discovered these long forgotten items their condition varied from very bad to unrecoverable. Because the whole lot were stored in an out-building much of the material, which dated back as far as 1949, had succumbed to damp, while some of the acetates had a thin layer of white fungus eating into the surface. Even

270

so, Doreen quickly realized what she had and contacted the BBC who discovered that most of the material was not in their archives and set about restoring what they could to broadcast quality. It was a comedy fan's treasure trove. There was a complete series of Morecambe and Wise's very first radio series from 1953, *You're Only Young Once*, which previously had been thought lost, also one-off appearances in *Variety Bandwagon* and *Variety Fanfare* from 1949.

The boxes also contained some priceless recordings of Eric and Ernie's stage work. It was hardly hi-tech stuff: Ernie's method was to simply place his tape recorder in the wings and leave it running. He also recorded programmes from the television by putting the recorder next to the speaker; in some clips you can hear Ernie laughing in the background. Comedy fans have much to thank Ernie for his hindsight in preserving material which otherwise would never have been heard and simply passed into oblivion.

THIRTY FIVE

FLORIDA SUNSHINE

For a good many years Ernie and Doreen had holidayed during the winter months in a home they owned in Boca Raton, Florida, located just south of Palm Beach. It was on a stretch of sand known as Broken Sound, which Ernie delighted in calling Broken Wind.

He was able to relax there in a way he could

never do in Britain. 'One of the reasons we had a holiday home in Florida,' Doreen reveals, 'was that he could do all the silly, ordinary things he wanted to. We'd walk down the street eating ice creams and getting it all over our faces and we'd spend hours in McDonald's. We called it "playing kids". He couldn't do that at home. People would have thought it undignified, or they would have pestered him all the time. Whenever we were in America and heard an English voice we would disappear.'

Ernie also loved visiting Disney World and going on the rides, especially Space Mountain, the Klondike Train and the Water Splash. He took such simple, uncomplicated delight in it. In many ways he was free at last from the treadmill of work to enjoy all the things in life he had missed. 'He had spent so much of his life entertaining other people that he had forgotten about himself,' says Doreen. And that included being a kid. 'He'd never had the time to be a child. He'd been working non-stop ever since he was six years old. His childhood had been stolen from him. After Eric went, I tried to make sure Ernie caught up on all the bits of life that had passed him by.'

Doreen was also looking to spoil Ernie whenever she could. She'd ask him what he wanted for his birthday or Christmas and the answer was always the same, 'I don't need anything.'

Doreen would always respond, 'Not what you need, what you would like.'

In the end she bought new coffee machines which Ernie was happy to accumulate, as he loved making fresh coffee.

Their American home came about during a trip to do the *Ed Sullivan Show* back in the late sixties.

Joan by this time had got fed up with the New York weather so it was just Ernie and Doreen; Eric was making his own passage later. On the flight over they met an American businessman by the name of Fred Olofson. Doreen has always been a nervous flyer, but this time she was sitting next to someone who was even worse than she was, and it was Doreen doing the whole, 'Oh it's not so bad' bit to try and cheer him up. It didn't help that Olofson confessed to missing his wife and new baby desperately and was reading an article in a newspaper about a crack in the tail of a Pan Am plane. 'Look, if they've found the crack, all the other planes should be OK,' said Doreen, helpfully.

After a few gin and tonics Olofson grew more relaxed and Ernie and Doreen spent the whole flight swapping life stories and by the time the plane touched down they were all firm friends. In the arrivals lounge Doreen and Olofson were nattering away and walking towards the exit, with Ernie quite some distance behind with the luggage. 'So I'm walking along with Fred,' Doreen recalls. 'And I'm wearing a full-length mink coat and we're laughing quite merrily. And who's there standing in the gallery watching but his wife, carrying their new baby. Fred pointed her out and said, "That's my wife." Well let me tell you, she had a face like *thunder*! And I thought, Oh God. So she's looking at me, thinking God knows what, and I'm looking at her thinking, it's not what you think, and I'm trying to point Ernie out and say—"That one's mine!"'

In a bid to smooth things over Ernie invited Fred and Jessica to the show and afterwards they enjoyed dinner together. 'Jessica was a real New Yorker,' says Doreen. '*Very* abrupt, but absolutely gorgeous.

273

Everything had been explained to her so she was fine. When she saw me she said, "I'd been waiting three months to see Fred, and I was so excited, but when I saw him with you, I hated you!" And I said, "I know, I could feel it!" But we became friends for life.' Jessica also took to Ernie and found it amusing that she never saw him without a tie, once asking Doreen if he wore one with his pyjamas.

After that trip, whenever they were in the States Ernie and Doreen would make a point of meeting up with Fred and Jessica as often as they could. One time they all visited Jessica's mother in Miami who lived in a one-bedroom apartment. On hearing that a similar property was available Ernie snapped it up for $47,000. After a while they bought a bigger place in a more exclusive neighbourhood, with three bedrooms, and used to let friends like Norman Vaughan borrow it.

On early trips to their home in Miami one of the channels was showing *The Morecambe and Wise Show* on TV late at night, so the gate keeper always used to shout, 'I seen yer on there tonight!' Much later when *The Benny Hill Show* became enormously popular on American television people would say to Ernie, 'Are you Benny Hill?' Ernie would bite his lip and reply, *'No I'm not!'* Actually Ernie loved Benny Hill. 'We got on very well with him,' says Doreen. 'In the old days we used to stay in the same hotel in Manchester and have drinks together. I remember the last time Ernie ever saw Benny. He was driving through Hyde Park in the Rolls and saw Benny sitting on a park bench, so he stopped the car and said, "Do you want a lift?" And Benny said, "No, I'm having my lunch." And he took out a salad from a plastic bag and started eating, so Ernie sat there with him chatting away, sharing his salad. He had to go in the end as he was illegally parked.'

The couple made a lot of friends out in Florida, and among the closest was Eddie Plumley, a Chief Executive at Watford Football Club, who had a place out there with his wife Fran. They met Ernie and Doreen at a party, and Eddie reminded Ernie they'd previously encountered each other when he was a young professional footballer at Birmingham City back in the sixties. 'Eric and Ernie were on at the Hippodrome and they came to advertise the show at St Andrews, which is Birmingham City's ground. In those days most clubs had a snooker table, and so Eric and Ernie turned up and started fooling around with the snooker cues and the balls and everyone was chatting and laughing. And that cropped up in the conversation in Florida and Ernie suddenly remembered the day. He even remembered the snooker table stuff.'

The first time the Plumleys were invited to Doreen and Ernie's home in Florida Eddie was witness to a revealing moment that harked back to Ernie's underprivileged childhood. When the inevitable tea was served both were asked if they wanted a biscuit. Ernie got up and went to the kitchen and came back with a tin. He took the lid off, Fran and Eddie took a biscuit each, and then Ernie put the lid straight back on and returned it to the kitchen again. 'It was hilarious to watch,' recalls Plumley. 'You see, Ernie was an extraordinarily generous man. He was always first to the bar and he and Doreen were always hosting parties and events, but when it came to handing out biscuits Ernie was obviously doing what he'd done when he was a kid.

There was no leaving them on the table then. You took one, and that was it. It was just habit, I think. Very funny to watch, though.' On subsequent visits Ernie always made a show of slamming shut the biscuit tin lid after Eddie and Fran had selected their solitary biscuit.

Another close friend was John Mackie, who actually lived in Toronto where he was president of Jaguar cars. Mackie's son lived near the Wises and they were introduced one day and swiftly became friends. 'Every American Thanksgiving we would all take off, the whole bunch of us, on a cruise out of Miami or Fort Lauderdale and cruise around the Caribbean,' Mackie recalls. 'And Ernie and Doreen were part of that bunch of people and we used to have great fun. And of course he was recognized everywhere we went on the boat because there were a lot of Brits on board who were very fond of letting him know how much they appreciated his talent. So many of them were armed with their cameras and wanted to take pictures of those little hairy legs. And he was very very good, he always appreciated their interest and he always found time to chat with them and let them take their pictures. He was terribly modest, he was always very grateful for what he had achieved.'

That was something Mackie found particularly endearing about Ernie; that he rarely spoke about his achievements and success. 'Only when asked, he was extremely modest, he would never push forward who he was or what he was.' When Ernie was awarded the OBE by the Queen someone gave him a baseball hat with those initials on it. But he would only wear it in America where most people didn't really know what OBE stood for.

Of course, Ernie took great personal delight when confronted by fans—well, sometimes. Ernie held shares in Townsend Thoresen ships and often sailed abroad in them. Returning from a short trip to Cherbourg, a little boy kept following him all over the deck, his eyes like saucers at seeing a real-live TV star. Wondering how to get rid of the little chap Ernie told him that he was off to his cabin for a sleep and would he kindly keep guard outside the door. The hope was the little beggar would soon lose interest and go back to his mum. Several hours later Ernie awoke, only to see the boy still stationed outside. Feeling guilty, Ernie took the boy to the bar and treated him to a Coca-Cola.

Ernie also never refused an autograph, even in the direst of circumstances. Driving home one day, suddenly up ahead in the fast lane was a parked police car with the officer in the road breathalysing another motorist. Ernie couldn't stop in time and hit it. Clambering out Ernie immediately pleaded his case, 'No wonder I hit you. You shouldn't have been parked in the fast lane.' The policeman remained solemn. 'You're not obliged to say anything, sir. But anything you do say will be taken down and may be used as evidence.' There was a pause. 'Oh and by the way, Ernie, can I have your autograph?'

A similar incident occurred after he and Eric had done a live show in Newcastle. Eric was being driven home when his chauffeur noticed the unmistakable image of flashing blue police lights in his rear-view mirror. 'What have you done now?' said Eric. 'Have you been speeding?'

The chauffeur, Mike Fountain, who'd worked for Eric since 1969, pleaded his innocence as he calmly nursed the car to a stop. The policeman came over and peered in through the window. 'Excuse me, Mr Morecambe, can I have your autograph—we've just stopped Ernie down the road and got his, so we knew you'd be coming.'

There was another occasion when Ernie was driving home in his yellow Rolls-Royce. Stopping at some lights another large car pulled up alongside and there was some furious movement inside. Ernie was used to his car drawing attention, but this time it was from a most unexpected source. 'It's the Princess of Wales!' shrieked Doreen. 'She's smiling at you.' Erne looked across straight into the beaming face of Diana. Suddenly over-come he attempted a reverential bow, not easy with the steering wheel pressed up against him, instead he delivered one of his proud smiles. Just then the Princess grabbed a piece of paper and began writing on it furiously. Just about to hold it to the window the lights changed and her car pulled away. Ernie never got to know what message the Princess was hoping to deliver.

Living day to day in the close proximity of a boat, however large, Mackie got to know Ernie well and discovered that he was a keen reader. 'Many a time we bumped into him in the ship's library, he'd sit there for hours because he just loved to read, he loved the feel of a good book. It always had to be a hardback though. He refused to read anything in paperback. There was definitely a very serious side to him.' Naturally, Ernie got through a great deal of showbiz memoirs but according to Doreen his favourite reading material was military history, especially books about the futility of war. 'He could never understand why people made the same mistakes,' she says.

Often in the evening after dinner there would be a show and of course Ernie loved to attend and Mackie often accompanied him. They'd watch whoever was on the bill, usually a musician or singer of some kind followed by an old-time performer. 'I'll never forget those evenings because Ernie watched them very closely to understand their timing and would love to chat if you questioned him about how good they were and why it had worked so well. One show I particularly remember is Phyllis Diller because she would do a second show later that same evening and Little Ernie and I went back to watch it again, he just wanted to make sure that he picked up all the elements that made her so great and so funny and he would always point out if it was the timing or whatever that made the perform-ance so special. He was a great student of comedy. And he had impeccable timing as well, that's the thing people don't talk about. People think that it all came so naturally, it didn't, Eric and Ernie worked at it, and Ernie in particular, I think. I am not saying that he was Eric's coach but he was certainly very clued up on what worked and what wouldn't.'

Aware that Ernie was a fan of Noël Coward, Mackie delivered a surprise on the occasion the cruise ship stopped at Ocho Rios on the north shore of Jamaica. Mackie suggested that they all get in a cab and shoot over to Noël's house, which was nearby and had been turned into a tourist attraction since his death. 'So we arrived and we were greeted by this Jamaican guy in his dreadlocks singing 'Don't Put your Daughter on the Stage, Mrs Worthington'—unbelievable—and little Ernie's face was a picture, he couldn't believe it.'

Next they were confronted by a little Jamaican

279

girl who asked if they were all going on the tour, yes was the reply. 'Fine,' she said. 'Would you like tea afterwards?' Everyone nodded. 'Would you like some cake?' That was agreeable, too. So off they went, into the house. 'We saw the studio where Noël used to do his painting,' says Mackie. 'We saw his bedroom and the pineapple bed in which he died, the two grand pianos in the living room and the garden where Noël is buried. He's buried right there outside his house, overlooking this unbelievable view of the Caribbean. So we spent some time at Noël's grave and then we had a look at the little amphitheatre the Jamaicans have built where they put on little excerpts from his shows. So we finished and went back to the cottage area, which is a sort of museum, and then tea and crumpets and chocolate chip cookies and scones were duly served. And we were sitting there overlooking Noël's grave and the Caribbean and Ernie turned to us and said in a very quiet voice, "This has been a very special day." He'd felt that he'd made the pilgrimage.'

THIRTY-SIX

AUNTIE'S REVENGE

Ernie had been so long in the profession that his public persona was to a large extent now set in stone. He knew that he couldn't mould himself Dustin Hoffman-like into any role, they had to suit him. Ernie even called himself, 'an off-the-peg entertainer,' someone producers could insert ready-made into a production. People like Ray Cooney and the producers of *Edwin Drood* had made imaginative use of Ernie; others less so, such as the obligatory and uninspiring offers to do panto.

The problem inherent in doing panto for Ernie was that he'd always done them with Eric, now he was being asked to play roles like Baron Hardup, characters that essentially acted like a straight man, feeding lines to others. Ernie had done that for Eric, of course, and wasn't sure he wanted to do the same thing for another performer.

Bryan Burdon had met Ernie many times at various Water Rats charity events and had also worked with Eric and Ernie when he was in variety with his father, Albert Burdon. 'Dad's act was basically based around cod conjuring,' recalls Burdon. 'He wanted somebody to assist him so he took me out of school and got me involved in a magic act where I played a schoolboy who came up onstage to help and ended up making a mess of everything. The trick being that the audience thought that I was part of the audience. Unfortunately, when I reached fifteen years old I looked a bit stupid in short trousers and a cap. My father never forgave me for that and ended up replacing me with Jimmy Clitheroe.' By then though, Bryan Burdon had got the taste for showbiz.

Firmly ensconced at the Theatre Royal, Windsor, playing the Dame there for something like twenty-five consecutive years, Burdon was delighted when the management said there was a chance of getting Ernie for their next pantomime. 'Do you think you two would gel?'

Burdon didn't have to think too hard about that

281

one. 'Yes, I'm sure we would.'

After turning down panto for years, the mere fact that this one was so very close to where Ernie lived prompted a rethink. There hadn't been many jobs around in any case and his desperate need to work, to perform before his public, had to be sated. He was then sixty-seven but feeling fit and healthy, although he was careful with his diet and took half an aspirin a day to keep his blood pressure down.

He'd also given up one of his main vices, smoking cigars. He used to enjoy smoking one a night and would be thrilled if there was a cigar featured in one of their TV sketches because the prop girl always bought two and he'd swipe the other one. He even bought a cigar for Penelope Keith when she was on the show, who at the time was a keen smoker herself.

Ernie smoked the occasional pipe too, until one day Doreen went out for a few hours and returned to a home that smelt of burning. Seeing a fire in the grate she asked what he'd burnt. 'My pipes,' replied Ernie, some of which were handmade and quite expensive. 'Filthy dirty habit,' he said. 'I don't know why I did it.' He never did smoke a pipe again.

Usually Burdon wrote most of the comedy material for the Windsor panto himself but it was decided this time, given Ernie's experience and pedigree, he might wish to contribute. That was all fine but Burdon still needed to have a basic script to work from so arranged to go down and see Ernie at his house for a script conference. This was May. He arrived on an enormous motorbike which took Doreen quite by surprise, and found Ernie relaxing outside in the garden. 'OK, you do the script and I'll go shopping,' said Doreen. Burdon sat down next to Ernie in the glorious sunshine and they started chatting. 'We seemed to get on very well. Then I suddenly noticed that Ernie had a swimming pool. "Ooh, wouldn't it be nice if we could possibly go for a quick swim." I suppose I was joking slightly but it did look so inviting and was in such a beautiful surrounding. Alas, I hadn't brought any trunks. Warming to the idea of the swim, Ernie suggested I might like to borrow a pair of his, so we both carried on chatting about the pantomime whilst getting changed.'

When Doreen returned and saw the two of them splashing about in the water she was not best pleased. 'What are you doing, you're supposed to be writing scripts!' In a manner of speaking they were. 'At least we were discussing them,' says Burdon. 'Anyway, we got out and carried on working when Ernie's little dog ran past and went off towards the bottom of the garden. As my gaze followed the dog I noticed a beautiful boat moored down there. "Whose is that beautiful cruiser?" I asked.

' "Oh, it's mine," said Ernie.

' "It's splendid. What a pity we can't take it out."

'Ernie said usually he would but needed somebody to help. "My dad used to have a huge boat so I've got loads of experience." So off we went in this beautiful cruiser, not too far but it was a beautiful day and we had such a nice time. As we were coming back we saw Doreen standing with her arms folded. "Aren't you two supposed to be working? First there was a swim and now a cruise, how much work have you actually got done?" Funnily enough, although we'd been having fun all the time, we had been talking shop and discussing plans for the pantomime so actually got a lot of work done. That was my first script conference with Ernie, quite memorable.'

When they met again it was at rehearsals, 'and he was absolutely superb,' says Burdon. 'We spent a lot of time together. We went to lunch and got on famously. Partly I think because Ernie was always comfortable around comedians. I'm not saying I'm in the same league as Eric Morecambe, good heavens no, but there was something instinctive with Ernie that made him feel relaxed and alive when he was in the company of comedians.'

Shortly before those rehearsals began the prestigious BBC2 documentary series *40 Minutes* approached Ernie to do a profile, following him as he returned to his roots in Leeds and performed in the panto in Windsor. On camera Ernie talked openly about his new show, which he insisted was not a comeback. 'I never left,' he said defiantly. And he gave his thoughts on the future; that he would be happy to perform or produce or direct, 'I have to have some purpose.' Ernie had felt the TV documentary an excellent idea, it meant exposure, an advert almost that he was still in the game. It would turn out to be a calamitous miscalculation.

The Windsor pantomime was a great success, playing to capacity audiences. Burdon and Ernie also worked well as a partnership. 'If you have been part of a double act for a long time you get to know what the other is thinking and that is obviously what happened with Eric and Ernie, they knew each other instinctively. There were things that Eric would put in off-the-cuff which Ernie would come back at, and vice versa. A lot of it has to do with fear. If either the comic or the straight man is scared for any reason the partnership won't work. Both need to be absolutely relaxed. If I'm working with a straight man and I'm not absolutely confident that he can react to an ad-lib then I won't deliver one. I'll stick to the script and probably give a very one-dimensional performance. Whereas, if no fear exists everyone's relaxed and you can go on and give the performance you want to give.'

That's exactly how Burdon felt with Ernie, completely relaxed and confident of his abilities. Here's a very good example. In the panto, Burdon was a very blousy Dame, with Ernie as the King. Their initial grand entrance was always to the line, said by a courtier, 'Make way for Queen Wilhelmina and King Cuthbert.' On this particular performance the actor suddenly changed the line to, 'Make way for Queen Wilhelmina and King Cuthbert the First.' As the pair made their entrance Ernie looked at Burdon and unscripted said, 'Am I the first?' Burdon paused and then ad-libbed, 'What do you think?' It got an enormous laugh. 'If Ernie hadn't come forward with that line, "Am I the first?" it wouldn't have worked. And I bet that if it had been a comic who'd delivered the line he would have taken it for himself, by saying something like, "I bet I'm not the first", and that wouldn't have meant anything or got the same reaction. And this is why Ernie was so great, totally unselfish and supremely talented. I have the greatest admiration for him. Ernie made enormous sacrifices throughout his career really. And if it wasn't for his lack of ego and general unselfish nature I don't think Morecambe and Wise would really have worked. And it was the same in a much much smaller way with myself and Ernie and this story proves it. Even at that time of life and after so much success he was still willing to feed his ad-lib to me: unbelievable professionalism and ability.'

Ernie felt pleased with the way the pantomime had gone and was looking forward to the possibility of more work. His hopes were to come crashing down when the BBC documentary, given the title *The Importance of Being Ernie*, was screened. There had been early warning signs. As the crew began to film during rehearsals Ernie started to regret the decision to allow them so much access to his day-to-day life, they really had become intrusive, prying into everything until it got to the point where he felt he had lost his privacy. 'It's almost too probing,' he told the *Radio Times*. 'About the only thing not asked is how much I have in the bank. I don't like being psychoanalysed.' Some wondered why he agreed to do it in the first place since he wasn't even paid. 'Ego,' he explained simply.

His misgivings about the programme proved to be horribly realized. When it was transmitted it drew some of the worst press Ernie had ever endured. The programme portrayed him, as the press in general had sometimes taken to doing in the last few years, as a sad, forlorn figure, lost without his partner, desperately clutching on for that last bit of fame, ever hopeful of being discovered by Hollywood.

The Ernie portrayed on that documentary was an Ernie that none of his friends recognized. Ernie's hopes of Hollywood fame had always been taken with a large pinch of salt, not least by Ernie himself; it was a hope more than a proper ambition. As he once remarked, 'There isn't a professional in show business who doesn't think, even if he is sixty-five

286

and still on the bottom rung of the ladder, that he isn't going to make it big tomorrow.' Yet the documentary took it all deadly seriously and he was ridiculed almost as a hopeless dreamer with an overinflated opinion that at his age he was Hollywood material.

In truth Ernie was a happy and contented man who despite everything had carved out a pretty successful part-time career post-Eric and without ever having to resort to trying to recreate or rehash what they had achieved. Not only was there the sell-out tour of Australia, the two West End shows, the specially written guest appearance in one of America's biggest sitcoms, the hundreds of charity events, the regular newspaper columns and myriad TV appearances—but on top of all this there was his life at home with Doreen and the pets. Sad? Forlorn? Lost? Doubtful, really. But one also has to ask the question, 'Why on earth shouldn't he harbour a few childhood ambitions?' The American singer Pearl Bailey once wrote, 'A man without ambition is dead.' Well, Ernie certainly wasn't dead. He was a happy and gentle man who had spent the best part of his life entertaining many millions of people. None of this made the slightest bit of difference though and in an editing suite somewhere in London Ernie was, as the saying goes, done up like a kipper.

Perhaps worse was the way press commentators began to belittle Ernie's contribution to the success of Morecambe and Wise, the inference being that Eric could have made it without Ernie. Perhaps the most brutal comment was one journalist's suggestion that, 'if the roles had been reversed and Eric had survived, would anyone bother to make a programme about life after Ernie?'

Other snide press comments followed after the documentary's screening. One reviewer described how it perfectly captured, 'the infinite pathos of being an "and".' The most savage was courtesy of the *Sunday Telegraph*: 'There could be no doubt, watching this programme, that "and Wise" was just as dead as Morecambe.'

That Ernie had agreed to the documentary being made at all perhaps demonstrated a degree of naïveté, an innocence about the fact that the game of show business had changed radically. But it didn't alter the fact that Ernie was left devastated by the programme and its aftermath. Doreen believes the stress and undue hurt placed upon him by it may have contributed to his first heart attack.

During this difficult time Doreen was a rock. 'I have to say that Doreen was wonderful with Ernie,' says Burdon. 'There was always a certain vulnerability about him, possibly since Eric died, and he'd had a really hard time from some quarters of the press and media. The Lord knows why, but there were certain sections that really seemed to hate him. In my opinion Ernie probably wasn't that aware of this and I think Doreen managed to hide it from him quite successfully. She was very much his guardian as well as his wife and he was lucky to have her. In fact I'd say they were lucky to have each other.'

Another victim of a similar but far more vociferous campaign was the author and presenter Jeremy Beadle. His role as a 'TV Prankster' meant he was once voted the most hated man in Britain. A fairly jocular exercise initially, until the tabloids decided to run with it. After a few weeks the whole nation loathed and detested Beadle, although nobody really knew why. Was it really the pranks he played on people? Maybe it had something to do with the £100 million he'd raised for charity, or the fact that he was actually, according to all who knew him, an extremely nice chap. Unlike Jeremy Beadle though, Ernie wasn't terribly conversant with the 'nuances' of the modern press, so this was definitely a time when Doreen's protective nature came into its own.

Marty Kristian observed how Doreen saw to it that Ernie was not only well looked after but protected. 'As far as I remember Doreen was very protective of Ernie, and they were both obviously very much in love. I think they really needed each other. Whatever he needed she would provide, and vice versa.' Doreen is anything but modest about the strong feelings she held for Ernie and that their marriage was based on a deep love for each other. 'Ernie was the only one for me and I was the only one for him. He'd put his arms around me and say, "I'd be in a right state if I didn't have you."'

Upset at seeing Ernie hurt and humiliated by the press, some friends began to wonder if he ought now to re-evaluate where he intended to go with his career. Others, like Michael Grade, believe that it was always going to be difficult for Ernie to carry on without Eric and find his own path. 'It was very hard for Ernie when Eric died. You see Ernie was quite a big star when he first met Eric and gave up a very promising career to work with him. So when Eric died he was back to how he'd been in his early teens. Except this time he was on his own after creating an unbelievable body of work with Eric. How on earth do you follow that? In my opinion

289

he should have retired. Maybe done the odd chat show. But then again how could he? He'd been performing professionally from the age of six and had achieved, with Eric, genuine greatness. He'd become one half of the greatest comedy duo this country has ever known, or ever will know. He was on a hiding to nothing really, but he just wanted to work and there was no way for him to work that wasn't hugely exposed and open to criticism and/or comparison. Also, in the public's mind they didn't want to be reminded that Eric was dead.'

THIRTY-SEVEN

SLOWING DOWN

In December 1993 Ernie suffered a minor stroke and had to spend Christmas in hospital. Another one came along not long after; he was driving at the time. 'It was a Mercedes sports car,' says Doreen. 'And there was so little space in it that they had to fight to get him out. We got rid of it after that.'

Ernie had decided he was going to give up driving anyway after his first stroke as he was afraid of making a mistake. His pride was such he didn't want people yelling at him things like, 'You silly old fool, what are you doing on the road?' It was a shame because Ernie loved his cars. 'He used to love driving them,' says Doreen. 'But after the stroke he couldn't manage it, so a lot of the enjoyment went for him. Eventually he conceded that it would have to go. I remember he went to the dentist once and when he arrived back he said, "I got halfway there and I couldn't remember if I had to turn left or right when I got to a certain section. I think I'd better give up driving." Naturally he was upset, but he knew it was inevitable.'

In August 1995 Ernie suffered another stroke, this time a far more serious one. And yet he still gamely spoke about his desire to carry on working. Bryan Burdon recalls seeing Ernie at a Water Rats event. 'He looked quite ill. He was also a bit slow with his speech. Even so, he asked me when we were going to do another panto and he really seemed to mean it. I of course knew that it wasn't going to happen but laughed along with him and said I'd see him for a script conference around his swimming pool soon.'

What Burdon didn't know, nor the public, was just how ill Ernie really was. 'He actually lost fifty per cent of his sight and hearing,' reveals Doreen. 'But we didn't let on about that. You don't want to bleed all over people, do you?'

Ernie also suffered more attacks, quite dreadful things for Doreen to have to endure and live through as well. 'The ambulance men would arrive and give him an injection straight into the heart. They call it Code Blue, apparently, which means the person has actually gone and they have to get them back. They go all stiff and their eyes stare. It was like that with Ernie.' These attacks could come at any moment, even when Ernie was sitting in his favourite chair in the lounge relaxing. 'I nearly lost Ernie in that chair,' Doreen confirms. 'Not once but three or four times.'

Sadly, Ernie had to face the inevitable and on 27 November 1995, his seventieth birthday, he formally retired from showbiz. 'I'd like to have gone on for ever,' he said. 'But I realized I was finished.'

Not long afterwards a woman spotted Ernie in the street, came over to him and asked, 'Don't see much of you on TV these days.'

'I have retired,' replied Ernie.

'Too bad,' said the woman. 'There are people on TV today much worse than you.'

Ernie loved telling this story, a mark of his endearing humility.

For a man who hated the very idea of retirement, now he had no choice. However, he seemed to take to the concept quite well. But all the time Doreen was waiting for another attack, which could come at any moment, an indescribable feeling, coupled with the stark reality that Ernie was now living on borrowed time. 'Mentally, you steel yourself for it. You know he could go at any moment. But we were determined to fill our lives with as much happiness as we could. We didn't care where we were as long as we were together.'

It was the simple things they loved, spending a lot of time in the garden or in the house, 'just lolling around,' says Doreen. They rarely went out now. 'But we were content. He'd go swimming or take the dog for a walk. They were great pals. She went to see him in hospital. She was a dog rescued from an appalling home where she'd been terribly treated, locked in a room for five days and then thrown out of a window. Sometimes Ernie would cook a barbecue. His were the only sausages I could never eat and that was because he would talk so much he'd forget about them and burn them to a cinder.'

In spite of his frailty, Ernie's sense of humour never deserted him. He had a speech therapist

292

because his voice was affected by one of the strokes and would often pretend to whisper so she had to put her head closer and closer to his. Then, when she was a couple of inches away, he'd yell, 'Are you deaf?' at the top of his voice. It was a running gag.

Ernie also had the good fortune, unlike Eric sadly, to live long enough to see *The Morecambe and Wise Show* continue to prove incredibly popular and attract whole new generations of fans. He was also moved by the respect shown to him by the then current crop of comedians. Ernie was always genuinely touched when the more modern comics, people like Ben Elton or Rowan Atkinson, approached him and told him they were fans. Remember, this was during the age of 'alternative comedy' when most other light entertainers were smeared or derided, and in the case of Benny Hill assassinated. Morecambe and Wise were left untouched. John Lloyd, producer of *Not the Nine O'Clock News*, *Spitting Image* and *Blackadder*, has a personal take on why this was. 'The thing is Eric and Ernie never really dealt with anything approaching real life. I mean, they shared a bed and they came from a kind of golden past that was actually totally fictional. It was a world all on its own. They also transcended class, gender, age, sex, everything! The amount of people, regardless of where they came from, who didn't like Morecambe and Wise was very small, and probably still is. So, even within alternative comedy I don't think I ever met anybody who wasn't a fan. In fact throughout my thirty-something years in comedy I never heard anybody have a bad word to say about Morecambe and Wise as an act. They were absolutely the gods for everybody, all of us, regardless of genre or age.'

Such was the respect comedians felt for Morecambe and Wise that when Lloyd worked on *Spitting Image* Eric and Ernie were never candidates for their sometimes biting brand of ridicule. 'For the first three years of *Spitting Image* the vast majority of the week was taken up with fierce arguments as to who we should take off. And we kind of decided that the only people who would have a puppet made were people who deserved it, so these were politicians or people who made fools of themselves. But when I left the show that kind of collapsed and they would do puppets of anybody who they could do an impression of. They even started doing puppets of John Cleese, which just didn't work. And that was the same with Morecambe and Wise. It never occurred to anybody that there was anything ever to joke about with them, and if they had, it would have flopped. There was nothing to parody.'

It must have been personally satisfying for Ernie to know that he along with Eric had left an indelible legacy upon the world of British entertainment. 'We were powerful together and some of our shows were so beautiful they still bring tears to my eyes. It's a wonderful legacy.'

Even to the new up-and-coming entertainers an aura remained about him, the fact that Ernie had now passed over into showbiz royalty. Ant and Dec recall attending a recording of *This Is Your Life* back in the nineties and seeing Ernie there. 'He was sat in front of us and we spent the whole time just staring at him. Well, the back of him. It's one of the first times we were genuinely star-struck. We were just in awe of him.'

THIRTY-EIGHT

THE ENGLISH PATIENT

In the winter of 1998 the Wises engaged in something they always enjoyed, a nice cruise that took them to the sunshine of their holiday home in Florida and away from the biting cold winds of England. On board Ernie was his usual jovial self, strolling the decks wearing a *Titanic* T-shirt. 'Do you think that's a good idea?' asked Doreen, but his fellow travellers enjoyed the joke.

During the voyage Ernie complained of not feeling very well. Once in Florida his condition worsened and he was rushed to hospital. It was serious, medical advice was that his only chance of survival was a triple heart bypass and even then it was 50-50 whether he'd make it. 'There's no decision for me to make,' said Doreen when confronted by the stark facts. 'Give him the chance of life.'

For the next few months Doreen stayed in Florida with Ernie living in a state of almost constant nervous tension as she spent every day at his bedside, clocking up something like 4,000 miles in a hire car just going backwards and forwards from the hospital. 'Every day, I lived with uncertainty. One morning he'd be up, the next he'd be down, but if he squeezed your hand it made your day. I'd go out of that hospital walking on air.'

The doctors looking after Ernie soon became concerned for Doreen's well-being, seeing how much of a trial it was for her, urging that she at least take one day off to relax, fearing otherwise she might have a breakdown. It was an emotional rollercoaster, and there were some disturbing times, not least an unexpected change in Ernie's personality. During their whole life together Doreen remembers Ernie losing his temper just twice. First, when he was teaching her to drive in his prized Triumph Mayflower and she smashed it into a post during a reversing manoeuvre. 'He got very angry then and all kinds of language came out. I got out of the car and hit him with my handbag. It was partly out of embarrassment, I think.' The second time was on Coronation Day. 'We were in Birmingham and I was very, very drunk. It was late and we couldn't get a cab so were walking back to our digs. We were halfway down this hill when I tripped and fell over. Fortunately I didn't hurt myself, and when I started to get up I got an attack of the giggles and said, "Ooh, that was lucky." At which point I think Ernie had had enough of escorting his drunken wife. He yanked me up and said, "Pull yourself together woman, you're showing yourself up!" That wasn't true because there was nobody else around!'

Now, his normally sunny disposition would sink into dark fits of temper and he'd hurl abuse around for no good reason. 'It was something I'd never known in him before. Someone would come in to take him somewhere and he would say, "Fuck off, I'm not fucking going." He hated those words. He was normally so proper.' So concerned did Doreen become that she talked to Ernie's doctors about it and was to some extent reassured to learn that it was quite a normal side effect to the treatment he was undergoing, either due to the mental stress or the chemicals in the drugs. 'Even little old ladies who you wouldn't think knew words like that began to eff and blind like dockers.'

More worrying was that Ernie began to exhibit irrational fears. 'Towards the end he became afraid of people,' says Doreen. 'It broke my heart to see it. He had spent his life making people happy, and now he believed they were out to hurt him. He wouldn't sleep at night. "They come in at night and mug you," he would say. He didn't know who "they" were, but to him they were real. He would lay awake until I arrived, and then I would hold his hand and he would drop off.'

According to Michael Barratt when he visited his friend Ernie's bedside the comic didn't know who he was. 'It was very, very sad. He didn't recognize me at all. He didn't recognize anybody. I was desperately trying to get through to this poor man. I was trying everything—every line of conversation I could think of. In the end I said, "I'm sure Molly's missing you"—and that was it, he suddenly came alive and all was well. He recognized everybody. His dog Molly was the link that brought him round.'

Even during these disturbing shifts in personality the real Ernie shone through, the funny man, the born entertainer, the prankster. 'He didn't suffer fools gladly,' says Doreen. 'He made his feelings known. If a visitor was boring him he'd get hold of his sheet and slowly pull it up over his head, like a dust cover.' And he took great cheer in the number of greetings cards and messages from well-wishers.

Friends Eddie and Fran Plumley often accompanied Doreen to the hospital and one lunch time explained that they were just popping out for a bit. Suddenly Ernie piped up and said, 'I want to come with you.'

Everyone was a bit taken aback. 'Don't be daft,'

297

said Doreen. 'You can't.'

'Yes I can,' said Ernie and started to push himself up.

By this time everyone was getting very concerned, considering Ernie's frail condition, and didn't really know what to do. Then as he was pushing himself up Ernie asked, 'By the way, where are we going?'

'We're going shopping,' said Fran.

'Oh, I don't think I'll bother,' said Ernie and fell back on the bed like a sack of spuds.

One of the most poignant moments occurred as the couple celebrated their wedding anniversary. Ernie, who'd been largely fed through a tube, managed to eat part of the cake that had been baked for the occasion. It was a great big square confection with white and blue icing on it that resembled shaving foam. Ernie had four forkfuls and it left a blue ridge of foam around his mouth. When the doctor came and saw the foam Doreen had to tell him, 'It's all right, he's not had a turn.'

It had been of great concern to Doreen that for almost five weeks Ernie had only managed to eat a little solid food, half an orange and that was about it. Medically, though, he seemed to be pulling through. 'But it's the depression,' she says. 'He could have a couple of good days where he's making progress and talking and then we'd get two days when he maybe doesn't talk at all.'

Nor could Doreen fault the help Ernie had received at the hospital, he was well cared for and all the nurses absolutely adored him. 'He's a lovely little fella, our English patient,' they'd say. But after almost four months Ernie wanted to go back to Britain, back home to the garden he tended for hours on end, home where it could be just him and Doreen. 'Nothing else mattered to him. I kept assuring him that we were going home soon and from then on, whenever I came through the door, he'd say, "Ready yet? Have you brought the cases?"'

Eventually, with help from the insurance company, Doreen hired a specially adapted Lear jet from Fort Lauderdale to New York. Then from New York they flew to Greenland and from Greenland to RAF Northolt. 'Don't be fooled by the name "Lear Jet" though,' says Doreen. 'We could only take one suitcase because there wasn't room. There were no toilets on board. I sat with a doctor on the back seat with my knees on some boxes, while Ernie was laid full length on one side where the seats were and there were two doctors and two nurses. We also took our own food that I'd made at the apartment.'

For the whole flight Ernie looked out of the window, saw the skyscrapers of New York and icebergs floating off Newfoundland, sights he must have seen during those trips with Eric to America for the *Ed Sullivan Show* so long ago, just memories now, fading.

When they landed at Northolt, the RAF station in North-West London, Ernie was taken off the plane and placed into an ambulance and driven to the Nuffield hospital in Slough. As they got underway Doreen lent across to Ernie and whispered, 'You're back now . . . you're home.' Ernie smiled.

He was allowed a few visitors. One night Jan Kennedy, her husband Tony and Doreen arrived. They'd also brought with them Ernie's beloved dog. Everyone sat on his bed and sang 'Bring Me Sunshine'. Even Ernie managed to muster the strength to join in. It was a hugely touching moment for everyone. 'I am quite honoured to have had that moment with him,' says Jan. 'Because we wanted to cheer him up. Doreen was wonderful throughout, she was very breezy, as Doreen is, she wanted to make Ernie feel relaxed. She was a fantastic girl and I have got such admiration for her. She gave her life to Ernie. I believe she gave up thoughts of having children so that she could be with Ernie, so they could be together without compromising the children's upbringing, so that she could give everything she had to him.'

The sing-along certainly seemed to raise Ernie's spirits and the doctors thought he looked well enough to be allowed out for a couple of hours the next day. 'We were going to have tea together, sitting in the hospital's garden,' Doreen remembers. 'He was so looking forward to it. It meant so much to him. He couldn't talk about anything else.'

That morning Doreen had woken up with an uneasy feeling she wasn't able to shake off. Outside it was raining. She made breakfast and then picked up the phone and almost instinctively phoned the hospital, sensing that something was wrong. 'He's fine,' said a nurse. 'He's the same as usual.'

Barely five minutes later the hospital rang back. 'We think you should come right away!'

Doreen leapt into the car for the twenty-minute drive to Nuffield. Pulling into the car park she knew by the faces of the doctors who had come outside to meet her that it was too late. 'I went into his room and he was lying there in bed. I so wanted to kiss him and cuddle him. So I did. I put my arms around him and he was still warm.'

For a few moments it was Ernie and Doreen

together again. She could barely break off the embrace, knowing it would be the last time she would ever hold him in her arms. Eventually she came out into the corridor where the staff had mingled. She thanked them for all they had done. After a few minutes a doctor asked if she wanted to go inside and say goodbye one last time. Doreen dearly wanted to see Ernie again, but it wouldn't be right. 'I had said goodbye and I realized that the person in that room was not really Ernie any more because he had gone.'

The last words they had spoken to each other had been the day before. 'You look so nice and comfortable. Do you want a little sleep?' Doreen had asked. Ernie had smiled, 'Yes, you go and enjoy yourself.' It was so very typical of Ernie, never thinking of himself, always of others.

One of the quirky things to come to light after Ernie's death was his will. For a man whose life was dominated by money—earning it, saving it, looking after it, the accounts he kept, the records and contracts he stored away—that he should have lapsed so badly when it came to his own will is very strange. Was it deliberate or plain forgetfulness, but his will hadn't been changed since 1965.

Ernie first drafted his will in 1958, then again in 1965, mainly to take into account a change of property. In the document he left £250 each to his mother, father and sisters; small amounts now but relatively considerable back in the mid-sixties. All Ernie's personal clothing was left to his brother, Gordon; as for the rest of his estate it went to Doreen. In the end none of Ernie's surviving relatives lost out, with Doreen making generous provisions for them.

Ernie's funeral took place at Slough crematorium, Buckinghamshire on 30 March 1999. Marion Montgomery, the singer and a good friend of Ernie's, was among the guests and in the car with Doreen driving to the church. She looked out of the window and saw two swans swooping low over the hearse. Turning to Doreen Marion said, 'I think they are the spirits of Ernie and you.'

Jan Kennedy also attended the funeral. 'I went to the house and we went in the funeral car and I said to Doreen, "I think we should take Molly. Ernie adored her." And Doreen said, "Well how?" And I said, "I'll take her, I'll take Molly." So I took the dog in the next car and when we got out Doreen took him from me and walked into the church with the dog and I thought it was just a lovely moment, Doreen going inside with Ernie's best pal. It was a silly soppy thing but very meaningful.'

The eulogy was read by Michael Grade, and with kind permission we reproduce a portion of it below:

There is an overwhelming sense of sadness that hovers over any funeral. But today, the tears are not just confined to this chapel, and the family and the friends who have come to mourn. Today there is a sadness across the whole nation as we all have to say our last farewell to Ernie Wise, the last half of a beloved British institution: the Morecambe and Wise comedy legend.

He was born Ernest Wiseman, seventy-three years ago in Yorkshire, in the humblest of circumstances, and went on to achieve what is given to very, very few of us: by dint of his

God-given talent, his hard work and his intelligence, he managed to leave an indelible mark on the rich cultural history of his country.

The nation's hearts go out today to Doreen as she faces a future without the man who was her devoted partner for forty-six years, through thick and thin, and let it not be forgotten just how much thin there was in the early days. I doubt anyone here could imagine a couple more devoted than Ernie and Doreen. They made and kept friends easily, they laughed together and, no matter what success came Ernie's way, they remained inseparable and unspoiled by the trappings of his glittering career. They delighted in each other's company both at work and at play.

The written tributes of the past week have gone some way to redress a rather unfair imbalance in the appreciation of the genius of Morecambe and Wise which has tended to concentrate more on Eric's dazzling contribution and not enough, in my opinion, not nearly enough on Ernie's. Let us be clear, they were equal partners in the comic genius department.

For us, his public, we have the videotapes to keep us in touch with the genius that was Morecambe and Wise. For you, Doreen, the tapes are not enough. Our hearts go out to you today and I hope that our hopes and prayers and our love, and the memories of that very special human being we were all privileged to know as Ernie, will, somehow, offer some comfort and in time soothe your grief.

Let us all, then, say farewell to Ernie Wise—and let us give thanks for the sunshine wot *he* brought us all.'

THIRTY-NINE

LIFE AFTER ERNIE

Doreen admits that she has never truly got over losing Ernie. They'd been together nearly fifty years and barely spent a night apart. Those weeks immediately following his death were the toughest, sometimes she'd be overtaken by waves of grief and anger. 'I used to go out to the bottom of the garden and scream.' Her early morning walks with the dog became an ordeal as she was repeatedly stopped by people. 'I am so sorry about your husband. He was wonderful. We do miss him.' Tears would well up in Doreen's eyes: 'Not half as much as I do.' It got to the point where she stopped going out. 'I know they meant well, but I couldn't deal with it.' Often she'd repeat to herself through scalding tears: 'Why him?' When so many horrible people survive and live long lives it was a question that had no answer. 'Ernie didn't have a jealous bone in his body. He was a gentle soul. He was kind to everybody.'

She blamed his job and found it difficult to reconcile the fact that her Ernie had succumbed to much the same thing that killed Eric. 'They never gave themselves a break and I'm sure the constant stress and tension contributed to both their deaths. They were very nervous people. Before they went onstage they kept going to the toilet. They'd stand around in the wings, checking to see if their fly buttons were done up and then, when the time came they'd say, "Here we go," then they'd feel that flood of warmth from the audience wash over them and they'd be OK. Even when they were getting unheard-of viewing figures, 27 million or more, they didn't bask in their success. They were busy worrying about the next show.'

Of course Doreen was surrounded by friends who tried to comfort her in her grief. Rolf Harris lived just across the river and four days after the funeral rang her up. 'Doreen,' he said. 'You and I are going to the cinema tonight. It's OK, it's a comedy, and it'll cheer you up.'

Doreen opened the local newspaper to see what was on. It was a film called *Waking Ned*, which told the story of a man who dies and his friends pretend he's still alive because he's won the Lottery. Doreen rang Rolf back.

'Rolf, do you know what this film is about?'

'Don't worry, you'll be all right, you'll be with me.'

They ended up going; it was a bit of an endurance test for a recently bereaved woman. 'I didn't appreciate it all that much when they put the false teeth back in the corpse, but there you are. Anyway I got through it, and I was glad I went. Afterwards we had fish and chips.'

The actor David Lodge also helped a great deal. He was a close friend of the couple and sensed that Doreen was drifting further and further away from the people she needed to be with at a time like this.

'When Ernie died I suppose I went into my shell a bit. I just wanted to be on my own really. I didn't go out much at all. After a while I wasn't really getting any better and David kind of took me in hand. He talked to me a lot and badgered me to get out and about. Eventually it worked and before long I was a lot better.'

And of course the industry itself wished her well. Doreen was invited by BAFTA to collect a special fellowship award on Ernie's behalf. 'I was nervous going up to make my speech, and then I looked down from the stage and Michael Grade was in tears, everyone was crying. I didn't feel so bad then. I thought, if I break down, I'll be in good company.'

But her friends and well-wishers couldn't be there all the time and the house, so alive and full of happiness when Ernie was there, was now a soulless, large rambling place awash with too many memories. The framed photographs of Ernie that adorned every wall were nice reminders of his career when he was alive, now they just reminded Doreen of her emptiness and the fact he was missing. So too his little dancing clogs that she couldn't bear to part with.

In the study was a life size bust of Ernie's head, a gift from a merchant seaman who on long sea voyages studied pictures of Ernie and chiselled it out of concrete. The likeness was uncanny. To a visiting reporter Doreen admitted that now Ernie was gone she often kissed it. When she popped out for a moment, the reporter used the time to observe the bust and sure enough there were little smears of pink lipstick all around the concrete lips.

What was worse was how cleaning up in the various rooms she would often come across little tokens of love Ernie had given her, like the card from a bunch of flowers he sent her one Valentine's Day. 'A host of golden daffodils,' Ernie had written, remembering the line came from a famous poem but unsure whether it was Wordsworth or Longfellow, in any case he couldn't stop himself signing it: 'Shortfellow'. He knew it would make Doreen laugh and it did. Underneath he wrote, 'Love, Ern' and there was a row of kisses.

It was in another of those quiet rooms that she discovered an old newspaper article in which Ernie had mentioned that his very favourite place in the entire world was the stretch of riverbank just outside their house. Doreen came up with a plan to scatter his ashes there. Inviting just close friends, Pearl Carr and Teddy Johnson, Fran and Eddie Plumley, Doreen prepared lunch, a cold buffet, and while enjoying a glass of wine everyone talked about Ernie.

After lunch Doreen announced, 'Come on, we'll go into the garden,' picked up Ernie's urn and everyone followed her through the back garden gate and towards the river's edge. 'It's not very nice,' she admitted, 'carrying your loved one in a pot.' At the towpath Doreen stopped and handed the urn to Eddie Plumley. 'I was a bit dumbfounded at first but she said, 'I'd like you and Teddy to do it. I'd like you both to scatter Ernie's ashes.' I said of course we would so Teddy and I with everyone following behind walked to where Ernie and Doreen's boat used to be, and we scattered Ernie there. It was the perfect place really—not least because they'd spent some of their happiest times together on that boat. I was so proud to have been asked. It was a very special occasion.'

The dust that was Ernie Wise blew among the alders and weeping willows, the rest gently seeped away into the calming waters of the Thames. 'It's tidal, you see,' said Doreen. 'Eventually it goes down to the sea, and then all over the world. So Ernie will be everywhere, everywhere I'll ever go.'

FORTY

GOODBYE ERNIE . . . AND THANKS

In comedy there's no such thing as just a straight man. Being a good straight man is an art in itself, even though sometimes they can come across as not being funny because they usually don't get the punchline or act in an amusing way. On the surface of it, it's rather a thankless task because the straight man usually has to set up the gags. He establishes nor-mality and convention, which the so-called funny one can then undermine or twist to comedic effect. 'The straight man is an absolutely vital component in the overall process of a double act working well,' says actor, Kevin Eldon. 'Ernie mostly played his role absolutely truthfully with full conviction and that's why he was so brilliant. Also when the material required it, he played the part of the vain pretentious artiste very well, and that provided pomposity, which was perfect for Eric's puppyish mischievousness to prick. He had a lot of energy about him. He was a proper showman and it made him very watchable.'

So to be the perfect straight man, and Eric described Ernie as the best in the business, you have to be almost subservient to the comic and totally without ego. Ernie was exceptional in his unselfish ability of knowing just when the perfect moment was to feed Eric a line. Along it would come timed to absolute perfection and Eric would hit it for six. It was like bowling under-arm to Viv Richards. 'POW!' as Eric would say.

'The thing I most admired about Ernie,' says Lord Archer, 'is that there appeared to be no envy to him and I thought that was amazing. His comedy partner was clearly bigger and more important in the public's eyes but that wasn't important to Ernie. Ernie's genius was his lack of envy.'

Because they had worked together for so long and professionally knew each other so well it wouldn't have been possible for Eric to have worked in the way that he did and to produce the reactions that he did without Ernie. Astute performers like Victoria Wood, who are also students of comedy, know this full well. 'Ernie was hugely vital. What he does is very clever, but it's very unnoticeable. If you replaced him with someone else, it wouldn't work. They do have chemistry. There's something about Ernie's lovability, and his pomposity—which is not his own, it's like an invented character. Eric's the daft, annoying child, and Ernie is like the grown up, trying to get on with something serious, like a play. And Eric is sticking his head round the curtain.'

Even Ernie's comical asides to the camera, his looks of exasperation when Eric was being the fool, were funny, and much like Matt Horne in *Gavin and Stacey* according to Miranda Hart. 'Matt was the master at giving a look off James Corden's character that would punctuate Corden's foolish behaviour with a laugh. Ernie did that too. He would often look at Eric then turn out to the audience with an air of desperation about what his friend had just said that was very amusing—perhaps more amusing than he thought. He could have given it more I think and been funnier, but he was so serving of Eric that he just gave enough to keep the focus on his funnier partner. What a gift. I love him for it!'

That's why the partnership worked. It was made up of two men who both had enormous respect for each other's talents and ability. And they liked each other; this friendship was possibly the most important component in their success. It's a camaraderie that has endeared them so much to the public; it's perhaps the main source of their appeal. 'I think that was very evident when you were working with them,' says Angela Rippon. 'They really did enjoy each other's company, they were good friends as well as a very great double act and I don't think that it would have worked as well as it did if they hadn't been such good friends.'

They did seem to feed off each other, too, use the other's energy to bolster their own. 'They were amazing to watch onstage,' says Michael Grade. 'If one of them ever had an off night, which did occasionally happen, you could see the other one trying to work on him—trying to coax him round and bring him back to speed. It's an almost indescribable professionalism which was born of this chemistry between them.'

This is evident in their TV appearances, too. Ant and Dec picked up on it while watching an old show of theirs on DVD. 'Ernie comes out and completely fluffs most of his opening lines. Then Eric comes out, takes the mickey a bit and then kind of picks him up. You can tell Ernie's having an off night, and you can see Eric helping him along. We can totally relate to that. We know instinctively if one of us is struggling and it's the other one's job to help them along. Watching Eric and Ernie do that though is amazing and quite touching really. The bond is so apparent. More so if you've ever been in the same situation.'

Ant and Dec are huge fans of Morecambe and Wise and can even pinpoint a few similarities they share with them, not least the fact they also got together at a very young age, thirteen, actually slightly younger than Eric and Ernie. 'All we wanted to do in the early days was make each other laugh. That was our purpose. We've even shared a bed on a few occasions; doesn't get any more Morecambe and Wise than that. We spent our formative years on tour, playing nightclubs. That was our apprenticeship, really. They were our variety halls!'

Incredibly Morecambe and Wise are as popular today as they ever were, winning over new fans and remaining relevant by inspiring the latest crop of comedy performers.

For some comedians like Miranda Hart, Eric and Ernie had a major influence on their career, in that they were the deciding factor in them choosing to go into comedy. 'I would watch them as a child and remember being mesmerized. I loved the singing and dancing and the sheer pleasure and sunshine that Eric and Ernie brought. And I remember being very grateful to them for the laughs and thinking what a wonderful gift that must be. I didn't consciously copy them, or learn from them, but inadvertently

I am sure there has been some comedy osmosis. They also influenced me in that, despite alternative comedy coming into play in the eighties and then the nineties, I would still always prefer their style. A style that might have started to be considered old-fashioned. But I never saw it as such. It was just funnier to me than anything new and always probably will be. It seemed like the highest art of comedy what they did. The hardest type too. The pressure they had, the live audiences, the amount they packed into a show—cross talk, guests, sketches, the bedroom scenes like small sitcom scenes—they did it all in one show. And they kept it up for many many years. Not many comedians put that much effort in to be their best at every opportunity.'

As Morecambe and Wise slip ever further into comedy past tense, it's more important than ever to cherish their achievements and celebrate what they brought to British popular culture. Watching their shows today one always gets the sense they're having fun, and they're enjoying watching the audience have fun, too; it's one of the infectious qualities about them that make them so endearing and well liked. What's also noticeable as you watch the two of them perform is that there never seemed to be an ego present, just a friendship. They obviously took the mickey out of each other, but the friendship transcended everything, on-screen and off. That was the key to Morecambe and Wise, and it was the key to Eric and Ernie.

In reflective mood, Ernie once took Eddie Braben, the writer who did so much to reclaim him from out of the comedy shadow of Eric, to one side and quietly said, 'Eddie, we would like to think that together we have given the public a lot of pleasure and never hurt anyone. To be stopped on the street and told how much our show has meant to people is the greatest joy in life.'

And some epitaph.

* * *

As well as doing our best to convey an extraordinarily rich and fascinating life story, we the authors have also unashamedly endeavoured to rejuvenate and, if you will, rehabilitate the reputation of one equal half of the greatest comedy duo that Britain has ever produced. Ernie was and is a genuine legend of British comedy and should indeed be treated as such. All that we ask is that the next time you sit down to watch Morecambe and Wise you shift the spotlight sideways a while, focus on Eric's little fat friend and in doing so revel in the timing, the patience, the understanding and the unquestionable talent of Mr Ernie Wise.

BIBLIOGRAPHY

Eric and Ernie: The Autobiography of Morecambe and Wise (W.H. Allen—1973)

There's No Answer To That! by Morecambe and Wise (Hodder and Stoughton—1982)

Still on My Way to Hollywood by Ernie Wise (Duckworth—1990)

Morecambe and Wise: Behind the Scenes by Gary Morecambe and Martin Sterling (Robson Books—1994)

Morecambe and Wise by Graham McCann (Fourth Estate—1998)

Eric Morecambe: Life's not Hollywood, it's Cricklewood by Gary Morecambe (BBC Books—2003)

Morecambe and Wise Untold by William Cook (Harper Collins—2007)

Picture acknowledgements

All photographs are from Doreen Wise's private collection,with the following exceptions:

Page 4, top left: © MirrorpixPage 6, top left: © Jack EmeraldPage 7, top: © Mervyn Berens; bottom: © *Daily Herald*Page 8, bottom: © *Press Association* (Barratts/S&G Barratts/EMPICS Archive)Page 9, top: © ITV/Rex FeaturesPage 11, bottom: © Mirrorpix, photo by Bill MalindinePage 12, top right: © PA/PA Archive/Press Association Images, top left: © Joan Williams, Page 14, top: © FremantleMedia

Every effort has been made to credit the copyright holders of thephotographs in this book, but where omissions have been made thepublishers will be glad to rectify them in any future editions.